D1450390

AMERICAN LABOR ON STAGE

Recent Titles in
Contributions in Drama and Theatre Studies

"Vast Encyclopedia": The Theatre of Thornton Wilder
Paul Lifton

Christopher Marlowe and the Renaissance of Tragedy
Douglas Cole

Menander and the Making of Comedy
J. Michael Walton and Peter D. Arnott

A History of Polish Theater, 1939–1989: Spheres of Captivity and Freedom
Kazimierz Braun

Theatre, Opera, and Audiences in Revolutionary Paris: Analysis and Repertory
Emmet Kennedy, Marie-Laurence Netter, James P. McGregor, and Mark V. Olsen

The Stage Clown in Shakespeare's Theatre
Bente A. Videbæk

Shadows of Realism: Dramaturgy and the Theories and Practices of Modernism
Nancy Kindelan

Fredric March: Craftsman First, Star Second
Deborah C. Peterson

Assessing the Achievement of J. M. Synge
Alexander G. Gonzalez, editor

Maria Irene Fornes and Her Critics
Assunta Bartolomucci Kent

Jekyll and Hyde Adapted: Dramatizations of Cultural Anxiety
Brian A. Rose

The Dramatic Art of David Storey: The Journey of a Playwright
Herbert Liebman

AMERICAN LABOR ON STAGE

Dramatic Interpretations of the Steel and Textile Industries in the 1930s

SUSAN DUFFY

Contributions in Drama and Theatre Studies, Number 72

GREENWOOD PRESS
Westport, Connecticut • London

Library of Congress Cataloging-in-Publication Data

Duffy, Susan.
    American labor on stage : dramatic interpretations of the steel
and textile industries in the 1930s / Susan Duffy.
        p.   cm.—(Contributions in drama and theatre studies, ISSN
0163–3821 ; no. 72)
    Includes bibliographical references and index.
    ISBN 0–313–29861–0 (alk. paper)
    1. American drama—20th century—History and criticism.   2. Steel
industry and trade in literature.   3. Textile industry in
literature.   4. Labor movement in literature.   5. Working class in
literature.   I. Title.   II. Series.
    PS338.S74D84   1996
    812′.5209355—dc20   95–46420

British Library Cataloguing in Publication Data is available.

Library of Congress Catalog Card Number: 95–46420
ISBN: 0–313–29861–0
ISSN: 0163–3821

First published in 1996

Greenwood Press, 88 Post Road West, Westport, CT 06881
An imprint of Greenwood Publishing Group, Inc.

Printed in the United States of America

∞™

The paper used in this book complies with the
Permanent Paper Standard issued by the National
Information Standards Organization (Z39.48–1984).

10 9 8 7 6 5 4 3 2

Copyright Acknowledgments

The author and publisher gratefully acknowledge permission to reprint the following material from correspondence, manuscript collections, books, and newspapers:

Theatre reviews from the *Atlanta Constitution* and the *Atlanta Georgian*. Reprinted with the permission of the *Atlanta Constitution*.

Excerpts from *The Cultural Approach to History* by Caroline Ware. Copyright © 1940 by Columbia University Press. Reprinted with permission of the publisher.

Excerpts from *Culture in the South*, edited by W. T. Couch. Copyright © 1935 by University of North Carolina Press. Used by permission of the publisher.

Excerpts from *Strike Song* by J. O. and Loretta Carroll Bailey, correspondence from J. O. Bailey, and correspondence to the author from Nancy B. Rich. Used by permission of Nancy Bailey Rich.

Excerpts from International Ladies' Garment Workers' Union documents and David Dubinsky Papers, International Ladies' Garment Workers' Union Archives. Labor-Management Documentation Center, Cornell University. Used with permission.

Excerpts from the diaries of Mary Heaton Vorse and *Strike!* by William Dorsey Blake and Mary Heaton Vorse, found in the Mary Heaton Vorse Papers. Used by permission of the Archives of Labor History and Urban Affairs, Wayne State University.

Excerpts from *Steel* by John Wexley and material held in the John Wexley Papers. Used by permission of the State Historical Society of Wisconsin and the Wisconsin Center for Film and Theater Research.

Every reasonable effort has been made to trace the owners of copyright materials in this book, but in some instances this has proven impossible. The author and publisher will be glad to receive information leading to more complete acknowledgments in subsequent printings of the book and in the meantime extend their apologies for any omissions.

This book is dedicated to the

memory of my parents,

Joseph and Betty Jacobelli

Contents

Acknowledgments   xi

1. Propaganda Plays and American Labor   5

2. *Strike Song* and the Textile Strike of 1929   25

3. *Strike!:* A Northern Response to a Southern Strike   57

4. *Altars of Steel:* The Steel Industry in the South   81

5. *Steel:* Militant Labor and Northern Steel   109

6. The Legacy of American Labor Plays   137

Bibliography   149

Index   153

Acknowledgments

The completion of this manuscript brought with it many personal rewards. The research over the last several years proved interesting and productive. Along the way I uncovered materials that will serve as the basis for my next project relating to treatments of labor in theatrical venues. I look forward to initiating work on these as much as I looked forward to completion of this book. Most rewarding to me have been the associations and conversations with archivists and special collection librarians, as well as scholars who have kindly taken an interest in my work. I relied on the assistance of numerous individuals and would like to acknowledge them with a deep sense of professional and personal gratitude.

As always, I must begin by acknowledging the love and support offered by my husband and daughter, Bernard and Elizabeth Duffy. Bernie read and reread multiple drafts and offered suggestions that helped strengthen the manuscript, while Liz patiently accepted my preoccupation with completing this project. My love and thanks to you both.

The invaluable assistance of many others needs to be recognized: Nancy Bailey Rich of Raleigh, North Carolina; Ruth Kerns, now retired, an archivist at the Federal Theatre Project Collection when it was housed at George Mason University; James Rush, archivist at the National Archives; Hope Nisly, archivist at the Labor Archives and Research Documentation Center at Cornell University; Harold Miller, archivist at the State Historical Society of Wisconsin; Margery Long, archivist at the Walter Reuther Archives of Labor History and Urban Affairs, at Wayne State University; Walter Zonchenko of the Music Collection of the Library of Congress, where the Federal Theatre Project Collection is presently housed; the librarians at the North Carolina Collection and the Paul Green Papers at the University of North Carolina, Chapel Hill; the librarians at the Billy Rose Collection of the New York Public Library; and the librarians at the Theatre of the Thirties Collection at George Mason University.

I would like to acknowledge the financial support awarded by the National Endowment for the Humanities, which chose this project as one worthy of

Federal backing in the form of a 1990 Summer Stipend. Additionally, I am grateful to the California Polytechnic State University in San Luis Obispo, where I teach, for its support of this project in the form of released time through Affirmative Action Faculty Development Grants in 1988 and 1989.

My thanks go to Rocio Alvear and Jane Brechler for their support and guidance through the vagaries of our temperamental office computer, and to Sally Hertz-Szelinski, and Juliann, and Michael Hertz, who welcomed us into their home during our stay in Pittsburgh. I would be remiss if I did not thank the readers who offered commentary on this manuscript, and Nina Pearlstein of Greenwood Press, who took an active interest in seeing it published. I am grateful to Maureen Melino, Pelham Boyer, Aimee Wolfinger and Jean Lynch of Greenwood Press, who helped prepare the manuscript for publication. To these, and to many others who have offered assistance, encouragement, and support of this project, I offer my heartfelt thanks.

Finally, I offer my thanks to the current readers of this manuscript. While I have spent years researching this project it stands only as a beginning. Any errors of fact or interpretation are attributable to me. It is my hope that future theatre historians will be able to fill in more of the details of the theatre's use by various groups for propagandistic purposes. I encourage all who read this volume to expand the investigation of labor plays and leftist theatre in the United States. I hope that my investigation clears a path that others will see fit to follow and thereby extend through their own studies of American labor and American theatre.

Susan Duffy

May 15, 1996

AMERICAN LABOR
ON STAGE

Theater is very much connected with the society, with the social situation. . . . A theater piece, of itself, demands a confrontation with an audience. It demands that you connect with other people; it demands a collective and social effort with the company and later with the audience.

Griselda Gambaro, translated by Alberto Minero.
In Kathleen Betsko and Rachel Koenig, eds.,
Interviews with Contemporary Women Playwrights (1987).

CHAPTER 1

Propaganda Plays
and American Labor

The propaganda plays that dramatized the plight of labor in the United States during the 1930s testify to the political power of the theatre. American labor plays are important in the study of American cultural history for two reasons. First, they provide us examples of rhetorical justifications for the militancy of labor, with which popular audiences were asked to identify, and second, they preserve dissenting voices instrumental in shaping American industry and society. The plays are representations of historical incidents and popular responses to them that might otherwise be forgotten. They are historical documents written from the viewpoint of the politically and economically disenfranchised. Despite the publication of several good studies of leftist plays, many significant texts from this period remain largely ignored. Admittedly, not every script would stand as a compelling work of dramatic art; many suffer from heavy-handed didacticism. But sincerity, an idealistic commitment to movements, and emphasis on educating ethnic groups at the bottom rung of the industrial ladder make every script compelling when viewed as social commentary. "Commentary" is a particularly appropriate word because the plays in production offer a unique opportunity for audiences to see and hear radical political thought in ways that would touch them emotionally and intellectually. The political plays of this period are often described with such loaded terms as "proletarian," "didactic," "Marxist," and "polemical;" yet the purposes, propaganda techniques, and effects of such plays, particularly those focusing on American labor, have not received the systematic examination that they deserve and that might justify these descriptions. This study reclaims four plays in a body of literature that has been too long overlooked.

The four plays analyzed in this study represent artistic responses to industries that epitomize the settings of American labor in two geographic regions: steel in the North and textiles in the South. *Strike Song*, by J. O. and Loretta Carroll Bailey, and *Strike!*, William Dorsey Blake's adaptation of Mary Heaton Vorse's novel, dramatize the Gastonia, North Carolina, textile strike of 1929. Documentary elements in both scripts parallel the actual incidents of violence during strikes, and the playwrights portrayed the bizarre incidents that transpired during the subsequent trials. The steel plays offer a different venue for theatrical spectacle and political militancy. *Steel*, a Labor Stage production by John Wexley, ardently promotes the rights of labor and underscores the virulent corporate attitudes toward radical labor. It also offers a unique view of the role and place of various ethnic groups in the mills and of the scabs and so-called "kitchen scabs" who stood as obstacles to the strikers. *Altars of Steel*, by Thomas Hall Rogers, a Federal Theatre Project play, is different in approach and somewhat in theme: it examines the steel industry in the South. Rogers's play promotes a more moderate view of management-labor confrontations while offering a particularly unflattering picture of unscrupulous efforts by "big steel" to buy up privately owned mills. In tone and tenor it bristles with regional pride and defiance. In both the textile and steel plays the analysis focuses primarily on union organizers and on the response toward them of ethnic outgroups who supported these two industries on their backs and fed them with their lives.

These plays are unique artistically and sociologically in their representation of issues affecting two industries not regularly depicted on the stage. The heyday of steel and textile production in this country occurred in the first half of the century. The far-reaching influence of these two industries in the North and South, and the labor battles they provoked, rocked the East and changed American labor practices. Both industries were affected by radical unionizing efforts, by the New Deal, by leftist political groups, and by substantial changes in the social milieu of the country. These changes are evident in drama-tizations of the struggle of American labor. At first glance these scripts seem isolated responses to social problems, but upon closer examination one recog-nizes a common skein of political militancy in the theatre of the 1930s up and down the East Coast. For fifty years national attention had been periodically riveted to violent responses to strikes in Lawrence, Chicago, Pittsburgh, and Gastonia.

The plays examined in the succeeding chapters were written in the context of a complex political world containing the seeds of New Deal social reform and the residual tensions of economic and industrial unrest from the labor wars of 1890 to 1920. The complexity of the 1930s is marked by the discernible economic shifts during the decade, a decade that began in poverty and ended with a display of industrial power as the nation prepared for war. The rhetoric of the 1930s reflected a myriad of political and ideological positions: radical groups promoted fascism, technocracy, socialism, and communism, while President Franklin D. Roosevelt appealed to traditional values of patriotism, loyalty, hard work, community effort, and community charity as he promoted the National Recovery Administration. The national cataclysm of the early years of the decade provided opportunities for reflective responses to the materialism of the 1920s. As the nation struggled to regain economic stability, the initiatives of the New Deal offered a fresh outlook on American labor. The Works Progress Administration institutionalized efforts to put Americans back to work. Art movements of the '30s helped change public perceptions of labor by sanctifying American workers in WPA murals in public buildings, and by dramatizing their moral fortitude in WPA sponsored plays. The worker became mythologized as a modern Atlas on whose back the security of the nation rested.

The national self-concept in the first half of the twentieth century relied on identification with industry. Popular magazines regularly published photographs of America at work. The industrial photos of these years, of steelworkers, welders, bridge builders, miners, riveters, puddlers, etc., were iconographic depictions of what we purported to be even in our poverty —strong, self-reliant, ethnically diverse, resilient. The national industrial image in the 1930s focused on an identification specifically with heavy industry, particularly steel. The shadow of this industrial giant looms over the plays in this study.

Concurrent with New Deal programs putting the unemployed back to work was the ongoing campaign for worker organization carried on by trade unions. The labor violence of the early part of the century casts its own shadow on the scripts in this study. The New Deal offered pragmatic, if at times utopian, solutions to a crippling national problem. Although the WPA programs succeeded in reducing unemployment, there was heightening tension between organized labor and industry. The scripts reflect this tension and play upon the audience's memory of the strikes, walkouts, and violence connected with the earlier drive for unionization. Historical conflicts such as the 1886 Haymarket riots and the Great Steel Strike of 1919 receive repeated references. The first two scripts function as a kind of *theâtre vérité* in their portrayal of the brutalization of workers by mill owners in the textile strike at the Loray Mill in 1929. The violence of the strikes is recalled and reenacted in these plays, and when not put literally on the stage, it is remembered bitterly in the dialogue. There were innocent casualties in all the conflicts. In the Haymarket riots men, women, and children were shot; one of the most prominent victims of the 1919 steel strike was a woman killed by a bullet while bending over her children to protect them; during the Gastonia strike Ella May Wiggins, a mother of five, was shot in the back at a labor rally. Loretta Bailey and Mary Vorse took advantage of the dramatic currency of eulogizing victims individually and collectively when they chose the Gastonia strike as the backdrop for their plays.

The steel plays examined in the final two chapters identify another kind of industrial victim—the American family. Both Rogers's play and Wexley's speak to the disintegration of the family unit: the former by showing the dissolution of independently owned and operated family enterprises swallowed by corporate conglomerates and confronted with absentee ownership; the latter by depicting the physical and emotional dissolution of individuals within families choosing between economic security in their total commitment to the mill, and personal freedom in breaking from it. Both scripts address issues of a single–industry town—the company town, where escape, economic and psychological, is thwarted by industrial control. The problems posed by industrial work and the concomitant social problems arising from life in an industrial state became a focus of academic inquiry during the '30s and receives continual reassessment in contemporary studies of labor history. The specific industry, whether steel, textiles, or rubber, was not as significant as the militancy of American labor that led to collective bargaining. The revolution in American labor was a cross-cultural, multiethnic, non-denominational civil rights movement. Injustices inflicted on workers in one industry were perceived as injustices by all workers. The rise of the American Federation of Labor and the Congress of Industrial Organizations, and their dynastic marriage as the AFL-CIO, created a new era in American labor history and American culture.

Collective bargaining in American industry was achieved, but not without discrimination, suffering, violence, and loss of life. In the history of American labor, the motifs of organizational heroes and common—man martyrs manifest themselves forcefully. These struggles were artistically represented in powerful imagery. The actions of heroes and societal martyrs are the soul of drama. Well remembered, canonical plays like *Waiting for Lefty* and *Stevedore* typify the dramatic interpretation of American labor struggles; they were not isolated artistic responses but part of a much larger movement. Many more playwrights and many more scripts used the labor wars as their theme than has been recognized. The theatre served in the '30s, as now, as a barometer of popular culture and unpopular politics. It points to societal problems often unnoticed or buried unheeded by the public, and it directs the thinking of its audiences toward allocation of praise and blame, as well as toward idealistic solutions. The study of propagandistic plays that attacked the bulwarks of American industry expands the investigation of significant social literature of the 1930s[1].

The approach of this study is historical/critical. It does not fall into a specific theoretical camp, though the academic battle lines have been drawn by the "new critics" and the "new historicists." In contrast to the recondite critical pyrotechnics of the deconstructionists, the treatises and articles written by historians and critics in the 1920s and '30s explicating a new approach to historiography are those I find the most cogent and their methodologies the most congenial. Caroline Ware's 1940 compilation of essays, *The Cultural Approach to History*, proved equally as useful as the works of recent historians and critics, such as Richard Harvey Brown's *Society as Text: Essays on Rhetoric, Reason and Reality*.

They, like others who identify issues in historiography, caution one to recognize the unconscious cultural biases of the historian as a primary hazard of historical analysis. Brown speaks to the inescapability of the "the culture boundness" of the historian, while Ware chooses to exhort historians to recognize their "own identification with groups in the past"[2]. My interest in these plays stems from a sustained academic commitment, borne out by a decade of research on how the political left used the theatre for propagandistic purposes. Yet I must acknowledge my own "culture boundness" as a Pittsburgh native who grew up in a "steel family" and who at an early age was imbued with a fierce regional pride and an idyllic notion of an industrial North that celebrated ethnic diversity and championed labor. Such notions, I would realize later, did not always square with reality. I began my teaching career at Clemson University in the Piedmont region of South Carolina, the nation's textile center. Though I lived there nine years, I remained always a cultural outsider. But I recognized there too a congruent regional pride and identification, as well as a mythos that surrounded the textile strikes. The strikers, many of them women, had opposed industrial inequities and helped to change society. While living in South Carolina I found references to plays about the textile strike in Gastonia.

Certainly the lenses through which I view these scripts are colored by my own experiences, values, and perceptions. Some readers will see the scripts as I did, might find the same lines of dialogue pertinent, might agree with my assessment of their artistic merit or lack thereof. Others will disagree, may even disagree vehemently. In either case, the reevaluation of these texts is important and may lead theatre historians and researchers in American studies and popular culture to continue the investigation of the forgotten political plays of this era.

Because the approach taken in this book is historical/critical, each chapter begins with a discussion of the historical background of the play, including an examination of the careers of the playwrights and, where possible, identification of their political leanings. This is followed by an analysis of the play scripts. A list of twenty-five questions helped structure the comparative and textual criticism. They offered a convenient framework for analysis and provided opportunities to interpolate historical detail. I hope that the interplay of literary criticism with historical analysis illuminates the significance of the scripts as social history. The questions that governed the textual analysis are listed here. There are no claims that individually these questions are critical innovations; rather, they are the questions anyone researching labor plays should ask.

- How are the characters defined?
- What ethnic groups are represented?
- What is the relationship of men to men? Men to women? Women to women?

- What are the symbols of success and poverty?
- Who are the heroes?
- How is management portrayed?
- How are strikers portrayed?
- How are scabs portrayed?
- What traditional dramatic conventions are used? Chorus? Fourth wall? Soliloquies? Music? Others?
- How are scenic elements used for rhetorical effect?
- Is there documentary detail in the scripts? How does artistic interpretation defer to historical fact?
- How do people suffer in the plays? Why do they suffer?
- Are there hegemonic elements in the presentation?
- What are the propagandistic techniques used? Slogans? Speeches? Songs? Audience participation?
- What is the influence of the industry on society?
- What metaphors are used? What is the commanding image?
- What are the urban (versus) rural values exhibited?
- Are there cultures in conflict in the plays?
- How are comedic effects used?
- What are the central tensions?
- On what does the plot rest?
- What is important about the climax?
- What effect would the final scene have on the audience?
- What groups are seen as subversive? What are the symbols of the groups?
- What prejudices are evident in the appeals to the audience?

The answers to these questions constitute the central chapters of this book and serve as the bases for the critiques of each script.

The success of each production is difficult to assess. Reviews of the plays seemingly provide the most compelling evidence of their success or failure, however, in assessing the merits of politically inspired drama one cannot neglect the political motivation of the critic who pens the response. Accounts of the production of *Strike Song* that appeared in textile management publications in North and South Carolina border on diatribe, while reviewers for *New Masses* or *The Daily Worker* were uniformly laudatory of most any script that championed the rights of the worker. Although such overt prejudices are problematic in that they obscure complete historical objectivity, they are often the only contemporaneous responses to the plays in production. All of the plays sparked animated responses, if not journalistic catfights, as was the case with reviews of *Altars of Steel* in *The Atlanta Georgian* and *The Atlanta Constitution*. When confronted with political art used rhetorically, critics characteristically employ their own rhetorical means to support or reject it. The reviewers' attempts to persuade their audience, either by extending the argument of the play or positing a counterargument, are pertinent to the complete analysis a play's persuasive effect. The critic builds a case for or against a production throughout the review. Citing snippets from individual reviews unfairly truncates the reviewers' arguments in a manner analogous to reducing political rhetoric to "sound bites," yet it is the method most appropriate in this study. Interspersing selected excerpts of reviews in the analysis allows the focus of the narrative to remain on the scripts, not belaboring tangential material provided by the reviewer. But, ultimately, these excerpts are selected to support points I wish to make. The reviews offer evidence on which to build a case for the merits of each script, and readers are encouraged to read the whole review in their own subsequent studies in order to judge the validity of the conclusions drawn here. There is but one instance when contemporaneous reviews of the original production were not available: the Provincetown, Massachusetts, performances of *Strike!* The Provincetown newspapers between 1919 and 1935 were destroyed by fire—before, unfortunately, newspapers were photographed on microfilm; that record is lost to researchers. However, entries in Mary Heaton Vorse's diary (held in the Reuther Labor Archives) provide her own critical comments and clues to the responses of the Provincetown summer crowd; also, reviews of a revised version produced in Boston the next year offer some critical commentary about the play in production.

The historical circumstances surrounding a text ought not to be disassociated from it. Various critics and theorists have addressed this issue. Two in particular, C.W.E. Bigsby and Paul Newell Campbell, offer insights pertinent to the analysis of political scripts. The reader's attention is directed to them not so much because they govern the approach taken in this study, though their ideas are indeed appropriate and applicable, but because they provide a good starting point for approaching socially significant literature. Bigsby's claim that each literary text contains not only the history of its own production but also the history of its critical assimilation is thought-provoking. For him the question of authorship of theatrical works is problematic, not for the lack of a name on the title page of a script but because of a belief that all involved in the production of a play, through their own interpretive strategies, leave their mark on the work. Thus, the director, the actors, designers, and technicians have critical functions that result in a collaborative altering of the script. What an audience views in performance then becomes a multi-authored endeavor that is arguably more rhetorically effective than the text provided by the author.

Paul Newell Campbell offers a means of theatrical analysis that complements and illuminates Bigsby's position. Campbell maintains that each script nudges the audience towards a particular attitude by three means: the rhetoric of the text, the rhetoric of the production, and by a convolution of either the text or production, a rhetorical strategy that essentially mocks the original intent of the literature by turning the text or production back on itself in an ironic twist[3]. Campbell, more than Bigsby, influences the approach taken in this book.

Political theatre can be analyzed in terms of epideictic oratory—oratory originally intended to mete out praise and blame, but also intended as display and entertainment. Although epideictic oratory does not ignore forensic oratory's intent of achieving justice, or deliberative oratory's aim of finding an expedient course of action, it achieves its ends through a kind of indirection, by deepening audience values, that would become the basis for right thought and conduct. Epideictic oratory deals directly with cultural mores and beliefs. One of its distinguishing feature is that it is not intended to inculcate new values in its listeners; rather it aims at reinforcing already held beliefs. Labor plays relied upon the audience's identification with the values held by the characters. They were plays intended for audiences who already believed as the characters did. They mirrored deeply held values of family and clan, and specific regional and ethnic pride. The lack of a like-thinking audience was a contributing cause of the failure of *Steel* in its 1931 off-Broadway run, as well as of its success in its 1937 production by the International Ladies' Garment Workers' Union's Labor Stage. The audience in 1931 was a casual middle- to upper-class off-Broadway audience, while those who attended the 1937 production were lower- to lower-middle-class union members, who watched the play in union theatres and in local union halls.

Similarly, the early playreader reviews of *Altars of Steel*, the Federal Theatre Project play, unanimously recommended to Hallie Flanagan and Emmett Lavary that the script be rejected. The readers, in Washington and New York, were physically and psychologically removed from the intended audience; they grossly underestimated the regional appeal of the script to the values of southern audiences. It had been written by a Southerner, who knew that the sympathies of his audience lay with regional ownership and were informed by subconscious acceptance of patriarchal attitudes in southern industry that fostered an illusion of family in the workplace. Flanagan and Lavery chose not to reject it, and *Altars of Steel* became the most significant production of the whole Works Progress Administration enterprise in the South. In spite of reviews that attacked it as communistic, audiences flocked to the production. They identified with its sympathetic treatment of traditional southern paternalistic attitudes in industry, and its eulogizing of southern labor.

Interestingly, each play perpetrates what political media analysts Dan Nimmo and James E. Combs would call a "prelapsarian" myth—one that idealizes rural life and nostalgically looks for salvation in an agrarian past from industrialization. The metaphors and symbols used in the dramatic discourse and carried into the visual designs facilitate a neat pairing that transcends their thematic treatments of two industries. "What" the plays mean politically is supported by "how" they mean it metaphorically. The physical presence of the mill is important in all the plays, but the commanding metaphors created in the scenic elements of the textile (versus the steel) mill, differ dramatically.

In the steel plays the mill is anthropomorphized. It becomes another character and functions as a cannibalistic tyrant, devouring labor both spiritually and physically in a perverted technocratic, sacrificial ritual. The noise of the mill in *Altars of Steel* and *Steel* is something to that critics of both plays responded. Whistles, acting as disembodied voices which control and command, summon workers in the morning and send them home at the end of their shifts; the workers respond as automatons to mechanical signals. The sinister air that pervades the steel plays is conveyed in the mill's darkness and grime. Wives fear their husbands' transformation into men with hearts of steel. The hellish, nightmarish atmosphere in the steel plays is an effective rhetorical tactic, for it reinforces Manichean divisions readily perceived and accepted by the audience.

By contrast, the southern textile mill in *Strike* and *Strike Song* is present, for the most part, at a distance. It stands fort-like and impregnable. It is the castle on the hill—signifying industrial redemption from abject poverty, something built as a family enterprise to carve a place in the wilderness, or an encampment of exploitative invaders who conquer and control men for their own ends. The mill itself is never threatening or open to moral judgment or condemnation. Unlike the cotton cloth produced in the mills, a product that grew out of the same red dirt and evolved from the same natural background as those who worked the looms, the problems in this industry are manmade—industrially synthetic. Such problems typify the artificial value systems imposed by technocrats on a transforming rural economy. The quality of the moral fiber of American industrialists, and how their values weaken the fabric of society are scrutinized by the playwright and revealed to the audience.

The union organizers in the textile plays tend to be depicted as ineffectual male would-be saviors. In the steel plays they are characterized as ordinary men caught in extraordinary circumstances that thrust on them the responsibility of leadership. The use of overt religious imagery appears especially in the textile plays, while images of family dominate the steel texts. Ironically, when one examines which characters move the action in all four texts, they prove to be the female characters. The women in the two textile plays move the unionizing efforts forward; they are the protagonists in both plays, and the work of the movement is carried on by the women who succeed them. In part this accurately reflects the predominance of women in southern industry as well as their concerns for their children and their families. In part, it reflects the attitudes held by Mary Heaton Vorse and Loretta Carroll Bailey, who witnessed firsthand the suffering of families at Gastonia and the attempts by women to challenge the industrial argosy. In the collaborations between Vorse and Blake, and Bailey and Bailey, the women are most certainly the primary authors.

The steel plays, as one might expect, feature men, accurately reflecting the industry's predominantly male labor force. Both (male) playwrights, Wexley and Rogers, use women as vehicles for popular response to the union. They place the most courageous, optimistic, and even the most violent responses in the female characters. Although female roles in the steel plays are few they are sympathetic roles. Whether they are Rogers's stereotypical belles lamenting changes in their community or Wexley's women organizing "kitchen scabs" the female roles are particularly revealing and insightful.

In the present book, each play is analyzed in light of the rhetorical strategies used to appeal to and move the audience. The analysis gives close attention to the attacks on political ideologies evidenced in the plays, particularly those directed against the American Communist Party, the American Federation of Labor, and the Congress of Industrial Organizations. Whenever possible, competing ideological positions that are promoted as political alternatives, such as technocratic positions advocating scientific management, or the paternalistic stance of the agrarians, are identified. The scripts dramatize American labor history; at times doing so with respectable historical accuracy, at others, recasting incidents with poetic license to advance political arguments. The analysis of each script indicates where the playwrights used documentary detail. The documentary nature of the scripts is what makes them worthy of study. A central question underlying much of the analysis is whether these plays were merely didactic or served a more controversial purpose. *Steel*, which has been called "the most militant labor-management play of the early Thirties," and which was at one point scheduled for a tour of the northern steel strongholds of Pittsburgh, Youngstown, and Chicago, is quite different from *Altars of Steel*, intended for production in the southern steel center of Birmingham, Alabama (but which opened in Atlanta, Georgia). The tour of *Steel* was planned by Labor Stage, the theatrical arm of the International Ladies' Garment Workers' Union, and it was to be co-sponsored by other leftist theatre groups, such as the New Theatre League, the Theatre Union, and Artef, as well as the United Mine Workers.

The analysis attempts to dissect the commentary each play makes on the human condition generally, and on southern textile workers and northern and southern steelworkers specifically. The cultural milieu out of which the plays grew is important. The three plays that focus on southern labor offer interesting insights into the modern cultural dilemma faced by the South in clinging to agrarian values while simultaneously seeking economic salvation in industrialization. The attitudes toward blacks, poor whites, Northerners, and foreigners, and to an industrial value system, are reflected in the dialogue. So too are revealing references to the paternalistic nature of southern industry as reflective of southern culture. Consideration of the use of stereotypes, stock characters, and regional types is also important in the rhetorical analysis of how an audience would accept or reject the bromides of political propaganda sweetened dramatically. The anti-northern sentiment in each of the southern labor plays represents interesting appeals to audience biases, as do all of the rhetorical strategies employed by the playwrights. The analysis of such labor plays brings to light the power of the theatre to attack monolithic institutions.

The decade of the Thirties was given to such attack. The plays reflect the domestic political turmoil of the nation. The 1929 Crash, a decade of economic depression, and the gathering storm of a war in Europe that threatened to destroy families at home and friends abroad, shook the nation. The public felt a need to assess what was happening and discover the causes. Responses to these problems were mirrored in academic studies in all disciplines. Two are particularly pertinent to this investigation: the rise of social scientific research, and the attempt by historians in the 1930s to analyze the interrelationship between history and psychology. One school of thought emphasized the psychology of non-dominant groups, essentially ethnic groups, who shaped labor history in the United States[4]. The interest in the merger of history and psychology found its way into non-academic literature as well, most notably in documentary texts like these plays, which redefined historical incidents and interpreted motives of individuals and groups. While scholars have identified these tendencies in the documentary plays of the Federal Theatre Project's "living newspapers," they have overlooked earlier examples of this same genre. The texts in this study provide evidence that documentary detail was an element of political theatre in the United States before its use by the Federal Theatre Project.

Documentary theatre employs an artistic strategy to stir audience emotions. The commanding metaphor of these scripts is embodied in the character of the common man. The audience identifies individually and collectively with the common elements of the individual's struggle to survive in an industrial world. There was a mythos about the character of Ella May Wiggins, who participated in the Gastonia textile strike of 1929, that superseded the actual details of her life. Like Rosa Parks of the black civil rights movement, the individual, Ella May Wiggins, came to personify a group. The struggle of the protagonist in many instances is the literal struggle of the audience watching the events. The scripts look past the specific individual in the labor play to the multilingual, multiethnic labor force watching it. In some cases audience members actually took part in the events being dramatized. Their collective story, told repeatedly in the guise of different characters fighting for personal freedoms against impersonal industries, serves as the central theme of these plays.

The characters in the plays occupy the bottom rung of the American industrial ladder. Ironically, it is a rung occupied by various ethnic groups who cling to their ethnicity individually yet rally 'round their collective identity as Americans working to move up the economic ladder through their labor. The idea that work would provide economic and social freedom was embraced by tens of thousands of immigrants who found themselves in American mills and factories. Any analysis of the social milieu represented dramatically in these scripts requires consideration of what has been called the mirage of "Americanization." Historians like Ware provide an analysis of the process of "Americanization" that is particularly pertinent to understanding the sociological interrelationships evident in these plays. In becoming "Americanized," potential leaders within the various ethnic groups, those who achieved a level of financial and professional success, were drawn off and subsumed into the general American community. The second generation of leaders exhibited a unique ability to exploit group consciousness for their own ends. Often they manifested a defensive posture towards the broader American community. The absorption of financially successful leaders into the dominant culture helped perpetuate stereotypes that denigrated the remaining members of the group, playing upon their low economic and social status. As Ware notes, "The Polish-American doctor or business man is an "American"; the Polish-American worker remains a "Polack." This is an implicit issue in the plays, particularly in those documenting the Gastonia textile strike. What becomes painfully evident in these plays is that the most abusive mill foremen are Southerners who rose through the ranks to management but have disassociated themselves from their own in the ranks of labor. The mill managers were "Americanized;" in becoming management they broke the bond that tied them to labor.

The laborers in the textile mills bore the stigma of "poor white trash." They were the hillbillies and agrarian refugees. In some minds, they ranked below blacks in the social hierarchy. Clearly evident in these plays are the social hierarchies at work in the steel and textile industries—hierarchies, Ware notes, that:

grew out of the process whereby each new immigrant group has come in at the bottom of the economic and social pyramid, raising by its new presence the last group which occupied that position. The story of the manner in which each new group has been characterized as inferior mentally, morally, and culturally, with a taste for the attributes of poverty, and poverty-producing habits of shiftlessness and irresponsibility, is too familiar to bear repeating (Ware 73).

That stratification, as it is portrayed and identified in what is traditionally considered the basic framework of cultures— family, city, corporation, and military—is the skeleton around which the plays are shaped. All take place in a company town controlled by an industry that, when pushed, uses private and state militias to keep workers in line. All feature a family and a single individual within the family who responds to industrial abuse by a commitment to political action[5].

The "labor wars" divided families as brutally as had the Civil War.

Immigrant fathers warned their sons to "show appreciation," a refrain heard in Wexley's *Steel*, wives cajoled husbands not to jeopardize their source of income by joining a union and were called disparagingly, "kitchen scabs" while women in the textile mills, abandoned by their husbands, fought tenaciously to keep their children out of the mills. A model for analysis of the theatrical representation of the labor wars can be found in the traditional approaches employed by historians to analyze war.

Looking at the labor wars as they are depicted dramatically, one must decide whether to concentrate on the propaganda that vehemently directed sentiment against managerial groups and big business, to focus on the dramatic vignettes of the chronic abuses and mistreatment of labor in the steel and textile industries vignettes that reinforce the view that chronic sociological tensions erupted in labor violence[6]. War and drama identify heroes. The playwrights elevate the protagonists in these labor plays to folk hero stature. Typically such heroes represent anti-industrial, agrarian values and function rhetorically as symbols of a group's perseverance in the face of industrial pressures to homogenize, or "Americanize." Considerations that govern the analysis of the specific scripts center on the role of the historian in the investigation of aspects of theatre history—thus cultural history; on the function of the text as rhetorical discourse—which encompasses traditional examinations of social order, ethos, and point of view; and on the audience, the final component, which not only accepts or rejects the arguments in performance but helps shape and structure the performance by its presence and response. The audience is of particular interest when one considers the literary responses to industry.

This study examines only a few of the unfamiliar questions and texts in a largely unexplored area. It attempts to reclaim a lost body of theatrical work by placing the plays in a social/historical context. Originally, I planned to include copies of the scripts, so that readers might assess the analysis themselves. However, reproducing the texts became prohibitive in terms both of production costs and in the final size of the book. Anyone interested in this area is urged to secure copies of the scripts so that the ground of academic investigation into labor plays can be broadened. The analysis presented here is offered for discussion. If there are misinterpretations, errors, or oversights, they are my own, and I welcome their correction by others who follow me. Including the scripts would have facilitated responses to the contentions presented here; they stand as the primary source material on which this study is based. Fortunately, the scripts are readily available to anyone requesting them. *Strike Song: A Play of Southern Hill People*, by Loretta Carroll Bailey and James Osler Bailey, can be found in the North Carolina Collection of the University of North Carolina, Chapel Hill. William Dorsey Blake's *Strike: A Play in a Prologue and Fourteen Scenes* can be obtained from the Library of Congress. The "revised version," *Strike!!! A Play in a Prologue; Thirteen*

Scenes and an Epilogue, is held in the Mary Heaton Vorse Collection, Archives of Labor and Urban Affairs, at Wayne State University. Thomas Hall Rogers's *Altars of Steel* is in the Library of Congress Federal Theatre Project Collection. Both the 1931 and 1937 versions of *Steel*, by John Wexley are among in the John Wexley Papers at the State Historical Society of Wisconsin. Each script offers unique insights into the labor movement in the United States as well as political responses to unionization of industry and individuals.

Examining for the first time such plays as *Strike, Strike Song, Altars of Steel*, and *Steel* adds to the continuing evaluation of the period and the social forces that shaped it. These plays are not isolated artistic statements of the period. One cannot consider labor drama without recognizing that it was part of a larger artistic response evident in other polemical arts of the period. One finds the same issues raised in songs of Woody Guthrie, or depicted in the paintings of Thomas Hart Benton and Edward Hooper, in the WPA murals commissioned for public buildings across the country, and embodied in the narrative literature of John Dos Passos or Langston Hughes. The consideration of political issues in all art forms of this period would result in an encyclopedia of cultural history of the Depression. The focus here is on the particular form that is perhaps the most transitory; dance might be deemed more elusive for historical reconstruction of the performance event. By its very nature, performance art exists for a matter of hours, then disappears. When it reappears in subsequent performances, it is altered by a myriad of changes which are slight when compared with the major alteration of each performance's audience and its unique responses. Because of the elusive and transitory quality of dramatic production, a search for constants is required. One such constant is the rhetorical intent of the script—though, of course, even this is open to interpretation and argument.

In analyzing labor texts from this period, one must try to assess the underlying motivations of the groups who produced them. In 1931, on the first page of the first issue of *Workers' Theatre*, Albert Prentis outlined several principles he believed should govern the writing and production of labor scripts. His premise, that the theatre was but one of the media that needed to be developed by organized workers to reach the unorganized, was supported by various leftist groups throughout the decade and is reflected in the scripts in this study. Prentis felt that for maximum usefulness, a workers' theatre needed to subscribe to three primary principles: "First, it must awaken to class consciousness leading to organization; second it must go to the masses rather than wait for the masses to come to it; and third, it must have mass appeal"[7]. It is with some wariness that I attribute these motivations to the plays presented here. Simply restructuring the past through the documentary evidence one finds is challenging enough; ascribing polemic motivations to playwrights and production companies and inferring their values more than fifty years after the fact places a historian or critic in a precarious position. Yet these are assessments that need to be made in the analysis of dramatic literature. In examining how these plays function as didactic vehicles and as entertainment, we interpret the political and moral values of playwrights and their artistic attempts to inculcate those values in the audience through a union of rhetoric and theatre.

This approach sees labor plays as a kind of political discourse. Michael Leff and Andrew Sachs, in their article "Words, the Most Like Things: Iconicity and the Rhetorical Text," offer a unique perspective on the rhetorical function of a text. Their claim that rhetorical meaning is "designed to reach outward to the world beyond the text and to guide the audience's understanding of and behavior within that world" is applicable in the analysis of political drama. For Leff and Sachs the criticism of a work must retain an audience perspective, but not necessarily one that relies on the measurement of audience response for its validity. The process of rhetorical criticism then "seeks to explain how the rhetorical performance invites certain kinds of response. Working from the evidence within the text, the critic proceeds to make inferences about what the work is designed to do, how it is designed to do it, and how well that design functions to structure and transmit meanings within the realm of public experience"[8].

In the four plays discussed here, audiences were continually asked to assess the primary source material: the historical incidents and attitudes that gave rise to labor disputes and violence. More than that, they were asked to assess the praise and blame articulated in the dialogue, and to take sides. The moral argument laid out in each script was one in which the audience was implicitly expected to participate. The plays were written to generate political discussion that would inevitably spill out of the theatre into homes and factories. The approach taken here in the textual analysis attempts to draw the inferences that Leff and Sachs suggest regarding the function of such devices as metaphor, analogy, and narrative in a text rhetorical in nature.

The interdisciplinary nature of modern literary analysis is reflected in the many academic disciplines engaging in such analysis—among them American studies, feminist studies, ethnic studies, and studies in popular culture. One cannot read leftist plays of the 1930s without recognizing that this core of modern dramatic literature is fraught with political issues that can be legitimately addressed by critics employing multidisciplinary perspectives. Yet approaching such issues in literary analysis is not without its methodological or political problems. An overarching motivation in the preparation of this book was to examine the significance of the plays in their social and political context. To do so today one is often asked to identify on which side of the theoretical table set by the "new historicists" and "new critics" one sits. Ironically, the debates engaged in by the new historicists, and the new critics are ones in which the theatre critic and theatre historian rarely partake. The body of new criticism and of the theory that establishes the tenets of historicism revolve around the novel; surprising little of historical/critical analysis is applied to dramatic texts by contemporary literary critics. These texts have been excluded from the canon of humane letters.

The canon itself poses problems for many who investigate and teach dramatic literature, but the exclusion of drama does not evoke surprise. Jonas Barish lays bare "the antitheatrical prejudice" in his book of the same title. How this applies to the current historical/critical debate was outlined neatly by Susan Harris Smith in her article "Generic Hegemony: American Drama and the Canon." Smith adroitly identifies "the many charges laid against American drama" and labels the "four sweeping generalizations [that] recur most often; . . . American drama is emotional rather than intellectual, subliterary rather than literary, theatrical rather than dramatic, and derivative rather than indigenous"[9]. It is useful to consider these charges in relation to the plays in the present study—first, that these texts are emotional. Effective theatre requires emotion: in the scripts, in the representation by the actors, and in the use of appeals to stir the audience and forge identification. But emotion does not deprive a production of its intellectual or philosophical substance.

The second charge, that American drama falls into a category deemed "subliterary," is condescending and suggests a bias that no doubt contributes to the paucity of academic analysis given to American plays of this period. Admittedly, the plays examined here are not well known, but they are not without merit. Each playwright enjoyed at very least, a regional literary reputation, and Vorse and Wexley's extended nationally. As for the third claim, these plays are most certainly theatrical, all have large casts, some numbering over a hundred people. The sheer size of the production company lent itself to mass spectacle, a device exploited by the authors. However, these elements do not diminish or retard the dramatic impact of the text in performance. The entertainment (versus the propaganda) qualities of each script are important factors in the analysis of the rhetorical statements made by the productions both aurally and visually. In the case of *Altars of Steel* the set design contributed to the rhetorical stance of the production by using scenic elements designed to simulate steel—right down to the proscenium curtain.

Finally, these plays are indigenous in their thematic treatment of American labor and ethnic groups, and in their use of a robust and uniquely American production style. The two Gastonia strike plays are notable in their use, which some might find derivative, of documentary detail from European agit-prop plays. But they seem to draw more from the documentary techniques of Elia Kazan and Elmer Rice in the '20s, which merged into the living newspaper techniques of the Federal Theatre Project of the '30s, than from other external influences. This may be the most important and compelling reason to examine these scripts. They are early examples of American docudramas.

Smith, in turn, finds Russell Reising's analysis of the "paradox of

American literature" useful. She asserts that "while many critics of American literature attempt to define the radical or oppositional nature of American literature, . . . the theorists tend to separate literary significance and reflection from social and political significance"[10]. This finding is true of these plays. Incidental references to them in critical studies of the period focus on the radical politics evident in the plays yet fail to place them within a larger context. They do not analyze the audience to which they played, the industries and regions which spawned them, the political predilections of their authors, the theatrical organizations which produced them, or the critical responses they evoked. Her claim is valid and pertinent. In the 1920s and '30s American drama resisted prescriptions about the style and function of literature and became the "enemy of literature" when it became a weapon for propagandistic ends. However, her contention that American drama during this period was "firmly rooted in historical and political consciousness, more often challenging than reaffirming received American values, and taking an adversarial and critical position toward dominant ideologies" is debatable with respect to the texts of labor drama[11]. A repeated claim in the present analysis of the four texts is that they do in fact reaffirm and appeal to received American values of a very specific group—labor. The assertion that drama, particularly propagandistic drama, became an "enemy of literature" strikes a nerve. One is led to speculate why these plays have not been subjected to critical inquiry before now. What has prevented historians and scholars in several disciplines from investigating the propaganda plays of the 1930s that focus on industry?

The theatre and the academy both suffered from the scourge of the communist witchhunt, first under the Dies Committee in the late 1930s, then during the McCarthy era. The lack of interest in leftist scripts for so long afterward may have been part of the political fallout. This notion receives support from Harold Clurman, who thirty years ago wrote that "there is a tendency nowadays to downgrade the Thirties. The reason for this is that the prevailing mood of the Thirties was what used to be called 'left of center.'" He charged that the "intelligentsia" retreated from the examination of such literature in the late Forties, when phrases like "Iron Curtain" entered our national vocabulary. "'Left of center,'" he wrote, "might be construed as something worse than liberalism. To be 'radical' implied that one might be tainted with some degree of 'pink.'" Caspar Nannes, in his book *Politics in the American Drama*, offers a more sanguine rationale. He feels that political plays had an immediacy that allowed their original audiences to identify the issues and side with political positions quickly. He maintains that this immediacy is the ephemeral quality that contributed to the success of the plays but that it is precisely this timeliness that evaporates, leaving few period political plays with appeal for later audiences[12]. Yet a convincing argument can be made not only for their timeliness but for their influence on political theatre today. The role of women as labor leaders in the textile plays is unique and overlooked in artistic commentary. American labor literature that dramatized social problems of the 1930s may well stand as part of a larger movement, or even impetus for documentary dramas of recent years that range in scope from Peter Cheeseman's scripts depicting British labor on the legitimate stage to television docudramas that regularly dramatize the extraordinary circumstances that befall ordinary individuals. The form and function of political drama, be it enacted on stage or electronically, is of unflagging interest to cultural historians and critics.

Whereas scholars today engage in discussion about the new historicism and the new criticism playwrights of the 1930s became part of a movement called "new theatre." The "new theatre" was labeled a "genuine people's theatre;" it was said to have sprung from a different philosophy of life, a "philosophy of hope and struggle"[13]. How a few playwrights responded to the political calling of the "new theatre" during the troubled years of the 1930s is the focus of this study. Their plays embody the spirit of the movement and the spirit of the times that led many to call their work radical, didactic, or to disparage it as propaganda. The "new theatre" was, in fact, a genuine people's theatre, one that strove to go to the masses and to have mass appeal, as Prentis advised. It was not a theatre that lent itself readily to Broadway productions or commercial success. To investigate the history of leftist dramatic literature in the United States, one must look past the commercial theatre in metropolitan New York to the side streets, the back alleys, and the dust-covered roads trampled by American labor. Leftist theatre was intended for a different audience, a working-class audience whose pieties and beliefs were reinforced by their very dramatization. I hope that in the analysis of the four labor plays presented here the reader comes to understand the commitment and sincerity of an artistic movement that championed the rights of American labor.

NOTES

1. Several studies in the last twenty-five years offer excellent examinations of how the theatre was used as a vehicle for social change and political criticism. Among these are: Daniel Aaron, *Writers on the Left: Episodes in American Literary Communism* (New York: Harcourt Brace and World, 1961); Malcolm Goldstein, *The Political Stage: American Drama and Theater of the Great Depression* (New York: Oxford University Press, 1974); Morgan Himmelstein's *Drama Was a Weapon* (New Brunswick, N.J.: Rutgers University Press, 1963); Ira A. Levine *Left-Wing Dramatic Theory in American Theatre* (Ann Arbor: University of Michigan Press, 1985); Caspar H. Nannes, *Politics in the American Drama* (Washington: The Catholic University of America Press, 1960); Gerald Rabkin *Drama and Commitment: Politics in the American Theatre of the Thirties* (Bloomington: Indiana University Press, 1964); Sam Smiley *The Drama of Attack: Didactic Plays of the American Depression* (Columbia: University of Missouri

Press, 1972).

2. Richard Harvey Brown, *Society as Text: Essays on Rhetoric, Reason and Reality* (Chicago: University of Chicago Press, 1987), pp. 110, 4; and Caroline F. Ware, ed., *The Cultural Approach to History* (Port Washington, New York: Kennikat Press, 1940), p. 12–13.

3. C. W. E. Bigsby, "A View from East Anglia," *American Quarterly* 41 (March 1989): 131–32. See also Paul Newell Campbell, "The Rhetoric of Theatre," *Southern Speech Communication Journal* 48 (Fall 1982): 11–21.

4. Goodwin Watson, "Clio and Psyche: Some Interrelations of Psychology and History," in Ware, p. 34.

5. Ware, pp. 73, 39, 64.

6. Ware, pp. 6–7, 9.

7. Albert Prentis, "Basic Principles," *Workers' Theatre*, vol. 1, May 1931, p. 1.

8. Michael Leff and Andrew Sachs, "Words the Most Like Things: Iconicity and the Rhetorical Text," *Western Journal of Speech Communication*, 54 (Summer 1990): 256. This particular issue of *WJSC* is a special issue on rhetorical criticism, edited by John Angus Campbell. Each of its articles has interesting application to analysis of theatrical texts, though their authors focus on rhetorical criticism of the texts of historically significant speeches. Of interest to readers in this study might be: Michael Calvin McGee, "Text, Context and the Fragmentation of Contemporary Culture," J. Robert Cox's "On 'Interpreting' Public Discourse in Post Modernity"; and Celeste Condit, "Rhetorical Criticism and Audiences: The Extremes of McGee and Leff"— all contained in this issue.

9. Susan Harris Smith, "Generic Hegemony: American Drama and the Canon," *American Quarterly* 41, no.1 (March 1989): 116.

10. Harris Smith, p. 117.

11. Harris Smith, p. 117.

12. *Famous American Plays of the 1930s,* ed. Harold Clurman (New York: Dell Publishing: 1959), p. 1; and Nannes, p. x.

13. "Editorial Foreword," *Theatre Workshop* 1, no.3 (April 1937), pp. 8–9.

CHAPTER 2

Strike Song and the
Textile Strike of 1929

The contradictory nature of the South, agrarian and industrial, genteel and violent, makes the task of analyzing southern literature a complicated one. Descriptions of the South are conveyed in binary, or dualistic, images that modern analysts identify as patriarchal or populist, aristocratic or democratic, cultured or rustic, sleepy or bustling. Richard Gray sees these contradictions as a "tug of war between two different political vocabularies, two separate mythologies which continued in Southern life as well as thought." The Gastonia textile strike of 1929 ripped open the political animosities of the region and, like the Scopes Trial of 1925, became the *cause célèbre* of the liberal press in the nation. The South was perceived as another country, where people spoke differently, lived differently, and thought differently. More significantly, southern textile workers were paid differently. Between 1849 and 1927 the wages of southern factory workers ranged from 30 to 40 percent lower than those of the rest of the country. By the late 1920s, the average annual wage for cotton mill laborers was $673.12, or $12.94 per week, which was approximately 65 percent of that earned by northern textile workers in New England. The cotton mills proved highly attractive to northern manufacturers, who migrated south for three reasons: low wages, limited legal restrictions upon the hours of work and age of workers, and the South's traditional opposition to unionism. By 1929 the textile industry was booming in the South, particularly in North and South Carolina, but some scholars of the period believed this financial success to be directly proportional to the exploitation of southern labor that festered in the mills and finally resulted in violent strikes that same year[1].

There had been strikes in the textile industry in the late 1800s, but they had been largely symbolic and there were no cases of damage to mill property, and few instances of harm to strikebreakers. Violence in the South was often racially motivated, but such was not the case in the textile strikes. Robert Ingalls notes that "the textile industry relied on a white labor force, which reduced the potential for industrial violence sparked by racial animosities"[2].

The Gastonia strike was not racially motivated in the sense that white managers abused black workers. It had a racial, or more accurately a class, motivation only in the sense that a largely white work force, composed predominately of women and children, was thought of and treated as "poor white trash," not merely by mill owners and foremen but by the middle class and gentry. These were individuals below blacks in the social hierarchy since Reconstruction. James Agee and others wrote powerfully of the struggles of poor southern whites in the late 1920s and early 1930s. The photographic portraits in Agee's *Let Us Now Praise Famous Men* look out hauntingly, while his narrative deepens our understanding of the despair and resignation felt by these individuals. Loretta Bailey would embark on a similar chronicle when she took to the hills with a noted southern photographer, Bayard Wooten.

The plight of such women and children who labored ten hours a day in the mills, and the violence wreaked upon them by marauding terrorist groups of "upstanding" businessmen and law officials, became a focus of the national press. The Gastonia textile strike prompted artistic as well as journalistic responses. The two plays examined in this study, *Strike Song*, by Loretta Carroll Bailey and J. O. Bailey, and *Strike!*, by William Dorsey Blake, are notable for their use of documentary detail—detail derived from eyewitness accounts of the Baileys and of Mary Heaton Vorse, the labor journalist who covered the strike for *The Nation*, and on whose novel Blake based his play. Other plays on this theme, such as *Let Freedom Ring*, by Albert Bein, toured under the sponsorship of the New Theatre League. (Interestingly, actors from this cast were later solicited to act in the company that was to have toured with John Wexley's *Steel*, the last play in this study.) The Gastonia strike served as a focal point for the dramatic representation of labor problems for a number of reasons. It was melodramatic; it involved a classic struggle between good and evil, the oppressed and the oppressors; it had music; and it had clear-cut heroes, heroines, and villains. The most important figure was Ella May Wiggins, a mother of five, shot to death at a rally. The story of Ella May Wiggins's death in the strike reached folkloric proportions soon after it occurred.

William E. Lightfoot points out that there are two kinds of murder legends in southern lore, one that focuses on the murderer, and one on the victim. According to Lightfoot, "Ella May Wiggins' story was retold so often that it was raised to the level of 'murder legend.'" Not only was Ella May Wiggins one of the labor movement's most prominent victims, but she helped to establish protest music as a separate genre rooted in the labor protests of the South. She, along with Aunt Molly Jackson, Florence Reece, and Sarah Ogan Gunning, is credited "with boosting the morale of striking workers while bringing nationwide attention to the living and working conditions in the South." Upon her death her songs were published in *The Nation* and *New Masses,* and they were sung at labor rallies in the North and South. Like the protest movement of the 1960s and '70s, which found a voice in music, "the protest song movement of the 1930s and 1940s was confined to a narrow spectrum of Americans—labor activists, radical intellectuals and some college students"[3]. The audiences of the strike plays generally reflected this same narrow spectrum.

Strike Song was written for the Carolina Playmakers, a university theatre group founded in 1918 by Frederick H. Koch at the University of North Carolina at Chapel Hill. The Playmakers far surpassed the amateurish standards of ordinary university theatre. Their productions were reviewed in *The New York Times* and in leading theatre journals of the period. The quality of their scripts and productions was extraordinary, as was Koch's innovative concept of what dramatic themes should be treated. He trained his students to write native American dramas, using the stories, dialects, songs, superstitions, and trials and tribulations of the mountain and coastal inhabitants of the rural South. From his group emerged several playwrights and actors who achieved national prominence, most notable among them Paul Green. An ambitious playwright who often shared billing with Green on the Playmaker's tours in the late twenties and early thirties was Loretta Carroll Bailey, who wrote *Strike Song*. Her story, her ability to dramatize the conditions and family circumstances of textile workers through documentary evidence, and her life-long dedication to raising the social consciousness of citizens of the "New South," reveal as much about southern labor strife as about the evolution of political theatre.

Loretta Carroll came from "sturdy Southern stock." Unlike many in the rural South in the early part of the twentieth century, she came from a well educated and prosperous family. Her great-grandfather, Eli J. Hine, was a prosperous miller and staunch church-goer. He and his wife Keziah Loretta Raper Hine raised eight children in the Moravian Friedland community. Their eldest child married a school teacher who taught in the first public school in Forsyth county, North Carolina. Her grandmother, Mrs. Hege, also raised her two daughters in the Moravian Friedland community. Of these, Loretta's mother, Connie, married Wiley Totten Carroll and subsequently had by him several children[4].

According to her eldest daughter, Nancy Bailey Rich, herself a professor at North Carolina State University, Loretta was born in 1908. As a young child she lived in Winston-Salem, about two blocks from the Moravian village of Salem, where she took music lessons. The Moravian motto, "Unitas Fratrum," United in Brotherhood, held special meaning for her. Tragedy and loss touched her early: When she was eight her father left for work one morning, never to return home again. Her mother supported her children by giving piano lessons. This seemingly innocuous and proper enterprise for a single mother shook the roots of the community—because Mrs. Carroll taught piano to the children of the "colored families" as well as the white. Loretta often said that her mother "'struck a blow for freedom' by doing what she thought was right, even if it meant defying social conventions of the day." Loretta attended R. J. Reynolds High School and this is where the seeds of her civil rights advocacy began to germinate. She quickly gained recognition as a talented debater. Her oratorical facility was an extension of her life-long love of writing. While in high school she worked after classes for the Winston-Salem *Journal* writing "high school" news. In print, as in speaking, she often took the maverick position and served as a student advocate, gently taking school officials to task for foolish rules. In her senior year her talent for compelling drama received accolades when her play won the state playwriting contest[5].

At R. J. Reynolds High School she met her husband, James Osler Bailey. She was a student in his class and probably participated in the plays that he directed there. Rich observes, "I rather think that he was fascinated with this remarkable student—and that if they had not married, he would not have been caught up in the liberalism that their marriage brought to him. He had a rather staid, Baptist up-bringing. Once caught, I think he brought his share of intellectual enthusiasm and literary expertise to bear on the relationship and productivity, but the real force for peoples' rights came from her"[6].

Upon graduating from high school Loretta Carroll went to the Woman's College, now the University of North Carolina at Greensboro, where, though she did not complete her degree, she caught the attention of Dr. Taylor, the sole drama professor. She married James Osler Bailey in January of her freshman year and went with him to the University of North Carolina at Chapel Hill, where he taught and pursued his graduate work while she continued her course work towards a bachelor's degree. Rich's assessment of her parents' early marriage reflects an idyllic academic community, supportive, friendly, and intellectually and socially alive. The Baileys lived in a tiny house referred to as the "Pratt cottage," later moving to a small two bedroom house at the end of Berman Court. Here at one point, according to his daughter, Bailey supported seven people (family and relatives) on his instructor's salary, working nights typing manuscripts to make ends meet[7].

Rich described their friends as among the most influential figures at Chapel Hill during the 1930s. They included Anita Nix, Archibald Henderson (the biographer of George Bernard Shaw), Gertrude Coffin, Horace Mann, Olive Stone, Frederick Koch, Samuel Seldon, Johnny Booker and Paul Green, with whom they lived for a short period. Loretta worked for William T. Couch, editor of the University of North Carolina Press, and also of the landmark work, *Culture in the South*. Frank Graham, the president of UNC–Chapel Hill, was said to have stopped by to chat occasionally. From her daughter's perspective, Loretta C. Bailey was a "free spirit, confident of herself, but eager to learn from her 'elders.'. . . She would sit for hours talking with Mrs. Archibald Henderson. . . . This was an exciting time in her life for Chapel Hill was an intellectual center in the South, and she felt a part of it."[8]

Both Baileys became involved in the theatrical activities of the Carolina Playmakers. Loretta enrolled in courses at the university and often toured with the Playmakers. J. O. Bailey was a student in Frederick Koch's courses and also acted in many of the Playmaker productions. His one-act play, *Nat Macon's Game*, was produced by the Playmakers. While J. O. Bailey may have "had a passion for the theatre, especially the Little Theatre," it was his wife who possessed the greater interest in actually writing for the theatre. J. O. Bailey would later become nationally known for his *Pilgrims Through Space and Time*, the book which helped make science fiction an academically respectable area of investigation. He ended his career as an internationally recognized Hardy scholar[9].

However, it was Loretta Bailey who envisioned herself as a playwright and began to write her own scripts. Through her close associations with the Chapel Hill intelligentsia and her natural interest in drama, she became involved in the work being done by Frederick Koch and found his insistence that students write about the "folk" congenial to her political inclinations. Loretta Bailey, budding playwright, joined forces with photographer, Bayward Wooten. Wooten, who photographed the Playmaker productions and would later publish photographic records of Carolina gardens, had proposed to her that they interview and photograph the poor "mountain folk" to produce a record of "conditions as they existed in Appalachia in those days." However, as Bailey would later recount to her daughter, "things were happening in the Gastonia mills," and she became interested in them. There were stories of machine guns posted on top of the mills aimed at striking workers, and there was talk of strikes. By Rich's account, it was Frank Graham who suggested to the Baileys that a play be written about the trouble brewing at the Gastonia mill. "They were inspired by their evening's talk with Dr. Frank, and sat down that night to write the play. . . . It was written during a single night—at least in rough draft. . . . The purpose of this play's writing was indeed to provoke consideration of civil rights problems relative to mill workers"[10].

Loretta C. Bailey's interest in civil rights extended beyond the confines of the university. She became editor of *The Peoples' Rights Bulletin*, and in the early 1930s she used her editorial skills to assist William Couch with such University Press books as *These Are Our Lives*. However, Loretta Bailey spent her life involved in the theatre. She coached the dramatic club of the Durham, North Carolina, YWCA, and, more significantly, at the request of Koch and the president of Shaw University, a Negro college in Raleigh, she helped establish a group called the "Shaw Players." In the mid-1930s the president there felt it important to build a Negro Little Theatre, and in 1934 she produced for it three one-act plays and one three-act play. Like her mother who challenged convention by teaching music lessons to black children, she braved the repercussions against whites who worked with blacks during this time. She travelled at night by bus from Chapel Hill to Raleigh, and, Rich notes, a young black man escorted her to the bus "to be sure she was alright." On tour with the Shaw Players, Bailey was "the only white woman on the bus—and she was stoned in Henderson, North Carolina, by rednecks when they saw a bus full of black people, along with the students she was with on this tour"[11]. Unfortunately, little is known about her involvement in the development of this fledgling theatrical troop of black students in North Carolina.

More important, however, is her career as a playwright. Bailey wrote several plays. Arguably the most important are *Job's Kinfolks*, published as a one-act play in *Carolina Folk Plays* and as a three-act play by Walter Baker Company; *Cloey*, a one-act play published in *Carolina Folk Comedies;* and *Strike Song*, written in collaboration with her husband but never published. Both Baileys supported the Gastonia strike. Their interest and activities on behalf of the strikers permeated their home, and their connection with organizers, sympathizers, and strikers was more than casual. They knew strikers who were arrested and continued in their support after they were imprisoned. Their daughter recalls telling family visitors that her parents' friends lived in the state penitentiary, and also waiting in the car on Sunday drives when her parents would stop to visit these friends. "I can only assume," she writes, "that these must have been people who had been arrested during the Gastonia strikes. Who else? My parents were normal, peaceful people"[12].

The circle of friends in which the Baileys found themselves shared their interests in liberal, leftist, and labor issues, and this was reflected in their work. According to their daughter, their house "was always filled with people." Among them were some of the leading scholars in the South at the time, such as A. N. J. Den Hollander ("Nikki" to the Baileys), the Dutch scholar who travelled in the United States as a Rockefeller Foundation research fellow in social sciences between 1930 and 1932. His area of interest concentrated on rural whites in the South, and the results of his research were eventually published in *De Landelijke Arme Blanken in Zuiden der Vereenigde Staten (The Rural Poor Whites in the South of the United States)*. He contributed a chapter to Couch's *Culture in the South*. Molly Thatcher, who later married Elia Kazan, was also a frequent visitor. Rich attests that "Molly was interested in sociology and in particular interested in the Gastonia Mill problems. She (according to my mother) 'dropped in' to talk about the strikes—and went with my mother to observe them." Rich and her mother summered with the Kazans between 1944 and 1946; their common bond was an intense interest in civil rights and the theatre[13]. Bailey maintained contact with Molly Thatcher as a kindred spirit during trying times that included the collapse of the Baileys' marriage: Loretta left her husband to marry a man who had worked with her on *The Peoples' Rights Bulletin.*

The commitment to civil rights and other liberal causes remained a distinguishing characteristic of the new household. Nancy Bailey Rich speaks of her stepfather's commitment to civil rights and other liberal causes. Her description of his efforts to assist minorities in securing public housing in the 1930s moves easily to a tribute to her mother. As Loretta Bailey had said of her own mother, Rich reiterated of Loretta Carroll Bailey: "My mother always 'struck a blow for freedom'—she said—whenever she could. The people who were constantly in and out of our house were people from many places who came there because they, too, were liberals and concerned about either racism or labor problems in the South"[14].

Loretta Bailey was confident of herself and her playwriting. In approach, theme, and content her scripts were different from the others produced by the Carolina Playmakers. Her scripts were more political, and though like the others, they drew rustic characterizations from real life, hers were more documentary, more in touch with the violent undercurrent of a social movement. In 1982, when asked by her daughter to provide a record of her career, she wrote, "The story behind each play is perhaps of interest. The fact that my plays made a break away from the tenant farm plays that were the mainstay of the Playmakers needs recording but not in an 'I did this thing' manner"[15]. The transition from tenant-farm to political labor plays involved an innovative treatment of political events on stage using documentary techniques that theatrical historians have not addressed.

At first glance the friendship between Loretta Bailey and Molly Thatcher, based on shared interests and social consciousness, appears inconsequential. However, when one examines the evolution of propaganda plays, and more specifically documentary plays, in the American theatre, it is important to remember the early agit-prop scripts of Elia Kazan and Art Smith. Kazan and Smith's 1934 *Dimitroff* was the first of a series of anti-Nazi plays produced in New York in the mid-1930s. *Dimitroff* was the curtain raiser for the premiere of *Waiting For Lefty*, America's most famous labor play. In an earlier study I assert that *Dimitroff* was "a transitional work . . . that moved agit-prop toward greater realism and effect by basing its plot on a current political event." However, *Strike Song* was far ahead—four years ahead—of *Dimitroff* in its realism and political timeliness and therefore should be recognized for its role in the development of "revolutionary theatre" in this country[16].

Strike Song, written in 1930, predates other American labor plays of note by five years. What Loretta Carroll Bailey was writing in North Carolina in 1930 was tremendously innovative. This work, seen either as a direct result of the Playmakers' scriptwriting tradition or as an aberrant offshoot of it, nonetheless stands at the forefront of a native dramatic genre that employed documentary evidence in its treatment of current political issues. It is an interesting example of the early use of documentary technique in the American theatre. More importantly, it is one of the first documentary scripts to treat an American theme. Later attempts to use documentary detail, by Elia Kazan, Art Smith, and Elmer Rice in the mid-1930s focused on the documentary treatment of Nazi atrocities. The Federal Theatre Project would incorporate documentary techniques in its productions treating American themes, such as *Power* or *One Third of a Nation*, but *Strike Song* preceded the Federal Theatre Project's living newspapers. It and other labor scripts from this period have been overlooked as exemplars in the development of the documentary genre in the United States.

To examine *Strike Song* is to provide the record Loretta Bailey envisioned and illuminate its significance both as a theatrical history and an artistic representation of labor history. *Strike Song* had its first run December 10–12, 1931, billed as "a new play of southern mill people, in three acts." Loretta Carroll Bailey is listed singly as the author, although later productions would credit her husband, James Osler Bailey, with joint authorship. *Strike Song* was her second venture in writing plays about the life of mill workers in textile towns in North Carolina. An earlier play, *Job's Kinfolks* (1929), also on the subject of mill life, had met with critical acclaim and served as one of the Playmakers' touring staples for years, along with *Quare Medicine* by Paul Green. Of the nine full-length original productions listed by the Playmakers between September 1918 and January 1941, two are by Bailey; *Strike Song* and *Job's Kinfolks*[17]. *Strike Song* was entered in a play competition sponsored by the Theatre Guild in 1932, advancing to the final round of competition before losing there to another entry. This was not a loss taken easily by Bailey, who sat by Sherwood Anderson during the performance in competition; "She never wrote another play after that"[18].

The Baileys' association with Paul Green and his wife Elizabeth was a close one. The Bailey-Green correspondence between 1929 and 1938 indicates that they remained friends even after the Baileys were divorced. There is evidence that in the early years Green tried to help place Loretta's scripts with literary agents and production companies, but this too proved disappointing. A rejection letter addressed to J. O. Bailey, from Theodore Johnson, President of the Walter H. Baker Company of Boston, appears in the Green Papers. Johnson praises *Strike Song*: "It surely got under my skin. Why it's great. Its honesty is its big asset. There is a sincerity of purpose in its every line and your flag flies high and wide." But he rejects it, claiming that the Copley Theatre in Boston was "not doing any plays that have not had a Broadway production." A letter two months later reveals the Baileys' persistent efforts to have the script placed in New York. In it J. O. Bailey chronicles to Paul Green his efforts to have the play produced. He indicates that the script had been substantially revised after a two-month run, and that it had been considered by Vassar College, but was rejected there because they were producing another strike play by Tom Tippet, *Mill Shadows*. His letter notes that Barrett Clark had deemed the script "much tighter and more effective than its earlier version," and he asks for Green's assistance in "calling it to the attention of the group that did *The House of Connelly*"[19].

In October 1933 Frederick Koch, then a member of the Council of the National Theatre Conference (NTC), wrote to Rosamond Gilder, editorial secretary of the NTC, recommending *Strike Song* for inclusion in the NTC's newly organized play release service. During the 1930s the NTC tried to establish a vehicle by which "producers could reach playwrights who had unproduced scripts they would like to see staged." Essentially, it hoped to serve as a clearinghouse for unproduced manuscripts which would be highlighted in a newsletter sent to professional theatre groups. *Strike Song* had by this time been revised several times and the description of characters and incidents supplied by Bailey in a synoptic overview differs somewhat from the script extracted here[20].

Strike Song was not the only script that dramatized the strike theme in the early and mid-1930s. Strike plays were being produced at Vassar, and they were written and produced in the labor colleges at Brookwood, Bryn Mawr, and the Hudson Shore Summer School, to name but a few. Another letter from J. O. Bailey to Paul Green dated July 4, 1935, refers to another strike play, *Let Freedom Ring*, that toured through the textile centers, ultimately being produced New York[21]. Its cast would later be called upon to prepare the tour of John Wexley's *Steel* (examined in the final chapter). A linear evolution begins to reveal itself. One might chart the progress of the productions at Vassar, to Hallie Flanagan, educated at Vassar, and eventually to the documentary quality of the Federal Theatre Project plays, which seemed to rise up as a completely new American theatrical form. What becomes apparent is the relationship of the Federal Theatre Project scripts in form, tenor, and political leanings to the labor scripts being produced by university theatres and smaller, leftist production companies. These organizations were more closely associated than has been recognized.

Though it failed to be adopted by a major producing organization or to have a run in New York, *Strike Song* was produced throughout the 1930s in North Carolina including a production at the Raleigh Little Theatre around 1937 or '38. As an example of leftist southern drama it has several unique characteristics that distinguish it from other plays of the period. The most significant and innovative feature of *Strike Song* is the playwright's reliance on documentary detail. Documentary technique is ideally suited to the dramatization of trials and labor disputes; statistics, court proceedings, and documentation in the form of legislation and contemporary first-hand accounts establish the reality of the events and the factuality of the dramatic account. In short, it makes the drama credible and historically pertinent. What might be dismissed as theatrical polemicism is transformed with the inclusion of documentary elements, into persuasive performance. It is a dramatic form that relies on the audience's understanding of the event dramatized, often playing on the fact that its members may well have participated in the event and, in turn, recognize themselves as secondary characters. Audiences hear again speeches, statistics, and journalistic accounts of a political event they remember poignantly. The purpose of the performance is to remind audience members of the commitments they share and to reinforce deeply held attitudes that would lead to political action. A secondary motivation of such plays is to educate those who may not know the issues in the political concerns of the people with whom they share seats. *Strike Song* played to a collective consciousness of a region and a social class.

Reading the accounts of the Gastonia strike and the events surrounding it, one quickly realizes that the dramatic action in *Strike Song* parallels the actual incidents and characters associated with the strike. Only a thin veil of artistic license, in name changes, prevents it from becoming a literal reenactment of history. One need only read the newspaper accounts of the strike to recognize the accuracy with which the script treats the material. A more succinct chronicle of the byzantine intrigues associated with the strikes can be found in Samuel Yellen's version of the Gastonia conflict. However, it is important to remember that the details were known to every man, woman, and child in North Carolina in the late '20s and early '30s. Because southern labor plays were theatrical rhetoric, understanding them requires a knowledge of the history that spawned them. The fire of leftist theatre was fed by the volatile social and labor controversies of the late 1920s. To read Yellen's version of the Loray Mill strike, for instance, is to understand the historical basis of this theatre of social activism. The power of the scripts rests in the audiences' ability to identify the characters who speak the lines as individuals known to them, and to identify with them as workers struggling to break free of industrial oppression.

Strike Song uses the documentary details found in the accounts of Yellen and many other who wrote of the labor violence in Gastonia and Marion, N.C. But Bailey employs various rhetorical appeals to achieve the emotional and political effect desired. Character names are altered slightly to give an illusion of fictiveness, though anyone who knew the strike easily recognized Peel in Beal and Lily May in Ella May. Still, such close treatment of names and incidents regarding so volatile an incident in southern labor was courageous. It was especially courageous given that Bailey's play was produced in the very area where the violence occurred and that mill workers and management attended. The handling of the details that precipitated the violence is subtle. Bailey tends to veil the actual incidents of violence with fictional detail and ends her play before the sensational trial. (The second script in this study, *Strike*, by William Dorsey Blake, extends the treatment of the incidents past the strike itself into the court proceedings and chronicles the psychologically manipulative use of a lifelike plaster cast of the dead sheriff and the subsequent mental breakdown of one of the jurors.)

The violence depicted in the *Strike Song* is an important documentary element, as is that of the proselytizing efforts of the organizers. Both serve a rhetorical and political function in that they ask the audience to take sides. How these plays mirror the organizing efforts of American labor is as important as how they reflect American culture and specifically southern culture in the Depression. Beyond the violence the script articulates other inflammatory issues that stirred audiences and rankled the textile industry. The official response from the industry tended to focus on the use of union songs, which it felt would rally workers and boost morale. The vigor of the music and its implicit call for participation proved threatening: the songs were viewed by the mill owners as seeds of discontent blowing from the theatre on the wind of worker voices. Melodies filled with defiance and dissent took hold and like resilient weeds would not be uprooted. Ballads were a vehicle in the southern folk tradition that deified the lowly; they created a metaphoric rise in spirit, in unity, in determination, as voices rose in song. Labor songs, like hymns, offered solace and strength in their communal singing.

Textile management felt it necessary to respond to *Strike Song* soon after the play's opening, in a December 1931 issue of *Southern Textile Bulletin*, the industry mouthpiece. The review was short, but its proximity to two other articles on the same page is revealing. The article leveled criticism at the University of North Carolina for honoring Langston Hughes, who, *The Bulletin* claimed, had made insulting and blasphemous statements in an article in *Contempo*: "the radical publication of a group of former University students." The second article broadly indicted by implication and innuendo, professors and university students for being communist sympathizers. Looking at the whole page, one perceives immediately that the textile industry targeted intellectuals and students and identified these groups for their readers as the enemy. This antipathy is accurately captured in scenes in *Strike Song* and *Strike* (analyzed in the following chapter). In both plays, characters articulate mistrust of university associations, course work, and students: those who attended a university are immediately suspect, and liberal education is the handmaid of a communist plot. What the playwrights were responding to in their characterization had its roots in the industry. *The Southern Textile Bulletin's* review echoed the paranoid rhetoric of managers characterized in the scripts and takes offense at the lyrics:

COME ALL YOU SCABS IF YOU WANT TO HEAR
THE STORY OF A CRU-EL MILLIONAIRE.
ROB-ERT HENLEY WAS THE MILLIONAIRE'S
NAME,
BOUGHT THE LAW WITH HIS MONEY AND
FRAME,
BUT HE CAN'T BUY THE UNION WITH HIS MONEY
AND HIS FRAME.

What is the above? Just a verse from "The Strike Song," written by an instructor at the University of North Carolina and staged as a three-act play at Chapel Hill, N.C., last Saturday night. The play gives the public an untrue version of the strikes at Gastonia, N.C., and Marion, N.C., and it gives future strikers inspirational songs to sing just as the Communists sing the "Red International." We will have more to say when we get all the verses and lines of the play. They call loyal workers "scabs" and do not the professors have a union of their own known as the American Association of University Professors? To them everyone who does not join the union and pay dues is a "scab."[22]

One senses how accurately the plays caught the seething tensions when songs elicit such knee-jerk responses in industry bulletins. The play touched more than one nerve in the industry. *The Bulletin's* vituperation placed emphasis on the corrosive liberalness of university types, but the real danger of the production lay in its revelations about southern life and attitudes, revelations that surface in the script in an unselfconscious, almost accidental, manner. Loretta Bailey knew the workers, and she knew the South. Her ability to give voice to long-held, deeply seated attitudes regarding the paternalistic nature of southern industry and the rebellious responses of a class of workers disparaged in the industrial hierarchy, is unique in its authenticity. She followed closely Koch's admonition to write about "the folk" and this allowed them to see themselves as participants in a holy war for individual rights. Her play did more than give workers "inspirational songs" as *The Bulletin* claimed; it gave them heroes and a way to understand their place historically and emotionally in a complex political issue. In the days before television her script allowed them to see their story reenacted. They saw and heard themselves, their friends, and their enemies again and again, and they were able to take visceral satisfaction in the portrayal of their righteousness.

THE SCRIPT

The play opens in a store, the back room of which has been burned away. The rubble does not affect the store's interior, where the "store-front philosophers" sit on bins and take up sides on local politics. A simpleminded, childlike man, Henry Morris, sings "On Top of Old Smokey," continuing through the not-often-heard second verse, which is most significant for this production.

A thief they will rob you
They'll take all you have
But a false heart True lover
Will send you to your grave[23].

This theme of betrayal permeates the play. Henry breaks off his song to say that he is "pestered," because he believes "Mr. Steve's forgot me"—a statement that functions on two levels. Steve Baird, the bankrupt owner of the Saxber Mill, is selling it to outside interests. Though overshadowed by other characters in the play, Baird is actually the protagonist; it is he who undergoes the necessary recognition and reversal in the script. But in this opening scene he serves as the scapegoat for local frustration. Literally and figuratively, he has sold out. On the most superficial level, Henry is slighted because Baird has invited other musicians to entertain at the auction of the mill. More importantly, however, Baird has forgotten the town, which has for decades relied on the mill and his family for employment, compassion, and understanding. Mr. Steve has, for all intents and purposes, forgotten his cultural roots. This sense of loss and betrayal is underscored with the song and a subsequent discussion in the first scene of "dead folks." The central tension involves the selling of the Saxber Mill to the oppressive owners of the Caroleen Mills, thereby, in effect, selling the former Saxber employees to a new management that will not care for them as family in the tradition of southern paternalism.

Exposition embodied in conversation in the first scene identifies Lily May Brothers as a strike leader at the Caroleen Mills and Lije Bensen as another striker, who will feature prominently. The first act also reveals the presence in the town of a vigilante group called "The Committee of One Hundred," also known as "Black Masks," who terrorize the strikers. It was they who burned the back of the store where the strikers used to meet. Henry's refusal to sing strike songs because they are "songs designed to draw bullets." (Act 1, Scene 1, line 3) leads one quickly to recognize music as a powerful instrumentality.

Music and songs are vital as propagandistic elements in this play and underscore the documentary nature of the production. Lily May, a prominent secondary character, achieves notoriety not merely as a strike leader but also as a balladeer and composer of strike songs. Her unique ability to draw songs from the labor experience is one of the colorful threads running through this production. This parallels her real-life counterpart, Ella May Wiggins, whose "song ballits" rallied strikers at the mills and in the tent city outside the Gastonia city limits. Ella May's lyrics and those of other balladeers are changed slightly to reflect the names used in the play, and at times the lyrics of one song are combined with those of another. In *Strike Song* all the ballads are attributed to Lily May. The effect of the proselytizing songs of the martyred organizer would have been very powerful, since they were known to the audience. A comparison of the actual lyrics with those used in the plays makes obvious the use of documentary detail for effect, but it also reveals a subtle poetic alteration that reflects Bailey's use of many resources pertaining to the strike. The final verse of Ella May's most popular song "Chief Aderholt," serves as an example of the multiple wells from which the playwright drew:

We're going to have a union all over the south,
Where we can wear good clothen' and live in a better house.
Now we must stand together and to the boss reply
We'll never, no, we'll never let our leaders die[24].

In *Strike Song* these lyrics serve as the final verse of a song sung by Henry Morris and a group of strikers to taunt the mill owners. The first few verses, however, are taken from a ballad written by an eleven-year-old girl—a striker by the name of Odel Corley. The lyrics as sung in *Strike Song* (1:2) are virtually identical to Corley's original lines reprinted in a 1929 article in the *Nation*. Ballads about Fred Beal, the union organizer, were popular throughout the south during the early '30s, especially in North Carolina. They helped create a mystique and lore surrounding the strike leaders that elevated them to cult figures. In *The Nation* article, Margaret Larkin refers to another ballad about Fred Beal, commenting, "It is curious to think how the little handful of organizers from the National Textile Workers Union have passed into legend already. Fred Beal, Vera Buch, George Pershing are names which will be heard for many years in the South. . . .

Let me sleep in your tent tonight, Beal,
For it's cold lying out on the ground."

According to Larkin, the cotton mill itinerants carried "these names and the story of the union in Gastonia into every section of the textile South"[25]. Bailey uses labor and religious songs as persuasive devices in *Strike Song* (1:2). The potency of music as an agent of persuasion has long been recognized: Plato advocated banning music from the Republic because of the inherent danger it posed to the State. Labor songs fall into a category of protest music currently undergoing humanistic and empirical analysis. Generally, the persuasive function of such music is considered to be five-fold. The songs have as their intent the transformation of perceptions of history or society, the prescription of courses of action, mobilization to action, and the continuance or perpetuation of the social movement from which they stem[26].

As the first act of *Strike Song* progresses, there are brief references to Lily May's remarkable oratorical skills, which prepare those few in the audience who would not know of her to accept her as a strike leader while reminding the knowledgeable audience members of her dedication and skill. But the arrival of Lily May herself is delayed, to create tension; the audience must wait for her. Anti-northern sentiments surface early in the play and are carried by the use of analogy. Mr. Will compares the violence enacted in his store to the violence experienced in the Chicago Haymarket strike: "It shows they ain't no more law and order down here than there is up North, there, in Chicago" (1:1). The effectiveness of this allusion rests on the audience's knowing the violent incidents of the labor battles in the United States and its ability to make the connection the character expects them to make. Subsequently, the discussion turns to a wrapped portrait that Stephen Baird has brought with him into the store—a portrait of his grandfather, referred to by all as "the Major." Baird had removed it from the mill before its sale. Once again the discussion reverts to Yankees, and an analogy is drawn comparing defenses against northern industrialists to staving off northern aggression during the Civil War. "The Major" in the portrait was "a powerful Yankee-fighter" and led the battle against Union soldiers on the very ground on which the Caroleen Mills stand. This site is a sacred landmark to the locals because it reminds them of a time when they held their own against the North. Its sale to northern industrialists by a family member is tantamount to desecration. The bitter irony of the Caroleen Mills, a mill now owned by Northerners, standing on this ground approaches sacrilege and is not to be underestimated as a rhetorical ploy. For Stephen Baird, direct descendent of this quintessential Yankee-fighter, to take a position at the Caroleen Mills under northern management is treasonous.

Baird's response to the criticism directed towards him is defensive: "I wouldn't lead 'em wrong for anything on earth—they're like so many kids to me" (to which Will replies that Baird "can't give up being a daddy to a passel of mill hands") offers one of the first instances of a public discussion in the American theatre of paternalism as a cultural trait in southern labor. In its forthrightness this discussion breaks new ground, labeling a psychological predisposition for a popular audience. Paternalism recurrently surfaces as an issue in the play, like the "dead folks" alluded to early in the first act. In the dramatic representation of the historical facts Bailey writes deftly and knowledgeably. Where there existed a "lively paternalism" there was stronger opposition to unionizing efforts. The paternalistic protection extended by the mill owner to his employees went beyond assistance and indebtedness in times of hardship: it included a self-protective anti-northern bias that caused workers to feel that they were being shielded from external exploitation. The history of southern paternalistic attitudes became a subject of academic discussion and investigation in the late 1920s and early '30s. Harriet Herring addressed it in her chapter "The Industrial Worker" in *Culture in the South*[27]. While this source is dated, from a revisionist perspective, it does provide useful contemporary analysis of the labor force in the South. Paternalism was something recognized in southern industry by those who studied it, but not something discussed among mill workers, who were its beneficiaries and victims. Bailey identifies it, labels it, and expresses it in the play at a level workers would understand.

As the argument between Baird and Will over betrayal, paternalistic attitudes, and Baird's role as labor leader subsides, the plot moves forward with the entry of Thomas Peel, the northern strike organizer. His character immediately identifies another important cultural motif found in three of the labor plays treating southern industry: the religious overtones of the strike. "You know there's one thing that bothers me about this whole southern textile strike business—and that's the sort of religious flavor the thing takes on. Why, they join the Union like they join the church" (1:1). Peel lays bare cultural attitudes at work in the characters and in the audience. In these strike plays the union leader is depicted in messianic terms, usually as an idealistic young man willing to sacrifice his life for the union cause. His speeches and pronouncements are taken as gospel by loyal followers. The leader is most often an outsider; in *Strike Song* this proves to be an important distinction, for it explains the inability of the northern organizers to understand the southern mindset and cultural milieu. This liability, while treated overtly in *Strike* (see the next chapter) remains an understated concern in *Strike Song*, written with a southern audience in mind. Bailey recognized the dysfunctional properties inherent in a people's movement led by individuals who failed to understand the people, and she gives voice to this problem by having Peel's first lines articulate his inability to understand the workers he has been sent to organize.

The labor disputes and exemplary abuse depicted in the strike plays center on the use of "stretch-outs," a method to increase worker productivity. This exploitative chicanery, disguised as "scientific management," was introduced in 1927 at the Loray Mill at Gastonia, North Carolina. When confronted by Baird—what does he expect to "get out of all this trouble you're stirring up?"—Peel's answer eventually comes round to "shorter hours, better pay, and an end to the stretch out" This insidious practice brutalized the southern labor force in both the textile and steel industries and works is an issue in all the plays in this study. In the textile mills stretch-outs doubled the productivity expectations of the workers with no proportional increase in salary. Weavers who operated twenty-four looms were pushed to operate forty-eight, those running forty-eight looms were required to man ninety-six: "A weaver who operated twenty-four looms at $18.91 per week was stretched to one hundred looms at $23.00." Not only did stretch-outs result in brutal working conditions, but they displaced workers from their jobs. When one worker was forced to do the work of two, one lost his job[28].

The play combines documentary and poetic elements—as it were, Aristotle's inartistic and artistic proofs, evidence and invented appeals—in its attempt to build a case against the industry. Bailey reinforces the dark underside of mill life by employing ominous metaphors and prophecies throughout her script. In part this is done in the character of Hoffman, an elderly German printer, whose unusual analysis in the first act portends disaster. Pointing to a picture in the Sunday newspaper captioned "The Bridge," he establishes the structure as a metaphor for life: on one side was birth, on the other death, while the middle of the span held a trap door through which the unobservant fell. He declaims that "Lily May is to all of you a trap door! . . . Life is one long bridge. Not many will get across to a peaceful old age" (1:1). Such predictions in the first act created tension and helped establish the larger-than-life quality of Lily May. Hoffman's lines and the reappearance of the Sheriff and Bodenhammer serve as a drum-roll for the entrance of Lily May. She, more than Tom Peel or Stephen Baird, is the central character of *Strike Song*, but she is not the protagonist. She is the rhetorical model of right action epitomizing the southern labor movement led by women.

The spiritual significance of Lily May's character dovetails well with the religious-like concerns voiced by Peel. Her character acts as a rural spiritual medium, taking power from invisible forces in nature. She sees signs and is prescient in her knowledge of things, a gift taken seriously by her followers. Her character derives from a different mythology, a different folklore than does Peel's. She is part of the land, the folk; the social movement of labor is only important to her in so much as it improves living conditions for others, especially children. The interplay of religious and heroic attributes in her character, the combination of mother and metaphysician elevates Lily May to an Appalachian Jeanne d'Arc. Peel's character as an outsider, carrying the baggage of northern aggressor, excludes him from the spiritual communion of southern-ness. Lily May takes on more of the savior/martyr characteristics than does even Peel, which is unusual in a period of theatre that tended to cast women in melodramatic social roles.

That *Strike Song* focuses on the woman as a labor leader makes it truly significant, because of its fidelity to historical fact: the impetus for labor revolt in the South came from women. Their concern over child labor, working conditions in mills, education in the company towns, and families torn apart by low pay, night shifts, stretch-outs, and insecurity caused them to band together. The coalition of women in the textile industry made them easy

targets for derision and discrimination. Women were prominent in the labor
movement but were denied official leadership roles. More than one labor
historian has observed that though women led the strikes, men led the unions.
This is dramatized with piercing accuracy in the textile strike plays. It is
interesting to consider the plays as sociological icons depicting, in a blend of
realism and symbolism, the rise of industrialization that occurred in the South
between 1880 and 1920. What the plays showed, and what the audience knew
full well from first-hand experience, were the economic conditions that
prompted women from failing farms to seek additional income in the mills.
They brought with them their children, who were put to work in menial jobs.

By 1890 40 percent of the labor force southern textile mills comprised of
women and girls; this figure would rise to over 50 percent by the 1920s.
These uneducated, working-class women joined forces to demand shorter
workdays, education for their children, and a ban on night work for women.
They challenged the textile industry in the South and focused national attention
on their concerns. Women, as the bulk of the work force in the textile mills,
were particularly receptive to unionization and sought strength and representation under its aegis. The larger political leanings of the unions were not
always comprehended by those seeking their protection. Those who joined the
labor movement hoping for local reparations suffered, in many ways, from a
myopic view that distorted the broader picture.

The Gastonia strike was especially virulent because the communist-
dominated National Textile Workers Union was involved. Its leadership had
a different agenda from that of the more conservative American Federation of
Labor or the Congress of Industrial Organizations which ultimately succeeded
in unionizing the mills in the 1930s. Women strikers in the southern labor
wars, in their efforts to rectify offenses affecting their families, violated at least
two of the three criteria (class, race, and patriarchy) of a southern "lady."
This, again, is an issue that presupposes a tacit understanding on the
audiences' part of the agrarian, class-based value system that remained even
after Reconstruction. The threats to this value system posed by industry
proved vicious and more repressive; industry not only failed to adopt the
protective paternalism of the agrarian system but it viewed the workers as
impersonal units in the production process. Strikes in the 1920s and 1930s,
supported visibly and strongly by women, challenged the inhumanity of
unscrupulous mill owners. The role of women workers, especially southern
women, is an aspect of labor and social history that bears continual investigation. Betty Brandon identifies three southern phenomena that occurred in
political culture after 1920: "women as appointed male successors, women as
male proxies, and women as mirrors of male political authority." The women,
characterized in *Strike Song*, embody these characteristics in varying degrees[29].

The political inclinations of women in *Strike Song* provide an interesting
foil for the dramatist. However, Bailey could not alienate the audience by

having her female characters appear too masculine. For female characters to succeed in these plays, they must maintain some of the cultural attributes of femininity that the audience would expect. Lily May's character reinforces accepted notions of femininity by displaying exemplary maternal affection and keen intuitive traits. Throughout the play the signs, symbols, and superstitions of southern folk life, a tradition carried on largely in "old wives tales," help create the characters of the women. Lily May sees signs in nature from which she draws prophetic analogies; she speaks of her luck as something she particularly possesses; and other characters, especially the female characters, actively and vocally respond throughout to signs and mountain superstitions, such as birds in the house signifying death. Lily May believes the Lord has sent her a sign to lead the strikers in their walk-out, yet she fears the felt presence of something that "tain't a human person" following behind her. Folk beliefs, coupled with repeated references to fundamentalist religious precepts, create swirling images of divine presence and dark powers.

The final exchange of the first scene has Lily May walking into a rainstorm with a lit sparkler in her hand. As she steps outside the rain turns to hail but the sparkler miraculously continues to burn: Lily May, we are led to conclude, has special powers. This final tableau functions on two levels: she is an idealized mountain woman, earthy and intuitive, and a fitting foe of the culturally levelling industrialism; and she is also the image of a woman fighting for personal freedom with her torch held high and a proletarian statue of liberty.

One clearly senses the antagonistic power wielded over labor by the industrial argosy in the scenes that center on breaking the strike. The distinction between the idealistic "faith" of the strikers and the ruthless pragmatism of the mill owners is deftly implied. In a scene in which the mill bosses decide to evict strikers from company houses, Bailey adroitly dramatizes attitudes prevailing in the South during this period of transition from an agrarian-based society to an industrial one. The sociologic and economic underpinnings of the industrial problems facing the South are touched upon in flashes of revealing dialogue. In this scene, the paternalistic attitudes of southern mill owners are addressed more directly than in any other modern play. The dialogue, articulating Stephen Baird's naive paternalism and the industrialist, Henley's cynicism towards it, reflects accurately the attitudes and expectations of management and labor in southern mills at the time. The issue is introduced innocently, with Baird's defense of Henry Morris as "not right bright . . . [but] Henry rather feels as if he belongs to me." Henley's caustic response—"Good old southern paternalism here in our midst . . ." (1:2)—serves as a challenge on three levels, cultural, political, and economic.

Throughout the play, "Big Business" is synonymous with northern business, and the conversation between Baird and Henley that juxtaposes big business and paternalism is significant in that it underscores ethical and cultural differences. Henley's assessment that "Big Business is big because it goes its way without stopping for the individual toes it steps on" is followed by his acknowledgement that Baird is useful to them because of his vestigial paternalism: "The very fact that you are keenly interested in the people and see them as individuals makes you decidedly useful to the Caroleen" (1:2). After Reconstruction, when there was an economic shift from an agrarian culture to an industrial one, the southern industrialist was viewed as the hope of rural communities populated by starving tenant farmers. There was an active campaign by southern chambers of commerce to lure northern industry to their area by advertising, among other things, lower production costs, lower taxes, accessibility to raw material, freedom from stringent labor legislation and from unions, and most importantly, compliant "native American labor." At one point in this scene Ludlow remarks caustically, "We've advertised that the South has no labor troubles—it's up to us to see that it don't" (1:2).

The character of Ludlow is important in the play. He serves as a caricature of the southern worker who has sold his soul to an exploitative industry. He advances the theme of betrayal that runs as an undercurrent through the scenes. Ludlow is remarkably like Harriet L. Herring's 1935 description of the "Industrial Worker" in *Culture in the South:* he fits perfectly Herring's harsh characterization of a type of manager found in southern mills during the 1920s and 1930s. Herring's description commends the tenacity of the individual who has risen through the ranks, but it condemns those who turn their backs on their fellow workers. Herring wrote soon after the 1929 Gastonia strike, and Loretta Bailey was an editorial assistant for William Couch while he prepared *Culture in the South;* thus it is interesting to contrast the types from the point of view of a contemporary historian and social critic with the characters created by the dramatist.

Herring described one type of southern manager who rose by his own merits and initiative: a man who "learned by the trial and error method, or he watched his superior, or he actually paid a more experienced man to teach him." Such workers rose through the ranks and gained social position among workers and ultimately in the community. "He naturally believed that any man who 'had the goods' and was willing to work could do likewise. He wanted no organization that would limit the amount of work he was allowed to do, or slow up his progress by priority rules and set terms of service." While a manager risen from the ranks might offer assistance to a select few, "he certainly had no desire to be held down by the sheer weight of numbers in their ranks, no dream of becoming in any way the champion for them as a group." Herring concludes that as a result of this process that "the weaker members of the rank and file were left without their natural leaders"[30]. One sees this tension in the character of Ludlow in *Strike Song.* Herring's assessment of the social position of mill workers, and of the prejudicial attitudes directed towards them is also articulated in Bailey's script. Herring reports that mill workers were ignored or held in contempt: "To move to the cotton mill was step down from any situation. . . . Thus we have the amazing paradox of an industry exalted as few have ever been while the workers were despised as even cotton mill workers have scarcely been elsewhere." She writes that during the 1930s "intelligent, socially-minded citizens will tell you seriously that the people of the mill village on the edge of town are different—a 'sorry' type of folks, shiftless and nomadic, unambitious for themselves and their children, preferring isolation to mingling in the life of the community"[31]. This sociological distinction is made evident by Ludlow who articulates disparaging attitudes towards "poor whites." Here again, Bailey points to a central problem in a class system that placed mill workers on the lowest possible rung of a social ladder, a prejudicial predisposition that contributed to the controversies in the textile mills:

Ludlow: The poor fools. Working in the mill's a picnic to farming the kind of land they were raised on. I know; I came from a farm like that, worked my way up—proud of it. But, mind you, I didn't come from the class that goes into the mills—the lowest class we got in this state. It's a fine state, but it's got its scum the same as any other state. There's just one way to deal with 'em—they're like the niggers, helpless, don't know their own good. You got to set for 'em. And if they cut loose—if they're set on by these Yankee agitators—they've got to be dealt with." (1:2)

Bailey weaves into her dialogue many of the criticisms directed towards the strikers in newspaper and industry accounts of the day. To Baird she gives lines that take note of the union's "eye for the dramatic" in setting up a tent colony. This particular strategy consistently elicited sympathetic reports in the local and national newspapers covering the strike. But the dialogue between Baird and Henley about the tent colony serves to heighten the criticism of management, juxtaposing the suffering of the strikers with the callousness of the mill owners. Henley's indifference is the dramatic embodiment of the attitudes of the Loray Mill owners. Bailey synthesized it in Henley's culminating response to Baird, "The mill village is a perfect rabbit warren. That's the state's affair. We're behind in social legislation—the South's particularly behind—nobody knows it better than we do. That's why we built our mills down here." (1:2) The first act ends with the news that the sheriff has been shot in the tent village. This allows Bailey the riveting dramatic effect of having the mill management don the black masks of the vigilante group who terrorized the tent colony, as the "committee of a hundred."

The second act begins in the rustic setting of the tent village. The simplicity of the individuals is underscored by that of their surroundings. Lily May rejects warnings not to go to Pineville after the sheriff's shooting: she declares that she must go to "put backbone in these mill hands—backbone enough to make 'em walk out of the Caroleen Mill Monday." She rejects her daughter's fear that the Black Masks would attack her: "They wouldn't . . . cause I'm a woman." (2:1) In this line Bailey understates an irony that would not have been lost on her audience in the 1930s. Another character, Red Thompson, carries the theme of betrayal in this scene. He connives to get information about Peel and Lije in order to collect the reward posted after the death of the sheriff. With the arrest of Peel and the other male leaders, Lily May becomes the formal leader of the strike. Yet even as Bailey has her stepping into the masculine role of strike leader, she has the character respond with motherly grief to the death of a boy in the tent village. The death of the child prompts her to compose a song in his honor.

As Lily May goes to her tent to finish the song, disgruntled strikers fill the stage. There is a shift in sentiment: the strikers are rebellious and reluctant to attend a meeting that will surely lead to their arrest. The spokesman for this group is "Uncle Jake: who serves as the voice of pragmatism. He reminds the strikers that they are "living like brutes 'stead of like humans." He acknowledges Lily May's and Tom Peel's cleverness but maintains it is no match for the strength of the mill owners. Lily May appears in the middle of this insurrection, and when the trucks arrive to take strikers to the meeting in Pineville there is a stand-off between her and the strikers. Her rallying speech is interesting for several reasons: it appeals at once to the dignity and the racial prejudices of the workers before her—the poor white workers, so disparaged in the region—by comparing them in their submissiveness and servility to blacks. She reminds them of their mountain roots and ties them to a fundamental belief in the power and plan of God. The speech is militant and caustic. She goads the workers with stinging sarcasm, blaming them for their complacency in the face of management abuses. The speech succeeds and is drowned in shouts of laughter and of appreciation for Lily May's histrionics. But Lily May's spellbinding performance does not end with this speech. Prompted by a comment from the crowd, she relates her call to join the union in images of religious rebirth. Her call to the union is an epiphany, and her account of redemption is replete with trance-like swaying and talks with the Lord. She moves adroitly from performer to preacher in her style, giving the audience oratorical staples of southern elocution and fundamentalist preaching style:

Jess: . . . We've quit you.

Lily May: (*Climbing to the platform*) How many's quitting strike? (*Several answer up*) How many wants their jobs back—go back to the mill just like they was? Raise your hands up high so I can count 'em. (*the hands go up timidly—only a few hands*). . . That's all right now. Put your hands down. You all want your jobs back . . . and you can have 'em . . . (*Changing her tone—talking rapidly, leaning forward with eyes narrowed, nostrils quivering*) If you want to go ask for 'em. If you want to go crawling up there to President Henley—I see you now, going creeping and crawling up there to that fine house of his'n in Monclare Park—ringing his big doorbell. Then one of his niggers opens the door for you—don't let you in, jest let you stand there and wait—till by and by here comes Pres'dent Henley, a-smoking a big cigar—and he looks you up and down—like he was a-saying: 'What you doing here on my front porch—why ain't you off there on the mill hill?'—Then you commence to bow and scrape to him, like a nigger, and you say . . . (*She puckers her face and acts out the part*) . . .'Ef you please, sir—I'm jest one of them hands o' yours out at the Caroleen Mill, and I come here to 'ast you to take me back to work.' And then Pres'dent Henley, he rears back and laughs a little bit, and the big nigger woman holding the door open for him, she kind of grins back. (*She struts, like President Henley*) By and by he says: 'You got 'nough have you?' Then Holt Gibson down there he says: 'Yeah,' he says, 'I'm sech a big, hog-tying man (*She pushes out her chest and imitates Holt when he is boasting*) . . . I got to have me some work to do. . . . (*She suddenly alters her countenance and makes Holt appear a weak, deferential little man, she folds her hands on her breast and speaks in a whine, like Henry.*) . . . So I just tucked my tail between my legs and come up here to tell you I left the Union and I'm willing to eat dirt—men and Henry Morris, here, my pal. . .

The speech is drowned in a shout of laughter at Lily May's acting. The embarrassed Holt is slapped on the back by his neighbors.

Ben: O you make 'em laugh Lily May—but it's the truth I tell you, we're beat. We got to go back. We ain't going crawling—but we got to go, jest the same.

Lily May: (*Gravely and sympathetically*) I know—I know what's in your heart, Ben Levister—you got as good heart in you as any man I ever seen—you're all good folks—you got a heap of nerve—look there at Little Tuck—ain't no mor'n a boy jest seventeen and he's the main stay of the fam'ly. I know how you feel, you're low down in your mind. (*She paces the platform*) I been like that, too—like I was one Sunday when it was a-raining and I was lonesome, or that time my young'uns dies of the dip'therey—I set down in a chair and rocked. . . (*She sways a little*) . . . I rocked and rocked—and while I rocked I was a-praying . . . (*She closes her eyes*). . .'Lord,' I says, I'm sore with your scouring me—I'm tired of living, I'm wore out. Lay me in the ground and let that rain soak through my bones till they ain't no difference between me'n and the graveyard dirt.' (*She pauses, raises her head*) But my prayers run off the Lord like water sliding off a duck's back. By and by I began to pearten up—till some days I'd feel like—'Lily May, you got something inside of you that writes song-ballits—can't nobody shut your mouth.' Younder comes a line of men marching and little children and women follering after 'em. They're marching for the Union. We got to have a Union. If you got a Union, you ain't dirt under nobody's feet. Pres'dent Henley won't talk to you, but he'll talk to the Union—can't slam the door in the Union's face. I ain't no slacker, I'm a worker. I'm willing to work hard for my pay—(*She leans forward*) . . . But I come from the mountains, where I'm used to doing like I please. If I want to join a Union—ain't nobody on earth got a right to tell me 'No.' If I go on strike, ain't no men with black cloth on their faces and police on their side doing to stop me. You all come from where I do—you got the same feelings. Come on, now who's with me: I say—we're going to keep on fighting . . . (*She lays down the points by slapping her palms together*) . . . till they take off the stretch-out—till the laws fights some on our side—till they quit firing hands for joining the Union—and let the Union in. Cone on, you raised your hands a while ago to eat dirt—now raise 'em again to join the Union for good and all—Come on . . . *(Henry Morris shoulders his way through the crowd)* Here comes Henry Morris—he ain't right bright and he don't see clear sometimes—but the Lord's give him power to feel—he knows, same as a child, by jest feeling . . . Come on! (2:4)

The power of music and worker anthems to carry the striker's militancy begins to grow in this scene. As she concludes, strikers come forward and pick up the tune of Lily May's ballad, "Big Boss," sung to "The Battle Hymn of the Republic." Bailey uses music as social commentary and as a transitional device in this scene. As the strains of "Big Boss" leave the stage with the exiting strikers, Henry Morris picks out the refrain of "Old Smokey," the song with which the play opened and the second verse of which established the betrayal theme. The betrayal of individuals and groups is an evil that lingers hauntingly in the air. When chastised by Mammy King that he only plays "burying pieces," Henry breaks into a lively ballad about love that signals the arrival of Baird, come to warn Lily May of the danger of attending the rally in Pineville. But it is too late; the scene ends with the return of the strikers carrying Lily May, who has been mortally wounded by shots fired into the crowd. Henry plays his banjo as Lily May dies. A dirge closes the scene as Mammy King lifts her voice, "in the shrill, high keen of the mountain women over their dead." While the union songs serve as a means to achieve group cohesiveness, the most emotional use of music comes in the use of traditional laments and hymns.

The opening scene of the last act returns again to the issue of the predominant role of women in the union organization and in the textile industry. As Lily May's grave is prepared, Annie Myrtle, a young female striker, appears wearing an armband emblazoned with a 'U.' "Us girls are marching," is the refrain, used in the scene to indicate a new-found solidarity of women to the cause and to each other in these industrial clashes. The girl's discussion with Henry Morris functions metaphorically and powerfully, as they talk about the use of human bones as fertilizer. The synecdoche of grinding bones, of being systematically used up, is emblematic of the pattern of industrial exploitation. This is clearly an empathetic request that the audience recall its own sense of being ground down by both the mill and by the Depression. Lily May's funeral becomes the funeral for the spirit of all downtrodden mill workers, as the mourners, led by a "line of girls in rain-soaked white with 'U' on their sleeve-bands," appear and the service begins.

The words of the preacher's eulogy carry little importance in this scene; the argument is advanced emotionally, in the music. Music carries a rhetorical clout that overpowers the dialogue. As four girls prepare to sing a traditional hymn of mourning, their efforts are interrupted by the appearance of a young man, Saunders, wishing to speak. Saunders, the new organizer sent by the Union to replace the jailed Peel, launches into a rallying speech that ends with a call for the mourners to raise their voices in a political strike song: "I tell you we haven't lost that strike yet; this woman has not died in vain. Come on—it's not sacrilegious to sing over her grave the song she made—she that loved the Union, and died for it!" (3:1) Bailey's stage directions indicate that Saunders begins to sing "We're Going to Have a Union" and that a few people join in, but that they are not convinced it is appropriate at a burial service. At this point the stage directions have the old preacher begin to sing in "his shrill old voice . . . 'Jesus, Lover of My Soul,' a song so bound up with the emotions of these people that they cannot bear to hear it except on occasions like this." Bailey uses the song to create a climactic tension between the old religious faith in an omnipotent God and the new religious-like faith in the Union, whose saviors had feet of clay. She masterfully allows the scene to take the form of a duel: religion against religion, faith against faith. Her stage directions that make it clear the preacher knows the power of the traditional hymn and uses it to call the people back to him. One by one the people begin to raise their voices in the words of the hymn. "Without knowing why, only feeling the pull of the familiar, the crowd swings over to Lance and the preacher—the Union song dies—and the old hymn swells to a full chorus."

The use of dueling songs is a technique familiar to modern audiences of film: part of a score becomes identified with a group or character to heighten the tension of action. However, Bailey's use of this device on stage was most innovative and would have been extraordinarily effective, given the level of audience identification with each song. In effect Bailey asked her audience to choose a faith. The emotional pull of each melody in this scene is wrenching, as is the contrast between the political oratory of Saunders and his inflammatory choice of songs, with McChristian's emphasis on "Peace." Saunders lamely tries to regain the crowd by reminding them that Lily May died fighting and that the strike is not lost, but he fails. Like the others before him, he does not know his audience and is therefore unable to discover the appeals that will persuade them. An ominous sense of failure pervades the close of the scene. A tacit decision has been made, and the choice of peace over radical strife weighs heavily. Bailey brings her audience to the silent recognition that faith in the region's traditional values is preferable to sometimes misplaced faith in outsiders. In its epideictic effectiveness this scene is one of the most powerful in the literature of labor plays.

The final scene begins with a confrontation between scabs and strikers. The strikers march to the mill calling to the remaining workers to walk out, but they are met by mill-appointed deputies who brutalize strikers at the front of the march, then fire into the crowd. The transformation of Mary and Stephen Baird occurs in this scene. Mary rises to take her mother's place as a strike leader, transformed from a withdrawn, meek young woman to a courageous advocate for the union, while Baird's true allegiances to southern labor are revealed—he proves himself a son of the South. Rejecting the ties of northern-dominated management, Baird joins the strikers against the Caroleen Mills bosses, calling out to the workers looking out the mill windows to join the walkout. In the closing moments of the last act, Baird stands alone on stage staring at the mill. Slowly, his solitary form is surrounded by huge, grotesque shadows of soldiers looming against the mill wall. "Distorted to giants the shadows of the soldiers look down upon the scene ominously as the curtain falls." The metaphorical image of the human form of small labor surrounded by the shadows and darkness of big business is striking. The audience is left with a heavy sense of loss. Where the play began with music, it ends in silence.

Responses to the production from the textile industry were damning but not surprising. The *Southern Textile Bulletin*, the industry publication had given notice in December, 1931 that a review of *Strike Song* would be forthcoming; even in that first salvo the industry took umbrage at the use of radical union songs in the play. January 7, 1932, saw the publication of the awaited review; it again took aim at the playwright specifically and the academic community at the University of North Carolina, Chapel Hill, generally. Calling the Gastonia strike a "communist strike" that was "misrepresented and exaggerated" by writers from newspapers and magazines from all over the country, the review claimed that "never" had there been "such a gross, willful and deliberate misrepresentation of the textile industry as has been made in a play, 'The Strike Song,' which was written at the University of North Carolina and has recently been staged there." The reviewer acknowledged the documentary quality of the script, noting it was based upon the strikes at Gastonia and the United Textile Workers strike at Marion, N.C. He claimed that "every major incident in both of those strikes is featured in the play but is so colored as to represent the most extreme claims of the strikers. . . . Individuals upon the side of the strikers are painted in the best possible light whereas those upon the side of the mill are represented as unfavorably as possible"[32].

The production struck a raw nerve in the textile industry, as evidenced by the vituperation of its attack on the production and the university, and by its willingness to engage in posthumous character assassination of Ella May Wiggins. "The least said about the character and habits of Ella May Wiggins the better. She had worked in a cotton mill very little and had many times been asked to move out of a village for the good of the community. She cared little about the union but loved the excitement of a row or a fight and that was the only motive of the trip upon which she was killed, an incident which everyone regrets." The review refutes facts and incidents in the play, calling the "committee of one hundred" a fiction invented by strike leaders, and claiming that "the grossest misrepresentation of the entire play is the incident when twenty-one persons were shot, five of them fatally, early one morning at the Marion Manufacturing Company. By their account the sheriff and his deputies attempted to protect the employees and were attacked by the mob they tried to help. 'The Strike Song' deliberately represents the strikers as employees approaching the mill unarmed and peacefully, and being set upon and shot by an organized gang of men headed by the sheriff and employed by the mill"[33].

This review, like the first, held to the position that the songs used in the play were intended to "furnish participants in future mill strikes with inspirational songs." The reviewer objects to non-union workers being called "scabs" in dialogue and in song and calls this play "a stronger exposition of the cause of unionism" than any account that could be written, even by jailed strike leaders. A strong anti-university bias surfaces in this review; it speaks of "radical professors at the University of North Carolina who embraced unionism because they would profit from it. Evidence in the review indicates that the reviewer not only saw the production, but obtained a copy of the script and read the playwright's notations for characterization. The final line of the review deems the play and its production "a gross and willful effort and is contemptible." Clearly, this was an industry threatened by an amateur university production[34].

Though there are not many critical responses to the production; the ones that do exist are interesting for a number of reasons. While the *Textile Bulletin's* response is as one-sided as might be expected, it is interesting to note that it employed the same kinds of emotional appeal as Bailey had used in her script and other journalists had used in their accounts of industry response to the strike. The playwright and journalists painted the workers as unarmed, honorable, and victimized by the violence of the other side; the textile industry had reason to be chagrined by what it suspected would be a positive response to the play.

Strike Song attracted regional attention, and two years after the scathing commentary in *Textile Bulletin*, it was still being produced and reviewed, but this time in *New Theatre and Film*. Loretta Bailey's friend Molly Day Thatcher saw the play on her 3,500-mile tour of the South, a tour undertaken with the expressed purpose of viewing and criticizing the indigenous theatre. Thatcher recognized the strengths of the production but felt the play hampered by the emphasis that the Carolina Playmakers traditionally placed on "folk" elements. Her reservations, rarely expressed by other analysts and critics of the Playmakers, were astute, for in them she identified an elitism that is, indeed, apparent. "Its weakness," she wrote of *Strike Song*, "is contained in its first approach which builds on the educational and social gap between the authors and the people they write about. It has led to an unformulated, probably unconscious feeling of superiority; a 'studying' of 'types' which notes them, however sympathetically, as quaint; an aesthetic appreciation of phrases old in the mother tongue, of folk customs deliciously anachronistic." She notes insightfully, "A real art cannot grow down"[35].

Recognizing what Loretta Bailey knew about her play—that it was different from the others the Playmakers had been producing, Thatcher claimed, "*Strike Song* . . . is a first groping toward a new perspective." She identified a central tension created by this break from the Playmakers' tradition, one that emphasized character types over issues. The material of *Strike Song* was, in her assessment, "too strong for the accustomed folksy treatment." Thatcher may have preferred a more propagandistic approach in the play, more proselytizing, and clearer statements of the political and social issues involved. Her preference would have been to let the material "have its way" without the constraints and emphasis on local color that had become the hallmark of the Playmakers. In her estimation, "when one must show . . . the union tents being destroyed by a mob, there is a raw contemporaneity about the fact that does not tolerate detachment. . . . The material pulls toward stronger situations, demands fuller humanity and maturity, clearer understanding of what the issues are."[36] What Thatcher called for was a political shift in the productions of the Carolina Playmakers. Bailey implicitly concurred and wrote scripts that did not wholly conform to the representation of "folk" and regional types; they were, in fact, issue-oriented, rather than character-oriented scripts, and their existence and production in North Carolina puts them at the forefront of a larger artistic documentary movement that took shape in the 1930s in the United States.

Strike Song was the first dramatic response to the Gastonia textile strike of 1929. Others would follow. The Gastonia violence would be the subject of sociological and artistic investigation for many years. As an example of American political theatre, of American documentary theatre, this play is historically significant. Its political effectiveness is readily discerned from the responses in industry publications. *Strike Song* and plays like it were part of a movement in the early 1930s that used documentary evidence in dramatic productions for political effect. They are an important evolutionary link that ties the political theatre of the '30s in the United States to the agit-prop drama of Eastern Europe in the early part of the century, to the documentary drama of Britain in the '50s and '60s.

The domestic strife and political turbulence of the 1930s was captured in scores of contemporary newsreels and films. Theatrical responses to these same events tend to be overlooked, because they are not as readily accessible, or as easily viewed; but they are no less important. Conversely, they may be more important, because the theatre depends on an interaction between performer and audience that can be likened to the participation and exchange between preacher and congregation, or teacher and student. The labor wars prompted dramatic reenactments of turmoil in several industries. The labor plays of the 1930s exhorted workers to militancy and action, they were plays that taught a history and tried to reinforce a political position. The greatest technical innovation of these plays was the use of documentary technique for rhetorical effect. While many suffer from pedantic crudeness, they, were for the most part, effective and controversial. Reexamining these forgotten scripts allows one to hear again the voices of dissent that shaped American labor and American theatre.

NOTES

1. Richard Gray, *Writing the South: Ideas of an American Region* (New York: Cambridge University Press, 1986), p. 40–41, 72; and Broadus Mitchell, "A Survey of Industry," in *Culture in the South*, ed. W. T. Couch (Chapel Hill: University of North Carolina Press, 1935), pp. 85, 89.

2. Robert P. Ingalls, "Industrial Violence," in *Encyclopedia of Southern Culture*, eds. Charles Reagan Wilson and William Ferris (Chapel Hill: University of North Carolina Press, 1989), p. 1485.

3. William E. Lightfoot, "Murder Legends" (p. 512), Lynn Weiner, "Aunt Molly Jackson" (p. 1597), and Bill C. Malone, "Protest Music" (pp. 1023–1024), *Encyclopedia of Southern Culture*.

4. All references to Loretta Carroll Bailey's personal life are taken primarily from correspondence the author has had with Loretta's eldest daughter, Nancy Bailey Rich. Letters to author from Nancy Bailey Rich, June 22, 1989, and Sept. 7, 1995. There is as well some correspondence from J. O. Bailey to Rosamund Gilder on the National Theatre Conference, in the Billy Rose Theatre Collection of the New York Public Library

5. Rich to author, June 22, 1989, and Sept. 7, 1995.

6. Rich to author, June 22, 1989, and Sept. 7, 1995.

7. Rich to author, June 22, 1989, and Sept. 7, 1995.

8. Rich to author, June 22, 1989, and Sept. 7, 1995.

9. Rich to author, June 22, 1989, and Sept. 7, 1995.

10. Rich to author, June 22, 1989, and Sept. 7, 1995.

11. Rich to author, June 22, 1989, and Sept. 7, 1995. See also J. O. Bailey to Rosamond Gileler [sic], February 5, 1934, Billy Rose Theatre Collection of the New York Public Library.

12. Rich to author, June 22, 1989, and Sept. 7, 1995.

13. Rich to author, June 22, 1989, and Sept. 7, 1995.

14. Rich to author, June 22, 1989, and Sept. 7, 1995.

15. Letter from Loretta Carroll Bailey to Nancy Bailey Rich, Saturday, July 3, 1982. Xeroxed copy in possession of the author.

16. Susan Duffy and Bernard K. Duffy, "Anti-Nazi Drama in the United States 1934–41," *Essays in Theatre* 4:1 (1985), 41.

17. *Carolina Folk Plays*, ed. Frederick H. Koch (New York: Holt and Company, 1941), p. 359.

18. Letter, Rich to author, June 22, 1989, and Sept. 7, 1995.

19. Letters, J. O. Bailey to Paul Green, May 5, 1932, and Walter H. Baker

Company to J. O. Bailey, March 7, 1932. Paul Green Papers #3693 in the Southern Historical Collection, University of North Carolina Library, Chapel Hill.

20.   Correspondence,   F. Koch to Rosamond Gilder 26 Oct. 1933; R. Gilder to Baileys, 2 Nov. 1933, 30 Jan. 1934, 9 Feb. 1934; and J. O. Bailey to Rosamond Gilder, 25 Oct. 1933, 5 Feb., 1934, 12 Feb. 1934, all in Billy Rose Theatre Collection, New York Public Library, MWEZ + n.c. 23, 052.

21.   Letter, J. O. Bailey to Paul Green, July 4, 1935, Paul Green Papers #3693 in the Southern Historical Collection, University of North Carolina Library, Chapel Hill.

22.   "The Strike Song," *Southern Textile Bulletin* (Dec. 17, 1931), 19.

23.   *Strike Song*, by Loretta Carroll Bailey and James Osler Bailey. All references to the script are taken from a copy held at the University of North Carolina, Chapel Hill.

24.   Margaret Larkin, "Ella May's Songs," *The Nation*, 129 (Oct. 9, 1929): 382.

25.   "Ella May's Songs," pp. 382–83.

26.   Charles Stewart, Craig Smith and Robert E. Denton, *Persuasion and Social Movements* (Prospect Heights, Ill.: Waveland Press, Inc., 1984), pp. 137–159. This chapter on the "Persuasive Function of Songs" concludes with a useful bibliography that addresses the rhetoric of music.

27.   Harriet L. Herring, "The Industrial Worker," *Culture in the South*, ed. W. Couch, pp. 346–347. Herring writes, "when political leadership was restored, after reconstruction, the old class was as completely dominant as ever. Perhaps more so, for the economic substitute for slavery, the tenant system, gave it just as much control of land and credit as it had in the old days, and the new system was by no means limited to Negroes. The poor man came to the planter or landed professional or the new supply merchant for the means to make a living, for guidance in managing his rented land, and for aid in emergencies, very much as did the ex-slave. . . . We have only to make a brief sally into the countryside today and become acquainted with the contemporaries of the present generation of industrial workers and their relation to their more prosperous and influential neighbors to see the very same forces in operation. The latter are members of the school board though the former supply the bulk of the students. They are the leaders and chief support of the church and it is at their homes that the circuit riding preacher stays the night or the resident one is entertained for Sunday dinner. If there is sickness or need in a poor family, the wife of the prominent citizen goes on an errand of mercy to her neighbor. Other contacts between the families, especially the women of the families are limited to gatherings at school or church. Now this social grading based on economic status is common everywhere. In the South it has more force because it was based on so many more factors than economic possession alone, and because it is of longer standing. Families have lived next each other for generations on this basis. We need make only a brief study of the history of southern industry to learn that industrial statesmen saw this type of small owner of landless farmer as a class to be saved from a narrow and ignorant existence, and the entrepreneur saw it as a group to be exploited for handsome profits. The effort to build a textile industry in the 1840s and later from the 1870s onward produced a vast literature of propaganda and argument, orations, pamphlets, articles, editorials without number. All the advocates of mills got around sooner or later to the potential industrial workers to be gathered from tenant farm and mountain cove. They portrayed them as a people with a standard of living so low that a most modest wage would attract them; as

accustomed to community advantages so scanty that the supplying of the simplest church and a single teacher, four months' school would be a patriotic and Christian philanthropy."

28. Samuel Yellen, *American Labor Struggles* (New York: S. A. Russell, 1936), pp. 299–300.

29. Betty Brandon, "Women in Politics," p. 1561, Other references to the role of women in this section are taken from Carol Ruth Berkin, "Women's Life," pp. 1521–22, 1524; Anne Goodwyn Jones, "Belles and Ladies," p. 1529; Mary Frederickson, "Working Women," pp. 1567–69; and David Corbin, "Workers' Wives," p. 1566, in *Encyclopedia of Southern Culture*, eds. Charles Reagan Wilson and William Ferris (Chapel Hill: University of North Carolina Press, 1989).

30. Harriet L. Herring, "The Industrial Worker," in *Culture in the South*, ed. W. Couch, pp. 350–51.

31. Herring p. 348.

32. "Their Latest Effort," *Southern Textile Bulletin* (January 7, 1932): 18–19.

33. *Southern Textile Bulletin,* 18–19.

34. *Southern Textile Bulletin,* 18–19.

35. Molly Day Thatcher, "Drama in Dixie," *New Theatre and Film* (Oct. 1934): 18.

36. Thatcher, p. 18.

CHAPTER 3

Strike!: A Northern Response to a Southern Strike

The emerging industrial South of the 1920s and 1930s held particular fascination for certain segments of the American public. Accounts of southern life ranged from the defamatory in H. L. Mencken's scathing commentary of the Scopes trial, to the heroic in Margaret Mitchell's *Gone with the Wind*. The labor strikes of the late '20's received considerable attention because of the regional paradoxes they revealed. The strikes attracted northern journalists, who wrote in most instances with a liberal northern bias. Northern interest in the Gastonia textile strike stemmed from a general interest in labor conflicts, from the need to analyze the increasing power of organized labor, and from a wish to compare southern strikes to their northern precedents. In most national publications the South was depicted as anachronistic in its formation of laws and violent in its upholding of them. These themes received treatment from social critics and artists who traversed the South chronicling and photographing the poverty, racism, backwardness, and violence of the region. Criticisms of the South were not solely the province of northern liberals; these same social themes were treated most powerfully and sensitively in southern literature. Another telling treatment of the same themes occurred in the works of two northern writers working in concert, Mary Heaton Vorse and William Dorsey Blake, whose play *Strike!* offers yet another literary response to the Gastonia textile strike.

Historically, Vorse is the more significant writer of the two. She was one of the foremost labor journalists of the period, but her tumultuous personal life often led her in search of literary opportunities that would provide greater financial security for her and her family. Her reminiscences on the labor conflict resulted in the publication of *Strike—A Novel of Gastonia 1930*. Her biographer recounts that Vorse lived with the union organizers for six weeks while she researched and wrote. "She reported the second trial and was present near the spot where Ella May Wiggins . . . was killed by a sniper in September"[1]. One wonders whether her path crossed that of Loretta Bailey during those turbulent days or whether she knew of Bailey's script. There is clear evidence in correspondence surviving in her papers at the Reuther Labor Archives that she tried unsuccessfully in 1930 to find a playwright to adapt her book to the stage. In the summer of 1931, however, she received a telegram from William Dorsey Blake asking to see her "about making *Strike!* into a play." This serendipitous missive resulted in not one but three versions of the play, all of which saw production in the early 1930s.

William Dorsey Blake is an enigmatic figure in the American theatre. His significance for this study derives from his associations with individuals and projects important in American theatrical history. He remains a shadowy peripheral figure on the edge of the limelight, never achieving the stature of those with whom he worked. Despite his lack of celebrity he was successful, and he developed a working relationship with some of the leading literary figures and theatre and film companies of the 1930s. One of those was Paul Green, the North Carolina playwright who knew Loretta Bailey. Blake's association with the Federal Theatre Project and his use of documentary technique in the scripts he prepared for it lead one to question whether the documentary techniques used by the Federal Theatre Project were rooted in labor plays or in the artistic treatment of labor issues in the South.

In August 1928 *Theatre Magazine* published an article by a noted critic, Benjamin De Casseres, entitled "Has the Drama Gone Sissy?" An answer to this question came in an October article, "Stray Shots at the Sissy Theme," by William Dorsey Blake. This is the earliest public recognition of Blake and the only instance where he is credited as being a psychologist[2]. Blake's criticism was aggressive, combative, and well written. He addressed the human condition and the function of art and began to articulate an aesthetic that one sees embodied in his plays.

Characteristically, Blake's plays are unusually poetic in their treatment of social themes. Beyond the 1928 article, documentation of Blake's career is fragmentary. Correspondence in the Green Papers indicates that Blake and Green knew each other as early as 1930, when Blake tried to produce Green's *Tread The Green Grass* while serving as director for the Provincetown Players Playwright's Theatre, on MacDougal Street in New York. That same year he directed Strindberg's *The Pelican* and a revival of *The Drunkard*, a nineteenth century melodrama. While working for the Provincetown Players he collaborated with Michael Gold and Virgil Geddes on productions of their plays. His career as playwright started in 1931 with the dramatization of Vorse's novel. This script saw production in Provincetown, Massachusetts in July 1931 and in Boston in December 1932. His *vitae* lists fifteen additional plays authored between the years 1932 and 1948, most of them unproduced.

In 1936 he was employed in what he described as "a not very momentous job" as a reader for Selznick International Pictures in New York. In that year, Blake wrote again to Green, to tell him that he had read Green's *This Body the*

Earth, when it was sent to Selznick, and had "recommended it for picture material." He also took the opportunity to ask Green to read his anti-war play, *Testament of Drums* with the hopes of having Frederick Koch and the Playmakers produce it at UNC–Chapel Hill.

In 1937 Blake secured a position as a playwright for the Federal Theatre Project, a position he held until the closing of the FTP in 1939. Initially Blake worked for the Project in White Plains, New York, where he wrote everything from historical plays for marionettes to radio plays. In August 1938 he requested a transfer to the New York City Play Writing department, where his assignment was to research and write *The Ten Million,* a living newspaper script about the history of unemployment. This script received high praise within the agency and was scheduled for production at the New York World's Fair. However, Blake's chance to achieve national recognition was thwarted: Congress closed the Federal Theatre Project in 1939 before the play was mounted and *The Ten Million* went unproduced. Had *The Ten Million* seen production, Blake would certainly have achieved national stature. Emmett Lavery, one of the FTP's chief administrators, found Blake's work compelling. His unpublished account of the Project, "The Flexible Stage," offers strong commendation of Blake's contributions to the organization. Lavery felt his contribution important for several reasons: "It marked the emergence of a young writer with equal parts of vision and energy. It marked the introduction of a poetic feeling to the living newspaper technique. The choral episodes devised by Blake, have strength and beauty and rare dramatic power"[3].

The closing of the Federal Theatre Project was a tragic turning point in Blake's career. Between 1939 and 1943 he worked as a freelance writer of radio commercials and scripts. He supplemented his income by writing condensations of books and "continuities for adventure and mystery comic strips," all the while continuing his attempts to place his scripts through his literary agent, Leland Howard. From 1943 to 1946 he was a story editor at Universal Pictures in New York, after which followed a stint as press agent and advance man for various film companies including United Artists, Universal, Paramount, and Selznick. He prepared promotional packages for United Artists' *Henry the Eighth* (starring Lawrence Olivier), Universal's *Hamlet,* Paramount's *Samson and Delilah,* and Selznick's *Fallen Idol* and *The Third Man.* In 1948 he wrote to Paul Green seeking support for a Guggenheim Fellowship, which, ultimately, he did not receive.

Correspondence in the Billy Rose Theatre Collection of the New York Public Library offers scant information about Blake's career through the 1950s and 1960s. A resumé indicates that from 1951 to 1954 he was employed by RKO Pictures in San Francisco, where he worked in publicity, advertising, and "exploitation/promotion" of RKO films. In 1954 he moved to MGM Pictures, where until 1962 he handled publicity and advertising for MGM films in Denver, Salt Lake City, Seattle, Portland, and San Francisco. From 1963 to

1966 he worked for Universal Pictures in New York as senior publicist, handling special media events and films. There is evidence to suggest he continued his work as a freelance writer, playwright, and director, moving back and forth between coasts. In 1969 a review in the *Hollywood Citizen-News* offers praise of his new play, *Spring Training*, then in a trial run at the Horseshoe Theatre. Correspondence in the New York Public Library for 1970 indicates that he was the Director for Public Relations and Advertising for the Allentown Summer Theatre. Finally, a 1976 citation in the *American Film Institute Catalogue of Films 1961–70* credits Blake with adapting as a screenplay, an original story by Joseph Jacoby[4]. He worked continuously in theatre-related enterprises all his life. However, his career moved along an inauspicious, albeit productive path after his work with the Federal Theatre Project, the early years of his career remain most significant in this study.

Mary Heaton Vorse was captivated by Blake's ability to "infuse enthusiasm into the Provincetown Summer crowd." Her interest in the theatre was more than superficial. It was she who donated her Provincetown warehouse, that "deserted old fish house on the wharf," for use as the theatre by the Provincetown Players. Her book, *Time and the Town: A Provincetown Chronicle*, provides anecdotal accounts of the personalities and politics of the groups who created the two theatres in Provincetown in the mid-1920s[5].

Blake worked for the Provincetown Players in New York, but how he came to appear on her doorstep, with an adaptation of her novel *Strike!* in hand, remains shrouded. She had sought the advice of friends, John and Katy Dos Passos, and had pursued several leads in seeking an author to adapt her novel and a production company to stage it. In December 1930 she solicited Lawrence Langner, of the New York Theatre Guild, to consider an adaptation of her novel, and she approached Emjo Basshe, who was more encouraging about production possibilities, especially in Germany[6].

In early July 1931, Blake contacted Vorse. Her diary entry for July 11 comments, "I was just working when a telegram came. A boy wanted to see me about making *Strike!* into a play. He came and [was] no sooner gone." A letter written to her daughter Mary Ellen in the same month indicates that Blake's visit had been agreeable. It becomes evident in the chronology of events that Blake had a script in hand at the time of his initial visit. Vorse consented to its production, and it went into rehearsals almost immediately. Vorse kept a record of the play's progress in her diary:

I went to Provincetown over the weekend. A boy named Blake had come to ask me if he could make a play of *Strike!* and I had said he could to use locally. I went rather steadily to rehearsals expecting nothing—and there it was something being created something alive a boy's enthusiasm having taken a Provincetown summer crowd and infused them with his excitement.—It will have all sorts of faults but there will be something. It is the nearest to *Bound East for Cardiff* when we just gave it—There was the real thing People working sincerely with enthusiasm to produce something instead of working to feed their egos.[7]

Another entry, dated July 28, reiterates these sentiments and extends her praise of Blake:

I went up to the rehearsal of *Strike!* expecting nothing almost forgetting and there it was the flame. Something being created. Blake having kindled a little glow of [involvement]—people with fire—a beautiful boy—He had seen past my words to people and is editing. I am [illegible] with excitement"[8].

An undated entry in late July leads one to believe that the excitement persisted through the opening of the play but did not prevent her from offering her own abbreviated criticisms:

I had not had a moment to write before they came for me to go to Provincetown. . . . It was time for my play. There it was exciting fresh good all the fun part. The last part will have to be done over again. The court house scene will have to be done again.[9]

The play was still in production August 12, when her diary entry records an unpleasant party whose guest list included the Dos Passoes, and William D. Blake, and "Langston," quite possibly Langston Hughes. Later entries refer to the "dirt," the gossipy conversations concerning the Provincetown summer crowd, including Blake.[10]

There is no evidence to indicate that Blake's treatment of social issues was derived from a personal commitment to leftist causes. While working at the MacDougal Street Theatre he worked with leftist writers like Michael Gold and Vergil Geddes, but his commitment to the theatre appears to be one of a professional, one who made it his vocation, rather than of an idealogue who used it for political ends. Blake's collaboration with Vorse was the relationship of a ghostwriter to an author. Blake's talent, in part, stemmed from his ability to adapt dramatic material to multiple groups. He was a talented craftsman. His plays on social themes display an awareness of classical theatre and its use of choral readings, and also a sensitivity that combined the poetic with the polemical. He perceived clearly that political material lent itself well to dramatization and that there was a market for it in the 1930s. The techniques he perfected in *Strike!* are resurrected in the scripts he prepared for the Federal Theatre Project at the end of the decade. In the examination of *Strike!* we begin to see yet another regional prototype of the dramatic form that became the living newspapers.

THE SCRIPT

Blake's debt to Mary Heaton Vorse went far beyond the slim acknowledgement "from the novel Strike by Mary Heaton Vorse" on the title page of his script[11]. It was her expertise, her first-hand account, her experience at the Gastonia strike, and the scenes, characters and dialogue of her 1930 novel, that Blake turned into a producible script. In point of fact, there are two extant scripts of *Strike!*, and they are different.   There is a copy filed with the copyright office of the Library of Congress, bearing Blake's Provincetown address; it is probably an early draft of the version presented to Vorse in July, 1930, being substantially shorter that the script found in the Vorse Papers which bears Blake's New York address. Vorse's diary entry states that she found the ending problematic, and the manuscript in her papers contains a radically altered conclusion. It is this copy that is reprinted here. Still a third version of the play was produced in Boston in December 1932, but this script remains undiscovered.   Evidence from reviews indicates that while some elements remained unchanged the text was transformed from a powerful labor play to a melodramatic love story. The notice of this production in the *Boston Evening Transcript* is the only extant review of *Strike!*[12]. The reviewer noted Blake's reliance on documentary technique complaining about the "utter faithfulness with which detail after detail is crammed into the narrative." During the Boston run of the play, Blake was invited to speak at the John Reed Club on the topic, "The Theatre and Propaganda."

When he worked for the Federal Theatre Project writing *The Ten Million*, his internal correspondence requesting statistical information and government documents to supplement his dialogue indicates that Blake had mastered the documentary form of the living newspapers. One is reminded that along with the use of documentary evidence and of the loudspeaker as a disembodied character, other distinctive elements of living newspapers revolved around choral recitation and innovative group staging of large casts. These latter elements are found in Blake's script. His "Note to Prospective Producers" at the beginning of *Strike!* addresses how the play was to be staged but also speaks to his concerns that simply reading the script would not do justice to the real power of the staging.

This play was tried out at Frank Shay's Old Barn Theatre in Provincetown, Mass., this summer with an almost amateur cast. It was directed by W. D. Blake, with Maida Huneker as Assistant Director. It was very well received there, got good notices, and ran for over three weeks. It was produced very simply; a single suggestive panel used against a black cyclorama was the extent of the scenery except for platforms and benches. In reading the play it is necessary to bear in mind that in mass action it is difficult to read the lines from the script with the same force and speed and 'tellingness' with which they are played on the actual stage. The Prologue and Epilogue may be difficult to visualize from the script but done on the stage they become one of the most powerful and effective parts of the play.

Blake's affinity for beginning plays in recitative verse is evident here and in his other work. The prologue and epilogue, which receive the cautionary notes, are written in verse. In its staging and tenor, *Strike's* prologue is reminiscent of openings used in living newspapers. Blake calls for "twenty-five or thirty [actors] placed in small groups on varying levels. . . . The mood . . . is a staccato brooding." A cast of over fifty characters speaks largely as choral groups. Stage directions provide choral orchestration, designating single voices, two voices, four voices, half-chorus, etc. The opening choral verse illuminates the central metaphor of the script by comparing mill hands to the bobbins they control daily. The audience is left with the image of weavers for whom the tenuous threads of life are breaking.

Bobbins running wildly
Threads that break and Loose.

The music of the script is carried in the voices of the individual respondents, who assume alternating solo roles. The effect is that of dueling voices. This dramatic technique, used by the Baileys in their concluding scenes, is used by Blake in the prologue. The verse underscores basic contrasts between the oppressiveness of the mill and the openness and healthiness of the hills. These motifs are developed and reiterated throughout the text.

Boss Schenck want to add another hour
with no increase in wages . . .

women men and children
a-working in the mills
a-working in the mills
night and day
night and day.

We come from the hills, we do
from the green red hills
a glinting in the sun
from the blue brown hills
a-shining in the rain.

This script significantly expands the thematic emphasis on children as victims of a system where their mothers are forced to work long hours in the mill to the detriment of their families. The handling of the emotional appeals in the script is masterful and prompted Vorse's comment that Blake saw through her words to the people. The leitmotif of the children, oppressed and growing old and infirm before reaching adolescence, is reinforced by the songs of Mamie Lewes, who is the Ella May Wiggins character in this play. Blake and Vorse incorporate the labor ballads for dramatic and documentary effect, but they combine the songs with classical choral reading to add another dimension to the music.

The opening scenes in *Strike!* resemble living newspaper productions in three ways: First, as Franklin D. Roosevelt's Second Inaugural Address spoke broadly of "one third of a nation ill-housed, ill-clothed, ill-fed," the prologue to *Strike!* establishes the suffering of mill workers quantitatively:

A hundred thousand other
held down like you.

There is also the use of direct address, which confronts the audience with the problem, implores them to understand, and ultimately transfers to them the responsibility for a solution.

listen world
you understand
we don't want no fight
but we gotta save ourselves
our kids, and a hundred thousand other souls
We gotta world that's all.

Finally, there is a clever use of choral chants and slogans intended to serve as rallying cries for the audience. It is easy to envision an audience being caught up in the simple rhythms of the poetry when the prologue ends with the chorus chanting:

Now the time has come to strike. . .
walk out and strike. (Prolg. 1–5)

The dreamlike quality of the prologue as the strike begins is very dramatic and aggressive without being wholly confrontational.

When *Strike!* was produced in 1931, the New England textile strikes were specters of a somewhat distant past. Even though *Strike!* is a dramatic interpretation of the Gastonia mill strike, the several references to the northern textile strikes would have been enough to resurrect a few ghosts of labor militancy. The audience who came to view *Strike!* was not a labor audience: it was a resort crowd, a summer crowd, a wealthy, artistic crowd who made the pilgrimage to Provincetown from New York each season. It was a crowd that reveled in its own liberal regional identity—an identity not underestimated by Blake. Blake's dialogue plays to northern biases. There are several instances where characters speak of returning to the North, and to New York. The North becomes a haven of repose and reason. Northern characters are depicted as less violent than the gun-toting Southerners. Negative regional stereotypes of the South are played upon fully for the benefit of the New England audiences. Implicitly, the South is judged and condemned, and the playwright expects and encourages the audience to participate in the judgment; the play is so structured that the audience is continually asked to pass judgment. This culminates in the final courtroom scene, where the audience participates as jury members.

The protagonist, Fer, is the union organizer. Like Peel in *Strike Song*, he achieves cult-like religious stature. Fer is a pacifist who opposes the use of guns and is himself the target of violence by men willing to hang him if he reappears in their town. Fer's character is larger-than-life: the crowd awaits his return as a second coming of a hero who will champion their cause. His efforts are supported by three female characters, one of whom is Maime Lewes, the ballad-writing equivalent of Ella May Wiggins who, like Wiggins, is shot in the course of the play. Her personal circumstances and the plight of her children dramatize the textile strike in yet another sociological arena. We learn early on that Mamie Lewes was abandoned by her husband and that of the eight children she bore, four died from ailments brought on by life in a mill town. She makes $8.40 per week in the mill. This background reinforces Fer as the savior of women and children.

As Mamie relates how her husband became discouraged and left, she is interrupted by the announcement that Fer is returning. The subtext clearly implies that, unlike other men connected with the mill, Fer will not abandon them. Blake chooses to keep Fer from the audience but allows us to participate as members of the crowd gathered to hear their leader. We see him through the eyes of the crowd, who strain to catch a glimpse of him in the distance. We hear the disembodied voice of Fer but never see him as he begins, "This is my sermon. It's the same old sermon. This is a strike, not a feud. A strike. I don't want any violence. Let the violence come from them not from us. You all keep cool. I talk this to you in private, and I talk it to you from the platform" (1:1).

Like Peel's opening lines in *Strike Song*, Fer's carry religious overtones. Fer's actual arrival is inauspicious and anticlimactic: he merely rounds the corner and sits down at a table in a restaurant. The disembodied voice that intones his sermons is reunited with its mortal source. His ensuing discussion about religion, union organizers, and the role of women gives shape to the perceptions of both northern organizers and southern labor. In large measure it reflects perceptions borne out in the press and by labor historians writing about the Gastonia strike; however, one must keep in mind that the source for Blake's script was the novel of a labor journalist. Fer recognizes that he stands as an outsider—dialogue early in the play speaks to this. Irma, Fer's co-organizer and lover, addresses the issue directly, noting, "We're much more comfortable with the foreign workers in the North. We understand them better. We even understand their religious background better." Fer echoes this in his own response. He recognizes too, that "these people think a Union is like a Church. They think its kinda like salvation. You belong to the union and somehow or other you are saved. They have a mystical feeling about the Union."

Irma and Ma Gilfillan take aggressive leadership roles in the strike. They are depicted as instrumental in maneuvering strikers and orchestrating crowds. Mamie Lewes is a simpler character and less of a political force in this play than Irma: it is Irma who speaks to the crowds and Ma Gilfillan who tells men to "join the Union . . . or git." Women dominate the first union meeting of the production; it is run by Irma, the northern organizer, who, more than Fer, pragmatically oversees the day-to-day organization of the mill workers and the implementation of the strike. Fer is a masculine figurehead symbolizing strength and protection but who, in actuality, is a sincere idealogue caught in a situation beyond his control. Irma is the spirit and intellect of the strike. She, not Fer, possesses the requisite political savvy to push the organizing efforts forward in the name of Fer. Calling the meeting to order, she first addresses the question of scabs. The solution offered by the women, in the voice of Ma Gilfillin, is aggressive and violent. She wants to "Get . . . some boys and girls and whip the scabs. And whip them so they won't want to go to no mill" (1:3).

Mary Heaton Vorse's revisions of Blake's original script reveal that she wanted a different role for the female characters. The version in her papers has a decidedly feminist approach: the female characters more fully developed, and in this sense the text is more historically accurate. All evidence indicates that Vorse had a strong hand in reshaping the script. Where Blake's original emphasized Fer and Mamie Lewes, Vorse's revision featured the strikers as a group more prominently. The female leaders, the characters of Irma and Ma Gilfillan, dominate; there is greater emphasis on the woman as activist than as abandoned domestic. There is far greater discussion of women's role as strikers victimized by industrial abuse and of their efforts to save their children from further abuse in the mills than there is of their victimization by irresponsible spouses. This political militancy is evident throughout the revised version of the script. In his first draft of the script, Blake had allowed the treatment of the militant role of striking southern women to be continually interrupted; the Vorse version provided for their development as protagonists.

Irma gives the audience an overt analysis of the South's labor problems and the inability of its workers to organize. The religious metaphors she uses resonate throughout the play: references to Fer alternate between a David battling a Goliath of the mills, and a Messiah. Irma's lines combine these images in one analysis:

The South's hard to organize. They don't understand unionism and the labor movement. You have to approach them thru their religion. They look on Fer as tho he were some David defying the Goliath of the mills. He's a Messiah to them. You heard them there on the hillside this afternoon. Fer'd been kidnapped and gone three days. When he came back they pointed him out to each other. 'That's Fer' they said. It was the way they said it. It was like saying, 'That's god'(Sc. 2).

Later references to Romans and Christians, Caesar and the catacombs, surface periodically throughout the dialogue to reinforce the martyr imagery. Fer's inability to understand the southern worker's unwillingness to separate the economic and political facts of unionism from their stalwart faith in a religion that will deliver them from hardship is attributed to cultural differences between northerners and southerners.

Fer: . . . You know, they'd do a lot better if they had a southern fellow for their leader. Oh, they like me, they came to me and asked me to lead the strike. But I don't belong to them, not really belong.

Irma: That's true. We're much more comfortable with the foreign workers in the North. We understand them better. We even understand their religious background better.

Fer: Yes. You know these people think a Union is like a church. They think its kinda like salvation. You belong to the Union and somehow or other you're saved. They aren't yet sufficiently educated to Unionism to use it as a political weapon in their fight against the bosses. They're not far enough away yet from camp meetings and religious revivals. They have an almost mystical feeling about the union.

Irma: Yes. And then the mill's company preachers are fundamentalists. Their salary is paid by the company that owns the mill. Naturally they think that Unionism in any form is the work of the devil. So that here in the south you get the feeling of two religions fighting each other (Sc. 2).

The idea of a jihad, or "holy war," is a term connected today with religious strife among radical muslim groups in the Middle East, yet the metaphor of a holy war can be applied to the union organizing efforts of the first part of this century. *Strike!* offers interesting comparisons between the Wobblies (i.e. the International Workers of the World, or I. W. W.) and other union organizers; comparisons taken directly from Vorse's novel. In a short speech, the character of Hoskins admonishes Roger Hewlett not to think Fer scared or to question his commitment. He refers to Fer as a boy, a young fellow, and characterizes contemporary labor radicals as "kinda stringy," reinforcing the perception that the organizing effort is a radical movement led by the young. At times, the organizing effort is evoked in images more reminiscent of a children's crusade, more than a political and economic labor movement:

Roger: . . . In circumstances like these the Wobblies were hell-raisers. We don't seem to have any cussing hell-raisers in the labor movement any more. There isn't a hard loined son of a gun among them all. They're little fellows, young fellows. You know, radicals run kinda stringy in America. I guess that's because most of them come from the cities while the Wobblies came out of the woods and prairies and mines. There's a real terror here, though, all right.

When asked if the terror is "worse than the Wobblies had" Hoskins offers another insight:

Roger: Different. Altogether different. The south's hard to understand. No one understands it, not even the southerners. Fer doesn't understand it and he knows he doesn't understand it. . . . People carry guns much more in the south than in the north. It's legal here. Only one thing people watching a strike don't understand is that in ninety-nine cases out of a hundred its the police that start the trouble, especially among the textile people. Get that into your head, if you want to report any strike, and get it into your head that the leaders want trouble even less. This small number of northern people naturally don't want violence.

When Roger learns that the northern organizers number only two men and three women, he is struck by the response they have generated in the press:

Roger: You mean that all this row in the papers about northern agitators is about two men and three women? All this hysteria, all this mob hatred, all these editorials. . . all about a handful of kids (Sc. 2).

The North/South contrasts evident early in this script grow stronger as the play progresses. Comments like "We ain't used to strikes like Fer says they is up North" point to a kind of cultural resistance to organize on the part of southern labor. This attitude of resistance is then juxtaposed in a discussion, continually buoyed by subtle reference to the Civil War, of the use of the militia against strikers   Mamie notes "The militia will be fighting their own kin if they go against us. They's hill folks, same as we." She recalls with some poignancy the national strife that split families, brother against brother, as well as political states. This is a theme to which Mamie returns in a later scene. Blake supplies groups with a collective identity that allows them to function as characters in the play. The mill laborers establish an identity separate from those they identify as their oppressors, whom they label as "the comfortable people." The lines Blake uses to demonstrate the collective consciousness of the groups manifest both group cohesiveness and group paranoia. The strikers see themselves as "hill people" possessing a common sense and decency violated by the industrialists who seek to exploit them; they claim the "comfortable people" think they "ain't ordinary people" and "hate them and will shoot them if they aren't careful" (1:1). This is supported in the violent reprisals directed towards the mill workers by the "comfortable" few. As in *Strike Song*, the Committee of One Hundred becomes the villainous force in the play.

A discussion of "the mob" is a primary focus in the dialogue. The conversations carefully chronicle illegal strike-breaking actions. While the nature of the mob is revealed in more detail, so too are "the movement" and the individuals in it. Fer laments that both his strikers and the mob that moves against them have violent tendencies that arise from their southern backgrounds. His line "I wish I were north. I wish I were leading a strike of people I was used to" (Sc. 2) would have been sympathetically received by northerners summering on Cape Cod. Blake extends this appeal to northern liberalness in later scenes, when he has Fer comment on southern sensitivity to critical northern newspaper accounts of the labor strife in North Carolina.

Scene 3 provides a scathing enactment of southern prejudices. The rhetorical device employed so deftly is that of antithesis, or sharp contrast. Three vignettes intertwine to produce a pejorative commentary on Southerners, both men and women. As the scene opens, a parade of striking workers appears, carrying banners with such slogans as "MUST OUR CHILDREN GO TO THE MILLS," "NO MORE NIGHT WORK FOR MOTHERS," and "WE WANT SCHOOLS." The argument here, as evidenced by the banners and evidenced in the ideas presented throughout this script, work on a level of pathos, continually lamenting the hardships inflicted upon families by uncaring mill owners. The visual argument of the placards delineates the problems of children and families affected by the mills.

Following this demonstration of need for the children, the script reverts to antithetically contrasting scenes in which townspeople complain about the presence of the union and its threat to their community. A young girl petulantly renounces the strikers for ruining plans for the apple blossom festival and "upsetting everything." Her shallowness and indifference to children and mothers working in the mill serves to reinforce a picture of southern women as self-indulgent and unconcerned. The characterization of southern men is even more odious. The scene concludes with a chilling discussion by two men about "hunting niggers." This scene is surely one of the most shocking and potentially volatile exchanges of dialogue from this period: two nameless predators discuss hunting human beings as though they were small game and, though they reach the conclusion that "there ain't many niggers here to hunt," they concede that it might be equally "fun" to hunt a strike leader:

Second Voice: Say, did you ever hunt a nigger?

First Voice: Naw, there ain't many niggers here to hunt. Ain't many niggers in Stonerton.

Second Voice: It sure would be fun to hunt a nigger.

First Voice: Yeah, it sure would be fun to hunt a nigger.

Second Voice: They say they're doing to hunt this here strike leader out of town.

First Voice: They ought to hunt him out of the state. Did you all know they was making a committee of a hundred? . . .It's for protecting the people. It's for stopping these here Union leaders from tearing up our city and inciting the mill workers to riot.

The scene ends ominously as the voices agree to assist the Committee of a Hundred in its efforts" (1:3).

The progression of scenes displaying in seriatim a crusading movement of ignorance, shallowness, and stupidity, and finally obscene bigotry powerfully depicts the emotional excesses of the period and place. Blake and Vorse's juxtaposition of scenes shapes the impression of a rag-tag group of labor revolutionaries, led by northern outsiders who will be forced to confront formidable cultural obstacles in an intransigent South. The devout hope and faith placed in the union serve as the fulcrum by which the workers hope to move the mountain of injustice.

Blake's reliance on religious imagery is carried throughout the scenes. Like the Lily May character in *Strike Song*, Mamie Lewes in this script assumes the role of a prophetess. Her continual comments on how the militia "come from the hills same as we" and her inability to accept that "kin" could turn against "kin" foreshadow the violence to come. In this script, as in the first, there is a reliance on superstition, as characters sense that "something is going to happen" and are told that "it's in the air." Blake creates an ethereal atmosphere that resonates with the qualities of classical tragedy. A refrain in the choral passages provides a litany of offenses suffered at the hands of the mill bosses. A prayer in verse offered by Brother Williams, evokes the scriptural analogy of Israel in bondage:

Brother Williams:
   Oh, how these people have suffered, Lord!
   Oh, Lord, hear them in their struggle!
   Oh, Lord, soften the hearts of their employers!
   Oh, I never heard anything like how they treat these folks!
   Oh, I come from the mountains where folks is free to breathe
   God's free air!
   Oh, I seen women and little, little children a-working in the mills where
   they wasn't meant to!
   Oh, the Lord sent the children of Israel out of bondage!
   Oh, the Lord softened Pharaoh's heart!
   Oh, ain't Basil Schenck's heart going to be softened!

Oh, this old man ain't never seen nothing like these militia with their tear
gas bombs and their bayonets!
Oh, they're a prancing all over the town!
Oh, they're arresting girls and women!
Amen!

The song of Mamie Lewes that follows within seconds of this dirge-like prayer
has a blues structure without the repetition of the first two lines:

Mamie Lewes: (singing)
> We leave our homes in the morning
> We kiss our children goodbye
> While we slave for the bosses
> Our children scream and cry.
>
> And when we draw our money
> Our grocery bills to pay
> Not a cent to spend for clothing
> Not a cent to lay away.
>
> How it grieves the heart of a mother
> You every one must know
> But we can't buy for our children
> Our wages are too low.
>
> It is for our little children
> That seem to us so dear
> But for them, nor us, nor workers,
> The bosses do not keer.

Blake's verse provides a poetic foil for the dialogue that relies on
documentary detail. A great deal of the dialogue is derived from that in
Vorse's novel. Some of it is transferred verbatim, as in the comparison of the
Wobblies to other union organizers. Other scenes reflect the novel's detail,
such as the discussion of overworked mothers, and the brutality with which the
eviction of strikers from company homes is carried out.

The eviction of families, even those with children with smallpox, from
their homes occurs in the mid-point of the play, scene 7. The eviction of the
strikers and their subsequent establishment of a tent city outside the boundaries
of the company town allow Blake to display techniques that would become
staples in living newspaper productions. He makes use of figures—the five
hundred who would be made homeless in the eviction—and notes with biting
irony that if five hundred people were homeless due to a natural disaster the
Red Cross would come to offer aid, while no one came to the aid of mill
strikers. The details given of the eviction paint for the audience a dark picture

of inhumane southern industrial villains, toward whom the audience was to respond with antipathy. The "smallness and meanness" of mill owners is proven positively when the house of a mill worker's house with a child with small pox is tear-gassed. In this documentary incident the child's disease led to an indictment of southern public health practices and its ignorant rejection of vaccination requirements and quarantine laws. Blake is able to articulate the real social and civil rights issues of the strike as being beyond better wages and living conditions: "It's bigger than that. . . . Its what all the workers is struggling for. . . . It's getting in a place where we ain't dirt under other peoples feet not more. It's fighting to have our own place in the world equal to other folks." The most poignant casualties of the labor wars, the old and the young, are shown against a backdrop of a deserted tent colony. The first half of the play lays out the evidence for the audience; the last half calls them to pass judgment on legal and ethical grounds.

It is in the final courtroom scenes that Blake makes the heaviest and most convincing use of documentary evidence from the Gastonia trials. The final scenes focus on a tainted judicial process. Here Blake creates one of the most interesting scenes of all the labor plays of this period. The trial of the union organizers is structured to make the audience part of the jury—a jury privy to the thoughts of other jury members. It is a rigged jury in many respects, because Blake has orchestrated it to be a northern jury, sure to reach the proper verdict. The scene offers a psychological *tour de force*, conveying the action from the point of view of the jurors who speak their private thoughts aloud. The exposition, as the jurors' thoughts are individually related to the audience, indicates that the jurors sense that their position is untenable because of the sympathy generated by the press for the organizers and strikers: "They's all gonna laugh at us if we convict. We ain't got no evidence." They recognize that the state lawyer is trying to play on their emotions by prominently situating in the courtroom the widow and daughter of the dead policeman. Despite their recognition of the manipulativeness of this pathos, it is nonetheless effective, and they succumb to it. Blake sustains his use of a technique that allows the audience to view the manipulation of the jury's thoughts as the trial progresses. One juror thinks of the widow and her loss: "They's looking at us as tho we could make it right." Another interjects caution at being manipulated by the prosecuting attorney: "We gotta be careful of this lawyer with his smooth ways and fine talk." The emotional instability of another juror surfaces as he begins to fantasize that he buried his wife alive and that the deputies will present his wife's coffin in the courtroom. This psychological study is effective in depicting the intellectual deficiencies of the jury, which again, played to northern stereotypes of rural Southerners. Blake recreates virtually verbatim one of the most extraordinary scenes in southern legal history, the incident that caused a mistrial in the Gastonia case—the presentation in court of a lifelike cast of the sheriff's body, painted with realistic accuracy, clothed in the uniform in which he was slain. It was this unprecedented event that led to the actual emotional breakdown of a juror, and the subsequent declaration of a mistrial.[13]

After Mamie Lewes is shot, Blake continues to prod his audience to a condemnation of the mill owners. The cowardice of the attack in which Lewes is shot in the back is reinforced for negative effect by the apprehended killer arrogantly asserting:

Man: Sure I done it. We gotta kill these union rats. Gotta shoot 'em down like niggers. . . . Sure, they're gonna arrest me. But it ain't gonna mean nothing. The judge knows we're fighting to keep you Union rats down. The mill bosses will see that I don't go to no jail. I'll be out in two days and I'll be back to get some more of you. (Sc. 11)

The philosophical and pragmatic justification for Fer's circumventing the law by jumping bail rests on his utility to the movement somewhere else, somewhere north. This particular scene plays directly to northern biases. Progressive northern efforts towards reconstruction, education, and unionization are shown to be thwarted in the South. The script expects the northern audience to participate in a self-righteous recognition of the stereotypes of conservative southern ignorance.

The concluding scenes are enacted on a massive scale, with bodies strewn about the stage in a manner reminiscent of the closing scenes of Shakespearean histories or tragedies. As a picket line of strikers chants "Strike!" the sound of a hundred guns rings out. In the melee Fer is mortally wounded. The final scene offers a dramatic closure to the play. The epilogue is poetic, and the use of a divided chorus of thirty-five to forty people on various levels evokes an air of ritual reminiscent of Greek tragedy. A mill preacher, one paid and controlled by the mill owners, refuses to bury the dead until the living "stop the strike." A chorus of mens' voices beseech Brother Williams, one of their own, to take over the service, and he does so using such ritualistic invocations such as "blood of my blood":

Men's Voices:
Brother Williams
preacher man from the hills
will you god let you come bury our dead
read the last prayer
sing the last hymn

Brother Williams:
  ay, workers
  my god send me
  to pray this prayer:
  Oh, Lord here are men in their coffins
  blood of my blood
  bone of my bone
  I trust, oh, Lord
  that these friends will go to a better place
  than this mill village
  or any other place in Carolina. . . . (Epilogue)

Where Fer's death is the chief focus in Blake's original version, the text altered to Vorse's specifications centers on the union and the audience. There is greater proselytizing in the final choral verses. The use of the rhetorical device of apostrophe makes this evident; "oh workers, . . . listen world." Where Blake's original script ended with voices intoning, "We gotta make a union. . . . We just gotta," and then singing the "International," the version contained in the Vorse papers is more militant, more aggressive, ending with the lines,

  . . . but now the time has come to FIGHT
  and fight
  and fight
  and fight
  go on
  and fight.

Discerning public response to the play is difficult. Reviews for the 1931 production in Provincetown are nonexistent. The Provincetown papers were destroyed in a fire that consumed copies of the runs of the newspaper between 1919 and 1935, and *Strike!* was not reviewed in the *Barnstable Patriot*, close to Provincetown. We are left with cryptic notes in the diaries of Mary Heaton Vorse and the opportunity to compare Blake's original script with the version in Vorse's papers, presumably the text she accepted after alteration for production. As noted earlier, the version of this play produced in January 1932 is radically different, based on a lengthy review of its production. That version seems to bear little resemblance to the text discussed here, but is interesting as a mutation of the other scripts[14].

Strike!, like *Strike Song*, offers a unique perspective on a radical incident in southern labor history. Its production undoubtedly helped Blake to secure a position with the Federal Theatre Project. The script, aided by Vorse's critical commentary, depicted the suffering and injustice endured by southern textile workers in a way that merged documentary detail with poetic form.

Blake was innovative in his use of dramatic techniques. The disembodied voices announcing verdicts and giving sermons, the psychological dissection of the jurors' thoughts, and the use of choral poetry were atypical of plays of this period that treated social themes. So too was the militance of the female characters. The collaborative inputs of Mary Heaton Vorse are evident in the revised script. Her literary efforts as a playwright have gone unheralded, though professional writers recognized clearly the potential of the theatre to give voice to their political positions.

The significance of leftist political theatre in the United States has long derived from the notoriety given a few dominant producing organizations, such as Labor Stage, the Group Theatre, the Artef, and Workers' Theatre. Also important were the efforts of less prominent writers and productions in the early 1930s in areas less accessible than New York, because they were the first to incorporate documentary detail. This production style would gain prominence much later in the decade, most notably with the Federal Theatre Project. The theatre is a derivative art, and the experimentation of such productions as both *Strike!* and *Strike Song* eventually became codified in the production style of the Federal Theatre Project. These were indigenous American productions treating indigenous themes through the use of documentary techniques that predate by almost a decade the documentary innovations credited to the Federal Theatre Project.

NOTES

1. Dee Garrison, *Rebel Pen: The Writings of Mary Heaton Vorse* (New York: Monthly Review Press, 1985), p. 113.

2. Editor's note to Benjamin De Casseres, "Has the Drama Gone Sissy?" *Theatre Magazine* (August, 1928): 7; and William Dorsey Blake, "Stray Shots at the Sissy Theme," *Theatre Magazine* (October, 1928): 52.

3. Emmett Lavery, "The Flexible Stage," unpublished manuscript in Theatre of the Thirties Collection, Special Collections and Archives, George Mason University Library, Fairfax, VA.

4. See correspondence and papers in Theatre of the Thirties Collection, FTP 000 254, and correspondence in Paul Green Papers, #3693, Southern Historical Collection, University of North Carolina Library, Chapel Hill, N.C.; and the Cherry County Playhouse Collection in the Billy Rose Theatre Collection of the New York Public Library. The screenplay citation is found in *American Film Institute Catalogue of Motion Pictures 1961–70*, ed. Richard P. Krafsur (New York: R. R. Bowker, 1976), p. 975.

5. See Jay Williams, *Stage Left* (New York: Charles Scribner's Sons, 1974), pp. 7–8; and Helen Deutsch and Stella Hanau, *The Provincetown: A Story of the Theatre* (New York: Farrar and Rinehart, Inc., 1931), pp. 7–17. See also, Mary Heaton Vorse, *Time and the Town, A Provincetown Chronicle* (New York: Dial Press, 1942), pp.

197–212.

6. Letter, Lawrence Langer to Mary Heaton Vorse, November 24, 1930, Box 60, Folder 1930-Nov., in Mary Heaton Vorse Collection in the Archives of Labor and Urban Affairs, Walter P. Reuther Library, Wayne State University, Detroit, MI. The reader should recall that Loretta C. Bailey also submitted her play on the same subject to a competition sponsored by the Theatre Guild in 1932, and it too was rejected. See also letter, Emjo Basshe to Mary Heaton Vorse, May 3, 1931, Box 60, Correspondence, Folder 1931-April-May, in Mary Heaton Vorse Collection; and Letter, John Dos Passos to Mary Heaton Vorse, undated, Box 60, Folder 1929-1932, in Mary Heaton Vorse Collection.

7. Daily notes June 1930-1931, Box 82, Folder 1931-July, and letter, Mary Heaton Vorse to her Daughter, MHV Collection, Box 60, Folder 1931-June-Sept. See also Daily notes June 1930-June 1931, Box 82, Folders 1931-July, and 1931-Aug, Mary Heaton Vorse Collection; and letters to Mary Ellen Waldman, from Marvin Waldman, undated, Box 61, Folder 1932-Aug-Oct., Mary Heaton Vorse Collection.

8. Ibid.

9. Ibid.

10. Ibid.

11. References to the two scripts cited in this study are based on the two extant copies. One was obtained from the Library of Congress: William Dorsey Blake, *Strike!: A play in a prologue and fourteen scenes*, dramatized by William Dorsey Blake from the novel *Strike!* by Mary Heaton Vorse, TS photocopy in possession of the author. The second script, referred to as the "revised version," is *Strike!: A play in a prologue; thirteen scenes and an epilogue*, dramatized by William Dorsey Blake from the novel *Strike!* by Mary Heaton Vorse, copyright August 25, 1931; it is held in the Mary Heaton Vorse Collection, Box 40.

12. "What Is Going On," *Boston Evening Transcript*, 16 December 1932, p. 2, col. 7.; and W.E.H., "A Strike Recorded for the Theater," *Boston Evening Transcript*, 17 December 1932, part. 2, p. 4, cols. 1–2.; and "Notes About the Players," *The Boston Sunday Globe*, 18 December 1932, p. 45, col. 2.

13. Blake's reenactment of the incident leading to the mistrial and of other incidents in the play parallels Samuel Yellen's account of the conflict and trial in his chapter "The Southern Textile Strikes" in *American Labor Struggles* (New York : S. A. Russell, 1936) pp. 311–316. Yellen writes: "When the trial was resumed on August 26 at Charlotte, a prosecution staff of 10 was assembled, including Solicitor Carpenter, Clyde Hoey, a brother-in-law of Governor Gardner; Major A. L. Bulwinkle, special counsel for the Manville-Jenckes Company; and R. G. Cherry, state commander of the American Legion. Among the defense counsel were Dr. John R. Neal, who had been chief counsel for defense in the Scopes evolution trial at Dayton, Tennessee and Arthur Garfield Hayes. The selection of the jury required a full week, and when completed it consisted of a steel worker, a news vender, a union carpenter, a grocer, a railroad clerk, a machinist, two cotton-mill workers, and four farmers. On September 5 the taking of evidence began. At the opening of court the prosecution wheeled into the court room a life-size plaster-of-Paris figure of Aderholt draped in a black shroud. Solicitor Carpenter removed the shroud to reveal 'an exact reproduction of Aderholt in uniform, including hat and badge, complete to the shoestrings.' while Aderholt's widow,

dressed in black, sat weeping before the jury." The defense, of course, protested, and Judge Barnhill instantly ordered the figure removed; but an effect had already been produced "unexpectedly in September 9 one of the jurors went violently insane. Judge Barnhill, to the disappointment of the defense, which felt certain of acquittal, declared a mistrial and ordered a new trial for September 30. The news of the mistrial set loose a reign of terror in Mecklenburg, Gaston, and neighboring counties. On the night of September 9 a mob of 500 men raided strikers headquarters at Gastonia and Bessemer City. Part of the mob surrounded the boarding house of Ben Wells, C.D. Saylor, and C. M. Lell, all members of the National Textile Worker's Union at Gastonia, kidnapped them, drove to Cabarrus County, and there flogged Wells severely. Another part drove to Charlotte and surrounded the county jail and the offices of the defense counsel, threatening to kill both defendants and counsel. . . . Meanwhile, the National Textile Workers' Union announced a mass meeting for September 14, at South Gastonia. A mob collected to prevent the meeting. When a truck bearing 22 strikers and union members from Bessemer City tried to enter South Gastonia, it was turned back and 10 or 15 autos set out in pursuit. After a five-mile chase one of the autos blocked the road and the truck was stopped. A volley of shots was fired into the unarmed strikers, and one of them, Mrs. Ella May Wiggins, mother of five children, was instantly killed. The following day Solicitor Carpenter held seven men on charges of murder, six of whom were employed by the Loray mill. Other terroristic acts were committed. On September 18, for example, Cleo Tessnair, an organizer for the National Textile Workers Union was kidnaped at King's Mountain by armed vigilantes, taken across the state line into South Carolina, and badly beaten. . . . After this sequence of kidnappings, floggings, and shootings, the trial of the defendants in the Aderholt killing reopened on September 30. By this time the prosecution had changed its tactics. . . . The State . . . began to press for admission of evidence regarding communism, atheism, and race equality. E. T. Cansler, of the prosecution requested that Judge Barnhill grant the State the same permission granted the State in the Sacco-Vanzetti case and in the Haymarket case of 1886 to introduce the radical views of the defendants as evidence of conspiracy. Moreover, Cansler maintained that Beal, since he was an avowed Communist, was discredited as a witness, and that Carter, another of the defendants, was likewise discredited for having preached race equality. 'If teaching racial equality does not tend to impeach a witness, I do not know what would,' said Cansler . . . .The intrusion of political and religious issues continued; and in the final summation on October 18 Solicitor Carpenter referred to the defendants as 'devils with hoofs and horns, who threw away their pitchforks for shotguns.' . . . Carpenter emphasized his plea 'by lying down on the floor of the court to illustrate some of the testimony, kneeling and praying before the jury box and holding the hand of Mrs. Aderholt, the slain chief's widow, who attired in mourning sat wiping her eyes before the jury box.' . . . While the seven Gastonia defendants were convicted with dispatch and given severe sentences all endeavors to convict the kidnapers of Wells and the slayers of Mrs. Wiggins ended in failure. . . . In no instance was anyone convicted of a crime against a striker in Gastonia and the surrounding region. . . . In order to avoid serving the sentences, all seven jumped bail; two went into hiding in the United States, and the others, including Beal, escaped to Russia."

    14. The only extant review of *Strike!* is to be found in the *Boston Evening Transcript*, and this was for the Boston production opening in mid-December, 1932.

An announcement of December 16, 1932, reveals that the Ford Hall Forum Dramatic Society would present *Strike!* at the Barn located at 36 Joy Street. The theatre was in an upscale neighborhood, just below the State House on Beacon Hill. The following day the *Boston Evening Transcript* published its review. What is most remarkable about the review is that it reports on a completely different version of the play than in either of the two extant scripts. This points to the existence of still another scripted version of *Strike!* that has yet to be found. The reviewer comments on characters not in either version. While some of the elements remain the same, there is pronounced emphasis on the love relationships of a textile heir and the sister of a New York labor leader. What had been a powerful labor play was most obviously turned into a melodramatic love story. Whether or not these emendations were made with Mary Vorse's approval or knowledge makes for interesting conjectures. These scenes are not included in the copy of the script Blake filed in the U.S. Copyright Office, nor are they in the script held in the Mary Heaton Vorse Papers. According to Blake, the Provincetown papers carried favorable reviews of the summer production. The Boston paper, however, found elements both to praise and criticize. The review is included here to allow readers some insight into the production.

A Strike Recorded for the Theatre

That he who would write for the theater must first accept the theater's stern self-discipline in composition is an age-old adage. Its truth was proven again, however, last evening during the performance by the Ford Hall Forum Players of "Strike," a piece drawn by William Dorsey Blake from Mary Heaton Vorse's like-named novel. Though nearly three hours–clipped only by twelve exceedingly quick changes of scene–the company labored with an actable, but essentially undramatic script. For it was Miss Vorse's original purpose emphatically seconded by Mr. Blake to record on the printed page the principal events of the recent strike in southern mills. Fictitious as may be the characters, they carry on their shoulders a full expression of all the subtler facts regarding an allegedly intolerable social condition. With credit to themselves the two authors avoid inflamed arguments. Not in the ordinary sense is "Strike" a propaganda drama. Yet the intensity with which it records a grievous "case" dulls much of its effectiveness on the stage.

The kernel of plot upon which the play is threaded holds more possibilities than the adapter apparently would admit. Following an impressively stylized chanted prologue, we spectators enter the drawing room of an ancient southern family–the Hadley's of Stonerton. There we learn that Mr. Hadley is the largest mill operator in town; that his son, far from dutifully falling in love with the girl of his father's choice, has gone to New York to pursue his taste for music; that young Dan Hadley has had the ill-luck to admire, marry and become the disciple of a remarkable labor leader's faithful sister. Returning to his home in the Carolinas, he therefore sides with Fred and Jean Bretting instead of his dad. Complications naturally ensue, and it is with the clash of three idealists against an enraged, armed township that the play has to do. Sabine Walling, the heiress, who had set her heart on Don, and the unwavering Jean, find themselves strangely united by the death of first Fred and then Don. Their mingled curses flow easily into a charged epilogue as inspiring but not so impressive as the opening scene. Without a quiver of doubt one may accept the human interest of both the problem and the play. A dramatist would not need to have the heart or the talent of William

Shakespeare to find here a subject ready made for poignant tragedy. By their restraint, their evident honesty of purpose and occasional flashes of technique, Miss Vorse and Mr. Blake at times almost mine the golden ore themselves. Practically every one of the eleven scenes is potentially viable in terms of stark, unadorned theatre. Drama marches for instance through the homecoming of the boy with his secret terrible for a loving father to hear. It rumbles again when in blind impudence that father attempts to buy off his unacceptable daughter-in-law [and] when the grim manhunt for Fred and later Don himself begins. Always off-stage, save only in one savage scene, are the forces of law and order. Yet we spectators thrill to the lurking fear of the workers, tremble lest a spark will set off the guns. And when the sheriff, followed soon after by the militia, does start his dread work, we know the meaning of despair.

Many of the scenes which under present handling do not completely take fire, convey nevertheless the feverish tension, the counter-plotting of two aides engaged in relentless warfare. For example we see the labor leaders consulting in a shabby restaurant, we watch the mill-owners plan reprisals; the evicted laborers stride aimlessly the streets; the furtive meetings on distant hillsides, and finally the desperate chase, the slaughter of innocents to the tune of the Doxology. A newspaper reporter familiar with every angle of his trade, could no better. But a dramatist seeking to tell a suspenseful story in terms of individual human beings, would know that in thus merely summoning grim scenes, engaging color, reality in the raw, he had not entirely fulfilled his contract. The latent drama should build with a swifter pace, less talk, more action.

Where Miss Vorse, the novelist, gained and Mr. Blake, the playwright, fails is in the utter faithfulness with which detail after detail is crammed into the narrative. Much of the dialogue is repetitious, words to an extreme. Yet at times it becomes sardonic, acrid in its straightforward values for those interested in social and economic philosophy. Even such ironic tad-bits as the labor leaders confessing that they save their own souls with high ideals, but those of others with the promise of wages doubled 100 percent, are not allowed to escape our observation. One hesitates to decry a play so closely woven. For in its least dramatic moments it somehow contrives to picture extremely well the dumb, helpless weight of the mob swayed hither and yon by successive waves of excitement.

To these matters the Ford Hall Forum Players brought last evening a large, and for the most part, well trained cast. The chanted prologue with its constantly repeated chorus, its strangely assorted voices leaping this way and that out of the assembled crowd, was a work of rare skill, moving theater-craft. To an occasional player, too, came moments of inspiration. Mr. Mark Gershon was a toneless, gestureless, but very effective mill-owner, with the clean, sure competency of utter self-confidence. Miss Sara Bailet sketched in the labor leader, Jean Brettling. In similar, but sterner more masculine terms Louis Balsam did a similar job for Fred while the nervous staccato presence of Mr. Morton Baerson's Don Hadely wove a persuasive image of the younger scion of wealth fitting himself to a strange unreal environment. Least sure of all the elements was Mr. Blake's direction. A small stage, [and] large crowds excuse many things but not the ineffective groupings repeatedly assumed. As playwright he should weave a tighter thread of action; as stage director he should build up his crowd scenes with a richer flow of meaningful action and emotional pantomime. Play and production would be the better for both. W.E.H., *Boston Evening Transcript*, 17, December 1932, part 2, p. 4 cols. 1–2.

The last mention of the play in this run occurs the following day, when the *Boston Sunday Globe* carried an announcement noting that "William Blake, author of 'Strike' . . . will be the speaker tomorrow evening at the John Reed Club, 823 Boylston St." His topic that evening was "The Theatre and Propaganda." In "Notes About the Players," *The Boston Sunday Globe*, 18 December 1932, p. 45, col. 2.

CHAPTER 4

Altars of Steel: The Steel Industry in the South

When Hallie Flanagan envisioned the regional contributions of the Federal Theatre Project, she saw the South as posing the "most fascinating problem." In her mind playwrights needed to exploit the rich indigenous material of southern culture and labor. She realized that for decades the South "had witnessed no professional theatre activity" and that in 1935 the time was right to extend the resources of a federally funded national theatre program below the Mason-Dixon line. Organizing theatre professionals from southern relief rolls posed a formidable problem. The original southern plan called for FTP companies in New Orleans, Dallas, Birmingham, Jacksonville, Tampa, and Miami using what Flanagan called a "flying-squadron method" of production. This plan entailed a core of individuals comprising a stage designer and technicians, a director and a publicist, to tour from one state to another organizing and mounting productions. "The whole south was planned as one schedule, thus permitting the use of some of the same plays, equipment and personnel, all under supervision of the regional director and his aides." They drew their ideas from the region, recognizing the diversity of the states and the ethnic groups within them.

The idea for *Altars of Steel*, which Flanagan called "our most important southern production," came from an address by John Temple Graves, lawyer and editor of the *Birmingham* (Alabama) *Age-Herald*, at a meeting of the directors of Federal Theatres of the South. Graves delivered a speech on October 7, 1936, that provided the impetus for the production of *Altars of Steel*, which, by Flanagan's estimation, was the most successful play written for and about the South[1]. Graves's speech, though brief, identified three major social problems facing the region. The first fell under "the problem of the tenant farmer, a problem of poverty, poverty of people and poverty of soil." Answers, he maintained, were being sought in "government loans, the development of industry, and the development of education, both liberal and scientific." In the conclusion of this discussion he mentioned the "problem of absentee ownership draining the resources of the South" and how in this "the dramatist should find material." The second problem was the "development and assimilation of the Negro in economic, political and social ways." This he felt would present "material for many plays." Finally he alluded to the third problem, the industrialization of the South, concerning which he reflected; "Steel and cotton are dictating a whole new political economy for the South. Why not a play about steel?"

Historians today attribute the transition of the South of the 1920s and 1930s to what has been termed the New South, to "the work of prewar liberal newspaper editors and the post-war crumbling of the Jim Crow era." John Temple Graves is identified as one of the individuals who helped to promote the "rise of southern liberalism." In a special issue of the *Mississippi Quarterly* that addressed the theme of "The South in Transition," John Michael Matthews considered the influence of Graves on southern liberalism. His introduction provided insight into many of Graves's positions:

Southern liberals would never have been able to agree on a definition of their own liberalism or on a coherent program of reform for the south;. . .Nevertheless, fuzzy and inadequate as were their solutions to the South's ills, southern liberals found larger agreement on what needed to be changed. In the 1920s they stood on common ground denouncing the Ku Klux Klan, racial lynchings, religious bigotry, prohibition, and other social ills and cultural shortcomings. By the following decade the depression had diverted their attention to the South's overwhelming economic problems—sharecropping and the one crop cotton economy, dire poverty, industrial backwardness, and sadly neglected public services. Many of them looked to the emergence of labor unions as one key to modernization; most, with varying degrees of enthusiasm, welcomed the New Deal[2].

The Federal Theatre Project was part of the New Deal that may well have appealed to Graves in its development of the arts in a culturally rich, though economically deprived, region. It seems obvious now that Graves knew of the existence of the script for *Altars of Steel*. In reconstructing the chronology of events that led to its production it becomes clear that the script was delivered to the Federal Theatre Project's southern Bureau soon after Graves's speech. His editorial published in the *Birmingham Age-Herald*, the morning of his speech reinforces his enthusiasm for the Federal Theatre Project and previews the sentiments he would express later in the day to the FTP directors:

The Federal Theaters of the south with their discoveries of plays, players and playwriters, with the encouragements and opportunities they are giving to the histrionic impulses of this section, with the entertainment, inspiration and education they are providing the southern public deserve surely to be written down as one of the New Deal agencies with which no one has a quarrel. The south is full of drama today, and of people with a precious urge to drama. The combination of momentous event and mighty imagining makes a natural theater of our southern scene. The Federal Theaters are giving manuscripts to the event and footlights to the imagining. They are helping the south to know itself and to express itself—and that, as all the philosophers agree, is civilization's *sine qua non*[3].

The process of having a script accepted for production by the Federal Theatre Project was not complicated, but given the slowness of mail delivery in 1936, it was time-consuming. As a matter of practice scripts were sent to the Playreading Department in New York, overseen by Francis Bosworth. Proposed scripts were then sent to reviewers, who submitted "playreader reports." These reports provided a brief synopsis of the play, followed by a detailed synopsis, then critical comments, and finally a recommendation to accept or reject the script. Graves's speech was given in the first week in October; the first playreader report of *Altars of Steel* by Thomas Hall Rogers was returned November 18, 1936, by John Rimassa to Francis Bosworth in New York. Rimassa recommended rejecting the play calling it "Very bad! This play isn't geared for emotional or character appeal. Except for a few mawkish spots it concentrates entirely, and in long-winded speeches, upon social comment"[4].

The FTP Play Bureau's southern branch was active in the mid-thirties, and despite the script's rejection in New York, *Altars of Steel* went into production in Birmingham where enthusiasm for it was high. Flanagan assigned some of the FTP's best personnel to the project. Joseph Lentz's set design, which he promised to keep under $500, called for all scenic elements to have the look of steel, even the proscenium curtain. Hedley Gordon Graham, who had been responsible for such Works Progress Administration plays as *Triple A Plowed Under* and *O Say Can You Sing*, was sent to Birmingham to direct.

Thomas Hall Rogers is an elusive literary figure whose very existence seems to depend on *Altars of Steel*; though he is mentioned in a few books as "a Birmingham author," there is no other physical evidence that he lived or died. There is no record of him in the Birmingham Historical Society, the Southern Research Department at the Birmingham Public Library, or the Alabama Department of Archives and History; nor is there any personal information about him in the Federal Theatre Project Collection at George Mason University beyond his name on the title page of *Altars of Steel*. "Thomas Hall Rogers" was, in fact, a pseudonym. While only one southern reviewer noted that Rogers was "obviously a pseudonym," much was made of the intrigue surrounding the identity of the author in northern papers. *The Philadelphia Inquirer* ran an article claiming that the Federal Theatre officials were "shielding the name of the author" of *Altars of Steel* at his insistence because of his "fear of personal violence to himself or family and loss of his position. . . . he prefers to be known only as Thomas Hall Rogers." The article went on to claim that "many believe him to be connected with a steel mill in Birmingham, Alabama." It cites the FTP publicity direcior, Sara Sanders Thomas, as saying: "We have instructions to keep the identity of the author an absolute secret. I don't think anyone in Atlanta and very few persons any where know who he is"[5].

One must consider the strong evidence that the editor John Temple Graves was, in fact, the author of *Altars of Steel.* Even if this contention is incorrect, it is still probable that Graves knew well the individual who did write under the name Thomas Hall Rogers. It is altogether too coincidental that he would suggest a play about the southern steel industry and that one should appear in the FTP Play Bureau's southern offices within days. During his career Graves's literary efforts extended to writing nationally syndicated columns and publishing articles in such respectable journals as the *Nation*; he even tried his hand writing novels. It is easily conceivable, if not probable, that Graves ventured into scriptwriting in the 1930s and produced the script that became *Altars of Steel.*

The time-lapse from idea to production was but five months. Even though the play was well into rehearsals in the South, the script was still being bounced interdepartmentally in the Federal Theatre Project offices in New York and, ironically, still meeting with rejection. The Experimental Theatre of the FTP received it, and in February 1937 their Playreading Department received two recommendations to reject Rogers's play from readers Munson and Solomon, who called it "too naive to merit consideration." For the purposes of this study, the most interesting rejection notice for *Altars of Steel* came from John Wexley, whose play, *Steel,* is the last script examined in this study. While his play, treating northern steel issues, was in production at Labor Stage in New York, Wexley was also serving as a reader for the Federal Theatre Project. Hiram Motherwell, then working for the FTP as well, sent Wexley the script of *Altars of Steel* to review. Wexley's critique of the play and his references to other assignments and meetings indicates a previously overlooked association between Wexley and the Federal Theatre Project. The evaluation of *Altars of Steel* he sent to Motherwell on March 27, 1937, found little to praise. "My most serious criticism of this play," he wrote, "is that it is hardly a play, but rather a narrative in the shape of a number of haphazardly related scenes. In my opinion the author would have had more success had he written it in the form of a novel. . . . I would venture that Federal Theatre audiences would find the play, in its present stage, very uninteresting and in many places ludicrously unreal"[6].

Altars of Steel opened a few days later, April 1, 1937, but not in Birmingham, where the production had begun. In what was touted as a unique effort to foster "community co-operation," at the invitation of the Atlanta Little Theatre Guild it was moved to Atlanta. It opened at the Atlanta Theatre with a combined cast of seven Federal Theatre Project actors from New York, twenty-eight from Birmingham, and the remaining sixty-five coming from the ranks of the Atlanta Theatre Guild and the drama departments of schools and colleges in and around Atlanta[7].

The production was artistically innovative in its approach. It culled techniques derived from living newspaper productions and blended them with more traditionally structured dramatic conventions. The simulated steel set, which called for massive steel doors instead of a proscenium curtain, extended out beyond the stage lip and incorporated the adjoining boxes into its design. Reviewers could not ignore the staging and scenic elements, calling them alternately "massive," "modernistic," and "impressionistic." It was a noisy production; music, sounds of the steel mill, and a cast of a hundred responding mob-like to political and labor propaganda created a din that critics found objectionable. However, it was the political and labor positions espoused in the production that caused the most controversy and made *Altars of Steel* one of the most discussed southern plays of the decade.

It most certainly was discussed within the offices of the Federal Project in New York. The week the play opened Hiram Motherwell, with some irony, sent an interdepartmental memo addressed to "Esther Porter, John Wexley & all who enjoy a laugh." In it he cited reviews from the Atlanta papers that called *Altars of Steel* "as great a play as was ever written" and the "best drama ever presented here"[8]. The in-house reviewers had been dead wrong about the reception the play would receive and the interest and controversy it would generate. The newspaper critics deemed *Altars of Steel* dangerous, but whether it promoted capitalism, liberalism, communism, socialism, or just out-and-out radicalism, was a matter of some disagreement among critics. Nonetheless, the play was an artistic and financial success unequaled in the FTP's productions in the South.

THE SCRIPT

Altars of Steel was written in sixteen scenes[9]. Though conceived as a continuous performance, the text includes a notation at the end of the sixth scene allowing for a curtain should it be "deemed advisable." The Atlanta productions played without intermissions. The script focuses on the evils of absentee ownership and the predatory nature of giant business conglomerates, devouring independently owned mills in towns and cities across the country. Like many of the WPA productions it pits the little man against a powerful industrial monolith. Like *Strike Song*, *Altars of Steel* portrays with nostalgic sentimentality the paternalistic attitudes of southern mill owners. As in other southern labor plays, an undercurrent of anti-northern paranoia surfaces among the reflections on southern culture. Rogers offers perceptive insights into traditional southern values, but he also contrasts the underprivileged labor force, which included groups excluded on ethnic grounds from mainstream southern culture. The first scene, in which mill workers arrive at the gate outside the southern Steel Company for the 3:00 shift, underscores this ethnic segregation. Blacks are present, as well as Poles and other poor whites, referred to as "hunkies." The ethnic mix of the workers contributes to a mistrust among the workers, creating social anomie. The air is charged: conversation is peppered with epithets about "informers," "sticking by your own class," "exploiters," and "lousy communists." Each segregated group directs its own bigotry towards other discriminated-against groups. Their dialogue throughout the play offers a continuous stream of sociological commentary.

The documentary elements of the script are not always readily evident. A great many surface as allusions to actual southern labor issues and incidents that cut across several industries—rubber, mining, and steel. Those familiar with southern labor history and national union organizing efforts will recognize these allusions immediately, as did the audience, who knew the events first-hand or from contemporaneous newspaper coverage of labor problems. An example of this comes very early in the script, in the discussion of the struggles of rubber workers. The exposition in the first scene reveals that work for mill workers is for most of them sporadic and uncertain. Angry exchanges between characters lead to analogies to a local rubber factory caught in the throes of unionizing efforts by outside organizers. One steel worker editorializes; "Them organizers ain't gonna get to first base with the steel men. Mebbe they can with the rubber necks. They're dumber." Another interjects statistical information in the form of racial slurs: "Might talk the miners into something—80% of them are nigger." When it is suggested that someone should inform "old man Worth [the paternalistic mill owner] about the seditious talk of millworkers, Draper, a new man, an outsider and unknown to the group, rebukes the speaker, "Turn informer, will you? Don't you know enough to stick to your own class?" (Sc. 1:4)

In the ensuing conversation Draper reveals his radical leanings by calling Worth a capitalist and offering a blistering indictment of steel management. In other labor plays Draper would have worked as a foil against management through his union organizing efforts; in this play, his railings against management speak to unionization but also reflect his anger and despair that the traditional values of craftsmanship and pride in work that gave the worker a sense of dignity are being replaced by technocratic principles of efficiency, mechanization, and profit-and-loss sheets. When a worker objects that he is a "skilled worker," Draper ridicules him, saying "No, you're not—your machine is skilled. . . . Anybody can do your job. That's why your bosses treat you like slaves." He launches into a cynical parody of the Lord's Prayer, beginning, "I believe in steel, the Father Almighty, maker of millions in bonus and in Jung, his only son, our chairman, who was conceived by wars and rumors of war, born of the blood of mankind; he suffered unto Herbert Hoover, was crucified in '29 " (Sc. 1:5-6).

This is one of the few plays in which workers from disparate backgrounds support local management. Worth, as the southern mill owner, is seen as a benefactor who upholds the very values Draper sees being eroded in modern business practices, whereas the industrial executives in the northern steel strongholds are viewed as diabolical and evil, cold-hearted technocrats who value the machine more than the individual. One Polish worker indicates that he worked in Pittsburgh, Cleveland, and West Virginia and went through the strikes, but that Worth gave him a job, and that he gets a bonus the same as the others. He implies that his union background is not held against him by Worth. Union literature falls from Draper's jacket and he is quickly labeled a "communist." The association of violence with the union efforts is implied when millworkers find a gun strapped under Draper's arm. *Altars of Steel* manages to appeal to southern laborers while cleverly supporting the traditional southern manager's antipathy and suspicion of labor unions. It does so by arguing for traditional paternalistic and community values that asked workers to trust in the decency and integrity of those for whom they worked. Draper and Worth, though contrasted in the play, are both idealists whom Rogers portrays as fighting the onslaught of northern industrialism.

When taken to Worth's office, Draper refuses to answer questions but makes a small speech indicating that he, "spent half his life rotting in jail because I dared to speak and will continue to speak in spite of laws you make for your own purpose." Draper continues to reveal himself as an ideologue. When Worth asks if he has come to organize a union, he responds;

I'll be satisfied if I open the eyes of one poor deluded fool who slaves his life away for a system which uses men to feed the machine for profits to the employer. Let him starve when the machine produces more than is useful. After a life time of toil discard him to die broken in body and spirit—a poverty stricken wretch, the garbage of your machine age" (Sc. 2:2).

Worth's generosity is met by Draper's accusation that Worth is engaging in "another experiment in human engineering" (Sc. 2:3). Rogers deftly turns Draper's suspicions into an affliction of the soul and develops the metaphors with which he will color audience perceptions. The dementia of the lost soul is described in Worth's assessment of Draper's outburst: "He's so young Mike. And he's a sick man—sick in his mind. I predict you'll Christianize him Mike. Try it for awhile anyhow." These lines reflect the religious overlay one finds in southern labor plays. The idea of accepting a union becomes analogous with a fight with the devil—a clash of ideological positions and moral principles. The efficacy of religious metaphors in the unionizing effort is reflected in these plays in their images of martyrs, prophecies, voices, and crusading clashes between good and evil. Whether the organizing efforts are directed towards textile workers or steelworkers, they are depicted in plays with southern themes as seismic fault lines beneath the terrain of a traditional culture—incipient cracks splitting regional industries and labor forces.

The plot advances on the dilemma posed when the southern Steel Company is unable to fill a sizable order because the mill needs new equipment. Two important characters are introduced: Frank Carter, a reporter from *United Steel News*, and Worth's son Jack, an engineer, placed by his father in a lowly laboratory position in order to learn the business from the ground up. In a discussion between Worth and Jack the playwright reinforces the genuineness of Worth's altruistic nature, giving him lines like "The great need of the hour is really courageous action in behalf of labor" (Sc. 2:6). Carter notes the "rumblings about changes" and marvels at the activity of the plant, comparing it to mills in Youngstown, Ohio, that are not producing as much. This gives Worth the opportunity to launch into the first of several comparisons between northern and southern industry, specifically between Pittsburgh and Birmingham. His comment about the South being a "steel man's paradise" and his boast, "Not only can I make steel cheaper than it's made in Pittsburgh, but its quality is the finest in the country," echo a regional pride that would have been well received by southern WPA audiences in the 1930s—which, again, would have understood veiled allusions to contemporary news and editorials.

The play's villain, Karl Jung, is an executive representing Pittsburgh Steel, a thinly disguised version of United States Steel, headquartered in Pittsburgh. At a time when the country, and the steel industry, were moving out of the Depression by preparing for a war with Germany, Jung's decidedly Teutonic name is noteworthy. He is clearly established as an outsider, literally a foreign oppressor, one incapable of empathy or understanding for southern labor. Jung seeks to acquire the holdings of the southern Steel Company, and his takeover becomes obvious when it is revealed that his bank has absorbed the bank holding Worth's notes.

A meeting between Worth and his banker on the terrace of Worth's house allows the playwright to advance his arguments metaphorically, through the set design. With the flames and roar of the furnaces serving as a backdrop to the garden setting, the visual elements in this play function rhetorically. One senses the omnipresence of the industry in the lives of laborers and management. The mill looms in the background, dwarfing the characters center-stage with its raw power and symbolic impenetrability. One cannot escape the mill in a company town, even when the town is controlled by so a benign ruler as Worth. The mill controls like a virulent giant, and the set masterfully creates this captive feeling by having the roar of the mill work as a character. Critics commented on the noise of the production: the sound of steel-making filled the theatre. The imagery of fire and furnaces, of hellish heat and open hearths, lends itself easily to comparisons of sacrifices, enslavement, and the devouring of human lives by a primordial force that cared little for the humanity of the individuals. When used as a scenic element, the metaphor of a fiery beast is undeniable.

The analysis of the takeover given to Worth confirms what the audience fears, the ruthless intent of the giant corporation to devour the independent owners: "They want your holdings. They were determined to get them if they had to buy out every bank in the state and you know how heavily obligated we were. They don't want our banks, they were after your notes" (Sc. 3:3). Worth replies, "Not only my notes—every small industrialist in the South will feel this." The South, and southern industry are depicted as purer, more naive, more honest than the North or northern industry. Worth takes pride in being one of the last independents and despairs at losing his mill. His rallying speech at the end of the third scene pits the little man against giant industry, one of the classic Federal Theatre Project motifs: "We can't let them do this to us. It means the end of freedom. They'll drain us dry, as they have every other region and then discard us. We'll simply be the local branch. Just another juicy morsel for United Steel. . . . I'm going to fight" (Sc. 3:5).

From here on the playwright intermittently, but purposefully, employs FTP techniques to cast the audience in the role of jury. *Altars of Steel* becomes an ethical debate, in which northern industrial expansion is placed on trial. It is a one-sided debate, with evidence favoring the negative position that called for the rejection of northern industry, but objectivity was not the motivating force in Federal Theatre plays that advocated social and political changes. The loudspeaker, a classic FTP device, is used to open the fourth scene. The script notes offered two production choices: either to place an announcer in a box adjoining the stage, or to have a disembodied voice announce the information from backstage over a microphone. Indications are that the Atlanta production opted for the latter. In either case, the news flash serves to set an ominous tone by conveying information of vital personal and regional interest in an impersonal, mechanical manner. Such symbolic coldness worked to persuade the audience members that big business is impersonal, that it is removed from them physically and spiritually. Although they have been prepared for this by Draper's speeches, they now see and hear clearly that industry is concerned with machines and that the working man has become insignificant in an industrial system.

This recognition moved the audience, which held culturally to agrarian values of communal effort, assistance, and charity, closer to acceptance of the play's argument—the protection of southern industrial independents. The conversation among characters in this fourth scene gives voice to many of the angry sentiments of independents in the South toward northern steel, particularly the U. S. Steel Corporation. While Rogers does not use documentary detail explicitly, as had Bailey and Blake in the textile plays, he creates a montage of allusions to real corporations and individuals. Throughout the play Pittsburgh is depicted as the center of violent labor disputes crushed by the steel company. The anti-Pittsburgh remarks serve as a catalyst for most of the anti-northern sentiments in the play. When one worker, Lane, indicates that he cannot stand the strain of not knowing if his job is secure, another tells him to get out of steel and start a hot dog stand. Lane replies, "If I did some bastard from Pittsburgh would come in here and put me out of business with a chain of hot dog stands" (Sc. 4:1).

Mill workers refer to the buyout of southern Steel by the United Steel and Iron Companies of North America in terms of bondage, slavery, loss of freedom. Freedom becomes the benefit to the workers of Worth's management, freedom that would be relinquished in a change in management. The union and northern steel are depicted as violating the honor of the worker and the integrity of the job. Interspersed among the angry sentiments are more figures: workers assert that Worth had $25 million in coal assets of which Jung appropriated $6 million to cover outstanding loans held by United Banks. The 1919 steel strike is alluded to with indictments of United Steel for paying men starvation wages and firing them in retribution when they tried to organize. Worth's public announcement of the takeover of southern Steel by United Steel and Iron Companies is supplemented with the statistic that United Steel's control of independent steel companies would now exceed 60 percent of American steel. Those familiar with the buyouts of independent steel companies by U.S. Steel would recognize the numbers and the criticism immediately.

The playwright extends the criticism by giving Worth lines indicting the government for failing to intervene and invoke antitrust and antimonopoly laws. His sentiments echo those of struggling independent steel companies during this period. In this scene Worth speaks passionately and pragmatically for southern industrial managers: he warns workers wanting to lobby Congress that it would only anger United and that their jobs now are "to do what we can to protect the workers of this section and the public from exploitation." He acknowledges the various counter-arguments of those who view the merger positively, that people would profit from the expansion—arguments that appeared in southern editorials as well. These are met with Hogan's rebuttal, which reflects an attitude found in all three of the southern labor plays, the fear of absentee ownership and control by individuals removed from the region: "They'll soon learn better. This District has never known the evils of absentee ownership—all the unfair treatment that goes with United's policies." Jung's regime is referred to disparagingly as "the first American dictatorship," and Hogan, a mill foreman, even proposes socialism as an alternative to escape such oppression (Sc. 4:5). This casts the labor issue into a broader political arena. Earlier in the scene another superintendent has commented ominously,

"Jung had better watch out. Anybody but a fool can see that sooner or later such treatment breeds a revolution. 'Scratch a steelworker and find a radical.'" The aggravation of lower management reflects the seething discontent of the mill workers themselves. Jung policies are painfully obvious and his character becomes a reminder to the audience of the myriad of unfair labor practices in various industries. Jung, the northern industrialist, becomes the antithesis of Worth, the southern industrialist who, in the closing confrontation of the scene, stresses his resolve to work for the economic freedom of the region.

A choreographed plant inspection set to Igor Stravinsky's *Firebird* Suite No. 3, establishes the surreal beauty, power, and sense of order in America's steel industry as orchestrated and controlled by skilled labor. A scene in Jung's office follows in which his crass attempt to control and manipulate the press is juxtaposed to the attempt of American labor to master and control gargantuan industrial machines through integrity and pride: while Jung poses for a photograph writing an order for a $40 million expansion, the audience recognizes full well that northern expansion will be financed on the backs of southern workers. Jung's flippant dismissal of strikes in Youngstown reinforces for the audience his disregard for the integrity and intellect of the worker. This becomes even more evident in conversations with Worth about company policy and a newly created "company union." The far-reaching manipulative nature of his proposal emerges incrementally in his description of company stores, or "commissaries—one for mill quarters and one for mine quarters." Jung's intent is tantamount to enslavement: "You know how difficult it is for men to pay cash for their supplies. We will sell them on credit and deduct it from their wages." Additionally, his plan calls for the replacement of men with equipment: "Worn out men have no place in industry—they are the logical ones to go first." When asked who is to solve the unemployment problems, the cold reply comes: "That is no concern of ours."

Worth's paternalistic nature and his concern for worker safety and regional productivity is contrasted sharply with the callousness of the new northern regime. Again, the lines echo actual criticism by southern industrialists and editors: Worth expresses dismay that the price of steel produced by the southern mill is being artificially inflated to match the Pittsburgh quotations, when the southern companies could produce it less expensively. As Jung's master plan unfolds, his control becomes absolute. The artificial inflation of southern prices reduces the southern manufacturers' ability to compete, thereby making them easy prey for takeover bids. Jung's response comes with characteristic arrogance: "United doesn't recognize the word competition." The playwright takes the opportunity to reiterate the Federal Trade Commission's order that all prices be based on the point of manufacture, only to have Jung laughingly dismiss it as not to be taken too seriously. As Jung's plan is revealed, it becomes apparent that the playwright is using it as a composite litany of industrial abuses. The plan calls for the abolition of the safety department and the replacement of trained safety inspectors with mill foremen overseeing safety in their departments. The scene is cleverly structured so that the audience is led to sense the catastrophic accidents looming in the future for mill workers. The tension in subsequent scenes is heightened by the audience's expectation of imminent tragedy.

The audience anticipates the effect of the plan in operation. Worker conversations reflect the xenophobia evident in many southern labor plays, the fear of the strangers who bring with them changes in group affiliations, attitudes, and ultimately in culture. The lines of Checkers expose the anxiety felt by many industrial workers in the South: "There's a hell of a lot o' new men coming into this town and into the mills too. They ain't softies either—tough guys, old time bohunks—and not a southerner in the lot" (Sc. 7:1). He fears that these strangers are labor organizers and compares them to buzzards, smelling out a merger. His fear was one articulated in newspapers of the period—the fear of local laborers becoming prey to union organizers.

The most revealing dialogue speaking to the deleterious effects of the plan takes place between three black mill workers. They are unable to escape a predatory company intent on devouring their wages, their life's blood. The hidden tentacles of Jung's control are revealed in the discussion of "clacker," company money, legal tender only in the company store, issued to workers as compensation for their labors. Workers paid only in clacker were completely under the mill's control. One worker relates how he tried to buy groceries in a regular store with company currency and could not: "You can't buy nothin up town with "clacker." You can't ride the street car—you can't even get in a decent crap game with the stuff." Another adds that a man buying clacker for real money only gives four dollars of cash for five dollars of clacker. The isolation of the workers and their dependence on the company is poignantly revealed here, as is the irony of Rogers's having the hopes of three black workers for financial independence denied by enslavement to northern industry. *Altars of Steel* is one of the few plays that exposes elements of the ruthless authoritarianism of the company town. In these towns, workers' aspirations were drowned in insidious indebtedness to the company store. Rogers's dialogue offers a unique conversation about issues not often addressed in the social scripts of the American theatre.

This scene about "clacker" allows Draper to take a more commanding role. Draper is really the political foil in this play. His perceptions parallel those of the audience, yet within the play characters view him as a doomsday prophet. His character is analogous to Peal's and Fer's. The description of Draper in the Director's Report, prepared as a production guide, characterizes him as a young, itinerant communist organizer. Like that of the other labor organizers in the textile plays, Draper's role is that of a martyr. The union leaders in these southern labor plays recognize the religiosity of those they are trying to convert to unionism without, however, recognizing their own proselytizing. The fundamentalism of the deep South is translated to a faith in the inerrant union. Draper plays the role of union demagogue. When the newspaper carries an announcement of a scheduled vote for the company-sponsored union, he again cynically employs religious metaphors to instill fear in his listeners:

It means you'll have to belong to Company Unions. That's to keep you from organizing yourselves. All this is part of United's system. Soon they will own your schools. Your children will be taught to bow down to the steel god. They'll own your churches, their ministers will be prophets of United Steel, forgetting their allegiance to Christ in a make fight for positions of wealth in Company churches. They'll own the law. Your police officers will be eager to suppress freedom of speech and freedom of assembly, eager to use the club and machine gun on workers who rebel against their unjust masters. I know this man Jung. I've felt the weight of his chains. They are steel chains. They cut into your flesh and into your soul" (Sc. 7:4).

Draper's role as a prophetic union evangelist melds with the audience's own sense of foreboding when, against a scenic backdrop of a hellish open-hearth furnace, workers recount a litany of injustices and unsafe working conditions. The list runs the gamut of major labor infractions from the steel industry's equivalent of the textile "stretch-out," where four men were forced to do the work formerly done by eight, to the intimidation of foreign workers who failed to vote for the company union and were punished with fewer days of work than those voting for the union. A detail that seems insignificant—loose bricks in the furnace, becomes a major point of concern. Workers comment on the condition of the No. 4 furnace, referring to it disparagingly as a "wayward woman" and a "hussy." Such incidental details contribute to the credibility of the dialogue, yet may pass unnoticed by those unconnected with the industry. Rogers, however, knew the steel industry well enough to realize that mill furnaces are traditionally given the names of women and are assigned female temperaments. It was not uncommon for mill workers to engage in conversations about attributes of capriciousness or fickleness of a furnace, calling it by a woman's name.

Draper forcefully asserts his role as the prophet as the litany proceeds: "Every prophecy of mine has come to pass." Even though workers dismiss him as a "damned Red Neck," some are persuaded by the cogency of his reasoning and begin the slow process of conversion. The audience contemplates a dark future when two men are appointed as labor representatives to talk to Worth in a scene that represents the mid-point of the play. All the problematic elements have now been identified, and they are expanded upon as the play moves to a conclusion.

As Jung plots to remove Worth's son from the company, his Machiavellian nature is unmasked further. Playing on the son's discontent with Worth's plan to teach him the business from the bottom up, Jung offers to send him to New York to begin work in a capacity above apprentice. Labor discontent is felt more keenly in this scene, as the inequities of the plan take effect. The preoccupation with machines rather than with men resurfaces when Jung wants to dismantle an old open- hearth furnace and replace it with a more efficient furnace that takes only ten hours to make steel. The playwright continually plays on this idea. When workers gather to storm the office, it is Worth who agrees to a meeting in which issues of worker safety and equity would be addressed. His willingness to listen is contrasted sharply with Jung's action of calling out two hundred "strike breakers" to "stand by for a strike." As the play progresses, Jung's character is seen as unredeemably evil. He summarily fires all workers and offers to reinstate them only if they sign a loyalty oath agreeing to work below scale for a year and "refrain from allying . . . with any labor organization not approved by the employee representative committee."

His intolerance and misunderstanding of his labor force are played out bitterly in lines in which he calls the workers "crazy southerners." The audience is reminded time and again that Jung is a cultural outsider a position that, coupled with his inability to understand the southern mindset, is exploited in a manner reminiscent of character development in *Strike Song* and *Strike!*. In *Altars of Steel* the offhanded indictments of "crazy southerners" surely would have rankled Birmingham or Atlanta audiences. This is a script written and intended for production below the Mason-Dixon line. The playwright intentionally angers his audience with the use of anti-southern sentiments in much the same way that Blake and Vorse appealed to the northern sentiments of their audience by playing to a perceived liberal bias. However, in *Altars of Steel* the appeal to regional pride is used to make a pro-industry, rather than pro-union, statement—provided it is southern-owned-and-operated industry.

The inevitable confrontation between Jung, the northern industrialist, and Worth, the southern industrialist, moves the action forward. When accused by Jung of going over to the side of labor, Worth replies in terms that identify him physically, psychologically, and spiritually with southern labor:

I've always been on the side of laboring men. I'm one of them myself—my father carved out a settlement in this valley with his hands. Have I gone over to labor! . . . there comes a time when I cease being an industrialist and begin to be a citizen. . . . I hold you personally responsible for the lives of those men out there. . . . There is a right higher than property: the Right of the Public Good! The law is not an end but a means to an end which is equity and justice. This can't be so long as men are intimidated by bayonets and coerced by starvation. Do you want those men dispersed? Do you want those mills to run? Then tear down your armed camp. Give the word and I'll put the plate mill in operation. Do you know what that word is? . . . Representation.

Representation for the men; for this region" (Sc. 11:3–4).

Unlike other labor plays, the conflict in *Altars of Steel* escalates within the managerial offices of the plant rather than in exterior scenes of union marches and violent clashes. It is in his office that Jung demands the resignation of a foreman who has shut down the No. 4 open-hearth furnace, citing safety concerns. This triggers a series of resignations climaxed by Worth tendering his own resignation from the company he started. In quick succession Jung's control is questioned; he becomes increasingly isolated and soon recognizes the need for outside protection, in scenes that depict in righteous terms the deterioration of evil. The action moves quickly in these final scenes, many of them short. Worth's son returns, and during the reunion of father and prodigal son a siren wails ominously: The No. 4 furnace has exploded burning most of the night crew to death.

As bodies are removed from the smoldering mass, tension mounts threateningly, and Jung is called a murderer. Led by Draper, the mob marches to Jung's offices. When his appeals to the governor for National Guard protection are rebuffed, Jung turns to Worth, who agrees to help only when he fears the men will destroy the mill and its property, so dear to him. The conditions of Worth's agreement dictate that Jung write a statement assuming full personal responsibility for the death of the men in the mill. The scene ends with Jung signing the confession, through subsequent mimed action indicates that his act of conciliation was mere subterfuge.

The final two scenes are exterior. At the blast furnace gate a large crowd screams for Jung. Confrontation between guards and workers subsides with the appearance of Worth. Draper blames Worth, but Worth responds by appealing to the workers on the basis of shared values and long-honored bonds of friendship: "We have always been friends. The power of greed and hatred can wreck us. Come, let us rebuild our friendship. Tomorrow we will go back to work together" (Sc. 15:3). Draper espouses a more violent, radical position, draws a gun, aims at Worth, and fires. Amid screams for ambulances the guards return fire on the crowd, and several fall. With his dying breaths Worth orders the guards to put down their guns—"Jung is no longer in command here. I am in command. Do as you're told"—then dies (Sc. 15:5).

The play ends dramatically, in near darkness. The final moments of *Altars of Steel* are very reminiscent of living newspapers. The last scene combines techniques of tableau and the loudspeaker to convey a sense of passage of time and to proffer a judgment: a news commentator sitting before a microphone brings the play to closure. Just as in living newspapers the loudspeaker commented ironically, the commentator's lines carry a political bite. The ending is structured to hit the audience with searing irony, forcing it to indict northern labor even though the lines provide a literal exoneration. They relate the facts of the acquittal but implicitly calls the audience to judge and condemn the deceit, the callousness, the injustice, and the inhumanity of northern business in the South:

Flash! The special grand jury investigating the tragic death of nineteen men in the fatal explosion of Number Four open hearth at the plant of the United Steel, Iron and Coal Company has returned a verdict absolving any individual from criminal guilt. The verdict recites that while the men were killed in the firing of a defective furnace, there is no evidence to prove definitely who gave the order to fire the furnace. There are charges and counter charges of political pressure and bribery to influence the verdict of NOT GUILTY.

PUBLIC RESPONSE

Notices and reviews of *Altars of Steel* appeared in *The Atlanta Constitution* and also *The Atlanta Georgian*, a conservative Hearst-owned newspaper published under the banner, "The Leader in the March of Progress." Notices of the production's premiere April 1, 1937, competed with the dramatic and social activity created by movie director George Cukor's "search for a Scarlett O'Hara" the week the play opened; from accounts on the society pages, nearly every debutante in Atlanta auditioned for the role in *Gone With the Wind*. However, once attention turned to more serious dramatic fare, *Altars of Steel* sparked a lively and heated debate. Ultimately it became front-page news.

The first publicity appeared in the two papers on Easter Sunday, March 28, 1937. *The Atlanta Georgian* chose to bury the notice as a reduced-type announcement in its "Social Calendar." In contrast, *The Constitution* printed a full-blown publicity release in a five-inch column leading its "News of Stage and Screen" section; the notice highlighted the cast of "100 players" composed of "all the Atlanta Federal Theater players, members of the Atlanta Theater Guild, seven people from the New York Federal Theater and 28 people from Alabama. Millwrights, furnacemen, welders, melters, bricklayers, guards, pipefitters and rollers are volunteers from the dramatic departments of the various schools and colleges in the city"[10]. While their sisters auditioned to play Scarlet, the young men of Atlanta with dramatic inclinations had auditioned for *Altars of Steel*.

The Thursday the play opened, *The Constitution* carried a short article announcing 'Altars of Steel' World Premiere Offered Tonight." The article noted that the play would be the fifth production of the combined Federal Theater and Theater Guild, that a number of prominent guests were already in the city for its opening, and that Hallie Flanagan and Frances Nimmo Green of Birmingham were expected to arrive in time for what was heralded as "the spectacular opening." *The Atlanta Georgian*, again, buried its announcement of the opening of the play on page twenty-six, saying that the "world premiere of Altars of Steel, a play dealing with the labor and capital conflict in southern steel mills, opens a week's run at the Atlanta Theater Thursday night at 8:30." It chose instead to give greater mention to a Theater Guild membership committee luncheon on the society pages, failing however to mention any of the "notable guests" who were in town as listed by *The Constitution*. Of greater interest is a *Georgian* editorial by Edwin C. Hill, an ode to the steel industry, which ran the day *Altars of Steel* opened. In his regular column, "Human Side of the News" Hill extolled the virtues of the American steel companies and engaged in capitalist tub-thumping like "As steel goes, so goes business. . . . Steel is more than fiery furnaces and cold figures. It is drama and romance. It personifies the age of the greatest material progress in the history of mankind. . . . Tonight the skies of the steel centers glow in the fire from the furnaces. Steel is king again. Long live the king!"[11]. With such posturing in the editorial pages one might postulate that *Altars of Steel* was creating some stir even before the production opened.

Reviews of the opening night in both papers praised the production. *The Constitution's* headlines enthusiastically called it the "best drama ever presented here," and Ralph T. Jones reiterated this in his review, saying, "This is . . . the most impressive stage offering ever seen in Atlanta." Jones speculates on the controversial nature of the production, concluding that only the federal government would have been courageous enough to stage it. He saw the thematic development centered on a classic the struggle between heroic labor and villainous industrial capitalism. While not as effusive in his praise, Dudley Glass, the reviewer for *The Atlanta Georgian*, found little to fault and was, at worst, equivocal at times in his praise, calling it "intensely interesting." His assessment of the politics of the script is also ambivalent: "The theme is the struggle between capital and labor. It has a strong touch of Communism, though Communism is not advocated. I wouldn't call it 'subversive' though I do think it rather one-sided." Glass concluded, "in view of the universal interest in sit-down strikes and labor disputes just now, 'Altars of Steel' is especially interesting and timely"[12].

Both reviewers commented on the staging, the set design, and the success of the large cast in the crowd scenes. Jones effused over the orchestration of the ensemble, and the overwhelming size of the set design that extended past the orchestra pit to the side boxes: "It is so massive it effectively creates the illusion you are actually in a great steel mill." Glass's review echoed these sentiments: "The most impressive feature is the manner in which it is staged. . . . Instead of a curtain, great steel doors rise and fall. At left and right are glimpses of vast machinery. In the center rises a tall modernistic set upon whose top takes place most of the dialogue. . . . Always there is the sound of the mill at work, the roar of furnaces, the clank of machinery." Jones concluded that it was "as great a play as was ever written. . . . It is superbly produced. Perfectly acted." While Glass surmised: "It . . . may some day reach Broadway, where it will be either a big success or a terrible flop. Certainly it deserves a national tour"[13].

The play did not meet with such overwhelming support on all fronts. The morning following the opening, several protests calling the play "dangerous and incendiary" were lodged with Gay B. Shepperson, the state WPA administrator, and John McGee, assistant national director of the Federal Theatre Project. *Altars of Steel* made front-page news on April 4, with a picture of Dorothy Hinman of the Atlanta Theatre Guild extending an invitation to S. J. Roberts, Captain of the Atlanta Police Department, to see the play. The headline announced victoriously, "Police Came, Saw and Wrote, 'Clean Bill.'" The accompanying front page article chronicled the official police response to several anonymous protests, as well as one by John M. Cooper, who felt the play was "full of dynamite." The second performance had in attendance two policewomen, euphemistically the "official reviewers" for the Atlanta Police Department; two detectives from the vice squad accompanied the policewomen to the performance. Captain Roberts's statements in the article reveal the institutionalized monitoring of theatrical productions in Atlanta. His comment that policewomen "see all the shows in Atlanta and submit written reports" lends itself to the inference that the police in Atlanta during the 1930s acted as municipal censors for theatrical productions. Laura Davis and Vannie McDonald, the policewomen who filed their report, found "absolutely nothing objectionable in the play." As the police department's official critics they maintained; "Of course it is strong drama, and some of the language is strong. There might be a few mild 'damns' scattered here and there, but they are in spots where emphasis is needed. It seems to me a person would have to be very narrow-minded indeed to find anything objectionable with the play"[14].

The Atlanta Georgian begrudgingly acknowledged that the play had been "okayed" by the police in a very small article at the bottom of page 10A. Its real position on the play became evident in the columns of two feature writers, Mildred Seydell and Tarleton Collier, both of whom saw much more in the production than had Dudley Glass. If anything about the play was dangerous and incendiary, it was that it prompted Seydell's commentary that ran April 4, which used much of the same language reportedly used in the complaints filed with the WPA. Seydell's rhetorical approach rested on her analogy to the specter of liberalism raised by another literary work, *Uncle Tom's Cabin*, a book, she believed "infested with germs of hate and war." Her commentary, remarkable in its tenor and in its latent fear of northern unionism creeping southward, evidenced a paranoid fear of political changes. She appealed to women as mothers to preserve the culture; goodness and virtue for Seydell resided in the status quo. Ironically, Seydell found the play very compelling, calling it "magnificent," "gripping," "perfectly cast," and "startling realistic." It was precisely the effectiveness of *Altars of Steel*'s political argument that she found most disturbing:

'Uncle Tom's Cabin' was infested with germs of hate and war. It spread them so thick around the country that there was no time to work out sanely the problem the book presented. The novel was full of dynamite, caused disaster and destruction. Those same germs I found in 'Altars of Steel' the play put on by the Works Progress Administration. When government finances such performances, it is schooling the people in Communism. The play is so written that you must be either for inhuman brutality or for communism. You have no other choice. If the play had been put on with less perfection it might not have been so forcible in its teaching. But I have never seen better acting nor better production. Magnificent. Gripping. Perfectly cast, with settings startling realistic. And lighting and music attuned in satisfying harmony. Broadway has never had a better-staged performance. It really reached heights[15].

Her objections, though many, tended to center on government-sponsored agencies, such as the Federal Theatre Project, producing social scripts that not only advocated a political position but asked the audience to be persuaded by the arguments it presented:

I think it a serious matter when hard-pressed tax-payers money is spent to inculcate hate, unrest, when only side of the picture is shown with any fairness. In 'Uncle Tom's Cabin' there were half truths; so there are in 'Altars of Steel.' And half truths are the foundations for revolutions. . . . 'Altars of Steel' is a dose that unbalances our emotions. If we require that, then it serves its purpose. But before we have other plays like it sponsored by our government, it would be wise to decide whether there would be more happiness and peace and contentment for a larger number in a communistic government than in a democratic one.

Though the director of the play issued a statement denying support of "communistic labor," reiterating that the play did not advocate any one solution to the problem, that "it was for the audience to form its own solution," comment on *Altars of Steel* did not stop with Mildred Seydell[16]. Two days later a slightly longer article on page three reported that the play had been approved by the police even though "complaints went unanswered that the play, produced by tax payers' money, is communistic in nature." That same day the most interesting analysis of the play appeared on page seven, in Tarleton Collier's regular column, "Behind the Headlines." Collier deftly placed the play within a its proper political context by addressing the exploitation of southern resources and labor by "alien interests." He identified as a common character in the southern labor plays the patriarchal mill owner, who served as a regional soulmate with his laborers. He commented on the play's "organic power to move" and explained why such movement was necessary in the South. Collier accounted for the rhetorical power of the play while noting that this rhetoric had been heard before—even in his own columns:

What he saw was an excellent stage production, a production which in numerous respects was unusual, and which had an organic power to move. That power was heightened by effective acting and naturalistic dialogue. He saw also a document that was as fundamental in its facts—and just about as Communistic—as a health talk. The exposition of 'Altars of Steel' is the thing that everybody by this time ought to know, that the enlightened industrialist has known for a long time, and that, if you pardon a reference to our poor work, that this column has been suggesting—perhaps a bit too demurely—for several years. . . . The observation has been pursued to the conclusion that the South has not yet acquired economic freedom[17].

Collier tied the script to contemporary Supreme Court rulings on industrial cases and new legislation governing workman's compensation, minimum wages, and safety and inspection in the workplace. His observations implicitly acknowledged the documentary nature of the script and its ability to mirror societal concerns regarding industrial abuses of American labor:

Twenty years ago, or even ten years ago, a play like 'Altars of Steel' and its picture of the tribulations and unrest of the working staff might have been regarded as dangerous, inflammatory, indeed, and unpleasant. It might have been deemed expedient at that time to hang the author and to rout the actors out into the alley. Today, however, the Supreme Court (which we are hearing is too conservative for anybody's good) has itself taken the spot away from such polemics as those of 'Altars of Steel,' making them seem almost trite[18].

He refuted Seydell's criticism of the political bias evident in the play, claiming that he found "both sides rather carefully delineated." He accurately noted that "the playwright got out of his system most of the stock grievances against industry, . . . But everybody has heard it before and its repetition shouldn't be an indictment against the play." Collier claimed that the power of the production rested in the case it made for economic freedom for the South and the development of regional resources to aid in its economic recovery.

Seydell, in turn, took umbrage at Collier's wording and felt compelled to have the last word on the play, in the columns of The Atlanta Georgian. Her review is a classic example of the language used in passive-aggressive responses, attempting to sugar-coat statements of condemnation and paranoia. Seydell, a popular daily columnist with a sizeable following in the Atlanta community, reiterated comments representative of the conservative groups who found the play objectionable and who stopped just short of having it closed. In her final salvo she said:

I believe in free speech and if private interests wish to put forward their grievances against present-day American institutions, I for one might criticize them, but would not say that the authorities should stop them. But when tax money is used for propaganda for the purpose of putting on plays that cause controversy and that give birth to hate, I think it is high time for complaint. And if you can sit through 'Altars of Steel' and come away without hot hate in your heart, hate against ruling capital as it is presented, then you are of sterner material than I, less sensitive to good acting[19].

While the Seydell-Collier battle waged on the pages of *The Atlanta Georgian, The Constitution* saw fit to remain quiet on the issue. After its initial review praising the production and the front page publicity that recorded the play's exoneration by police censors (while stimulating ticket sales), there were no further reviews or commentary. There was, however, one small article, which appeared Wednesday, April 7, a few days after Seydell's first diatribe; it proclaimed, "WPA Theater Drives Insane Back to Sanity" and went on to describe how psychiatrists at Bellevue hospital, after six months of research, found "that the drama as practiced by experts of the WPA federal theater project might be used as treatment for mild forms of insanity"[20]. One might conjecture why *The Constitution* chose to run this particular article buried discreetly among the obituaries on page 27; it may confidently be assumed that the humor, whether intentional or unintentional, would have been lost on the readers of *The Atlanta Georgian*.

Even though *Altars of Steel* surpassed all expectations of in-house reviewers of the Federal Theatre Project, the New York office still had problems with it in December 1937. Francis Bosworth encouraged the tour of the play into other regions, but this proposal met with some resistance. His letter of December 8, 1937, offered suggestions to assuage the criticisms still made by reviewers and staff in New York. He urged a revamping of the script with an eye to an adaptation that would make it acceptable to audiences in the East and Midwest. Bosworth's criticisms included the characterization of Draper ("the Communist organizer should never carry a gun. . . . It would alienate exactly the audience that the play would depend upon for its support") as well as Worth, whom he found to be "too spineless and wishy-washy for a big industrialist." Other objections outlined changes in the handling of Jung, who he advocated bringing to justice, and a name change for Kaplan, the lawyer: "It seems a little unfair that the double-crossing lawyer should be called Kaplan. There is no reason why he could not have a good southern name." He concluded that "with some small clarification of the loose writing, the play would be popular with Federal Theatre audiences"[21].

Bosworth's concerns were unfounded. The unaltered production moved to Miami in winter 1938, and, buoyed by an FTP-supported public relations campaign, interest was generated and sustained through the run of the play. To call it a campaign might be understating the public relations activity of the

FTP personnel and cast members—It could be called a 1938 media blitz. According to a promotion report filed by Emma F. Young, Promotion Director for *Altars of Steel*, two thousand letters were sent to the Junior League, Smith College Club, the Jewish Hadassahs, the principals of each school in the Miami area, attorneys, the Miami Woman's Club, and the Miami Music Club. Additionally, seven thousand ten-cent service passes were distributed over a three-week period to various civic clubs and high school drama clubs, and eight hundred 14 by 22-inch posters were placed in hotels and stores around Miami. Anyone coming to or leaving Miami saw advertisements for the production: one hundred seventy-one 12-by-24-inch posters were placed in the street cars of Miami and Miami Beach; plaster plaques holding announcement cards of the current production were placed in the Eastern Air Line Airport and Seaboard Airline Ticket Office, the Postal Telegraph office, and in leading hotels and drug stores; and two Miami radio stations, WKAT and WIOD, provided public service announcements each day during the run of the play.

The Miami FTP promotion staff drafted the director and actors to meet with various community groups. Roy Elkins, then supervising director of the FTP, gave talks and produced a one-act play entitled "The Home Coming" for the Miami Woman's Club. By Young's account both Elkins's presentation and the play were well received, and Elkins invited club members to attend *Altars of Steel* on service passes he provided. She reported that this was the first time many of them had seen a Federal Theatre play and that they were enthusiastic and promised to return. Cast members were also drafted for community chats: Gene Gehrung, who played Bill, the open hearth foreman, spoke to the senior class of Miami High school on theatre makeup. Young reported that his talk was interesting and "showed results." Christine Ricketson, a young actress who played a secretary in the production, spoke to various women's groups about the aims and ambitions of the WPA, and this too, Young noted, was interesting and seems to have garnered an audience. In the closing comments of her promotion report Young noted enthusiastically that "I feel for the first time that our theatre is in the public eye. The whole town is talking about *Altars of Steel*"[22].

As a matter of policy a Play Production Bulletin was completed after the run of each FTP play. Such bulletins included technical data on building sets and setting lights, as well as reports from directors and production staff noting effective production elements and identifying those that proved problematic. In a Play Production Bulletin sent to the Miami Federal Theatre with the intent of highlighting production problems encountered in the play's run in Atlanta, the controversial nature of the script is mentioned: "All this tends to create great controversy, especially as to which side is really correct,—Liberalism, Capitalism, or Communism. The strange part is that all three are wrong, in the methods they adopt. The solution can only be formed from the point of view of each individual audience"[23]. A few days before its opening, a short article ran in *The Miami Herald* announcing "Altars of Steel" will Open Monday." Headlines identified it as part of a "So-called New Theater." What reviewers found most striking about the play was not the ideological clash it depicted between labor and management, capitalism and socialism—but the modernistic production techniques and set design. Even in the previews, reporters commented on the set: "Altars of Steel . . . deals with the questions of capitalism, liberalism and communism in a startling and daring manner. The huge sets were constructed under the personal direction of Josef Lentz, assistant director of the south and rehearsals have been directed by Roy Elkins, supervising director of the Federal Theater"[24].

The first reviews of the Florida production appeared March 1 in *The Miami Daily News,* with another published in *The Daily News* on March 6th. Both reviews offered positive assessments. However, the reviewers noted with some pique that *Altars of Steel* was a welcome reprieve from the standard Federal Theatre Project fare in Miami. They complained that previous FTP productions had been characterized by "poor play selection, bad acting, obvious mediocrity," and were "a source of keen disappointment to most Miamians." The *Daily News* critic found it in his heart to forgive and forget the FTP for their earlier plays because of *Altars of Steel,* a production with which he believed the WPA theatre there could "earn for itself a reputation that will be the envy of other such national groups."

Responses to the propagandistic elements in the play were at odds in their liberal and conservative perceptions. It was called "the first modern controversial drama ever presented in Miami" and "a propaganda play . . . so obvious in its preachment that it ruins its own chances at sincerity." One review commented that "the battle of capitalism vs. socialism is drawn with such obviousness in dialogue and character that its own evangelistic fury kills its chance at credibility or realism." The March 8 editorial in *The Miami Herald* called the play "one of the most interesting stage experiments in America today" but drew attention to the propagandistic elements in the play and questioned the use of government monies through the WPA to support a play that criticized American business to such an extent and promoted "radicalism."

Here is Uncle Sam in the theater business, providing jobs for scores as well as a means of expression. . . . The other angle is propaganda, a factor that will lead to discussion, to opposition, to questioning the right of the government to use taxes to promote radicalism, to hammer away at monopoly and big business, to resent the giant octopus as swallowing the little independents in steel, as oppressing labor, as being completely inhuman to the extent of curtailing safety precautions and causing a disaster. . . . There is no doubt as to its power not its purpose in attempting to influence the minds of the audience against the impersonal big business, against trusts, and the need for labor to organize against this type of capitalism.

Virtually all reviewers noted the effectiveness of the ensemble's acting, and the modernistic set and lighting designs by Josef Lentz. The Miami reviews spoke of audience response to the setting, and comments by the reviewers gave some sense of the quickness and tightness of the whole production. *The Miami Herald* recorded, "The varied scenes in 'Altars of Steel' elicited spontaneous applause from the audience. The realistic stage settings are given added interest by the sound effects simulating the noise of a steel mill in operation." The paper editorialized, "Here is something entirely new in the way of a stage play—short as a feature film, no intermissions but changing scenes, well acted, exciting and powerful, and with romantic love entirely missing." *The Daily News* felt that the sets aided the actors "immeasurably in their parts" and noted, "The speed of the performances, the series of attention-arresting sets, the momentum of the play is so well maintained that the audience reacts automatically. Just as an old-fashioned audience once hissed the villain when he attacked the heroine, so does this modern-day audience hiss the capitalist when he rapes the workers of their rights and the question of one system against another is lost in the emotional drama." All critics commented on the assured orchestration of the hundred-member cast and the sincerity and intensity evident in the acting in the crowd scenes. At times, in fact, the amateurs in the cast were too sincere and intense; as a brief article in *Time* recounted with some humor, a week into the run of the play:

In Miami last week, a Federal Theatre labor play, Altars of Steel, had reached its 15th and climactic scene. The boss was barricaded inside his factory. A mob was milling outside the gates. A Liberal swung at a Communist, the Communist shot him, company guards shot the Communist. Ensued a terrific free-for-all which seemed like fine convincing stuff to the audience. And it was. Carried away by the action, the mob had suddenly taken violent sides, started swinging at each other in earnest. When the curtain came down, three limp actors were stretched out on the stage[25].

Contemporary references to *Altars of Steel* criticized it for offering a "view of management-labor confrontation from the middle of the road." This kind of criticism misses the point. If one views this play as promoting the integrity of southern industrialists, southern industry, and tolerance for an ethnically diverse work force, then one sees that the playwright was not fence-sitting. Rogers constructed the play's argument to appeal to both southern management and southern labor. Draper, the communist agitator and labor advocate, is not permitted the audience's complete sympathy, because the audience would find his politics repugnant. As the director's report indicates, "he [Draper] loses the effectiveness . . . when he adopts drastic radical tactics." The same report begins with a notation that "the play was selected as it applies to any section in the country, stressing the evil of absentee ownership, ruthless methods of trying to derive the utmost out of worn machinery and labor . . . regardless if it is an industrial center or not." This, too, may be soft-pedaling the intent of the play, which seems intended specifically for southern industrial centers. Worth, a southern liberal whose mill is populated by diverse ethnic groups for whose well-being he cares, is the vehicle by which the arguments against absentee ownership are presented to the audience. He is paternalistic, in the southern tradition, he possesses regional pride in the natural resources, tying himself to the ore and the strength of his steel; yet he represents a break from the agrarian traditions of the deep South. Worth epitomizes that which is good in American industry and ties it to southern values. His character reassures the audience that industrialization offers regional benefits and a means to increase standards of living. Essentially, Worth's character asks the South to accept industrialization.

The whole play makes a progressive case for the expansion of southern industrialization beyond textiles. When one recalls Graves's speech at the FTP's Birmingham meeting, with its specific call for a play about steel, combined with the quickness with which this play appeared in the hands of the Federal Theatre Project directors in the South, one might conclude that this play is designed to promote the interests of southern industry to a southern audience. It makes artistically the case that columnists like Collier in Atlanta, and Graves in Birmingham, were making editorially in their newspapers—that the South needed to use its resources to achieve financial independence through the development of competitive industries. Therefore, where many have looked at *Altars of Steel* as a pro-labor play, it should be viewed as a pro-management play—southern management[26].

Altars of Steel was not solely responsible for the success of the Federal Theatre Project in the South, but its performances attracted thousands of playgoers and revitalized the FTP in that region. Yet even if one places it within a larger context of government-sponsored theatre in the South, its contribution to the success of the program there is unquestionable. Financial reports for the whole southern FTP operation filed to the Works Progress Administration indicate that in Florida, by March 31, 1939, there had been 1,531 FTP performances of various plays, attended by 341,496 people, with admission revenues of $33,431. Georgia is recorded as having 315 FTP performances, reaching 88,487 people, with receipts of $10,758. Hallie Flanagan reiterates in a prefatory comment to this fiscal report that the "Federal Theatre was established to employ and rehabilitate human beings and not to take in revenue; at the beginning of the project no provision was made for the receipt of money, and at the end 65% of the productions were still free of charge"[27].

The uniquely modernistic character of *Altars of Steel*, and the author's willingness to make the case for southern industry offer a striking example of the political efficacy of the theatre. The rhetorical effectiveness of the play rests on the audience members' identification with traditional southern values, in the character of Worth. They were receptive to arguments supporting industrialization, provided it was regionally owned and operated. There is a progressiveness in this script that runs counter to traditional agrarian values yet is conditionally accepted by the audience. Technology, the play argues, is safe in the hands of southern industrialists who understand and value the land and its people. One cannot underestimate the effectiveness of the use of spectacle in creating a play that is lavish in technological design, arresting in its use of sound effects, and creative in its ensemble acting. Production techniques govern this play. In this respect *Altars of Steel* might be easily criticized on its literary merits, or on weaknesses in individual amateur performances, but this is clearly a case where the whole production and its effect were greater than the sum of its parts. For these reasons *Altars of Steel* stands as the landmark play in the efforts of the Federal Theatre Project in the South.

NOTES

1. Hallie Flanagan, *Arena: The History of the Federal Theatre* (New York: Benjamin Blom, 1940, 1965), pp. 81–82, 88–89.

2. John Michael Matthews, "Virginus Dabney, John Temple Graves, and What Happened to Southern Liberalism," *Mississippi Quarterly; The Journal of Southern Culture,* Special Issue, The South in Transition, Fall 1992, v. 45, pp. 367, 405.

3. John Temple Graves, "This Morning," *Birmingham Age-Herald,* 7 October 1936, clipping in Billy Rose Theatre Collection of New York Public Library, MWEZ + n.c. 20.374.

4. "Altars of Steel" Playreader Report, by John Rimassa, November 18, 1936, Library of Congress Federal Theatre Project Collection at George Mason University Library, Fairfax, Va.

5. TS copy of newspaper article, "Problem Play Author's Name is Kept Secret," *Philadelphia Inquirer,* 18 April 1937, in The Billy Rose Theatre Collection, New York Public Library, MWEZ + n.c. 20.374.

6. Letter, John Wexley to Hiram Motherwell, March 27, 1937, in Play Reports, Library of Congress Federal Theatre Project Collection. See also Reader's Reports filed by Munson, February 3, 1937, and Louis Solomon, February 8, 1937, in the same file.

7. "WPA's 'Altars of Steel' World Premiere in Ga.," *Variety,* April 7, 1937, clipping found in Title File, Folder 972, Theatre of the 1930s Collection, Library of Congress Federal Theatre Project Collection.

8. "Synopsis," National Service Bureau Play Production Bulletin, "Altars of Steel" found in Folder 972, Theatre of the 1930s Collection Library of Congress Federal Theatre Project Collection.

9. All references to the script are taken from the copy contained in the Library of Congress, Federal Theatre Project Collection.

10. "100 Players in Cast of 'Altars of Steel,'" *The Atlanta Constitution,* March 28, 1937, p. 15.

11. "'Altars of Steel' World Premiere Offered Tonight," *Atlanta Constitution*, April 1, 1937, p. 8, "Steel Conflict Dramatized," *The Atlanta Georgian*, April 1, 1937, p. 26; "Theater Guild Group Feted, " *The Atlanta Georgian*, April 1, 1937, p. 17; and Edwin C. Hill, "Human Side of the News," *The Atlanta Georgian*, April 1, 1937, editorial page.

12. Ralph T. Jones, "Altars of Steel Highly Praised As Best Drama Ever Presented Here," *Atlanta Constitution*, April 2, 1937, p. 14; Dudley Glass, "Timely 'Steel' Play Opens Run," *The Atlanta Georgian*, April 2, 1937, p. 26.

13. Ibid.

14. "WPA Play Given High Praise by Policewoman-Reviewer," *The Atlanta Constitution*, April 4, 1937, p. 1.

15. Mildred Seydell, "'Altars of Steel' Aids Communism With Tax Money," *The Atlanta Georgian*, April 4, 1937, p. 4D.

16. "Director of 'Altars' Denies 'Red' Charges," *The Atlanta Georgian*, April 6, 1937, p. 3.

17. Tarleton Collier, "Behind the Headlines," *The Atlanta Georgian*, April 6, 1937, p. 7.

18. Ibid.

19. Mildred Seydell, "Mildred Seydell Says—," *The Atlanta Georgian*, April 8, 1937, p. 13.

20. "WPA Theater Drives Insane Back to Sanity," *The Atlanta Constitution*, April 7, 1937, p. 27.

21. Francis Bosworth, Report, December 8, 1937, Playreader Reports, Library of Congress Federal Theatre Project Collection.

22. "Promotion Report," "Altars of Steel" Theatre of the 1930s Collection, Library of Congress Federal Theatre Project Collection.

23. National Service Bureau Play Production Bulletin, "Altars of Steel" found in Folder 972, Library of Congress Federal Theatre Project Collection.

24. "'Altars of Steel' Will Open Monday," *Miami Herald*, February 27, 1938, n.p.; "'Altars of Steel' Presents Modern, Controversial Drama," *Miami Daily News*, March 1, 1938, n.p.; "WPA Theatre Here Has Hit in New Play," *Miami Daily News*, March 6, 1938, n.p.; "Play and Propaganda," *Miami Herald*, March 8, 1938, n.p. "Steel Workers' Problems Shown," *Miami Herald*, March 2, 1938, n.p., clippings file, Library of Congress Federal Theatre Project Collection.

25. "Convincing Scene," *Time*, March 14, 1938, clippings in Theatre of the 1930s Collection, Library of Congress Federal Theatre Project Collection.

26. Malcolm Goldstein, *The Political Stage: American Drama and Theatre of the Great Depression* (New York: Oxford University Press, 1974), p. 254; and "Synopsis, 'Altars of Steel,'" Director's Reports, TS in Library of Congress Federal Theatre Project Collection.

27. Hallie Flanagan, *Arena*. p. 435; and Goldstein, p. 254.

CHAPTER 5

Steel: Militant Labor and Northern Steel

Of the four plays in this study, *Steel,* by John Wexley, received the most formal support and the most attention from organized labor when it was first produced, in New York. But unlike other labor plays produced there during this period, such as *Waiting for Lefty, Stevedore,* or even *The Cradle Will Rock,* the 1937 production of *Steel*—the first play produced by the International Ladies' Garment Workers' Labor Stage—is not well known. One finds only a terse assessment of it as "the most militant labor-management play of the early Thirties," in Malcolm Goldstein's *The Political Stage: American Drama and Theater of the Great Depression*[1]. It was this label, "most militant," that caught the author's attention several years ago and led to the subsequent investigation of labor plays that produced this study.

Three things distinguish *Steel* from the others labor scripts analyzed here: first, it had a long run in New York that the others did not; secondly, the amateur group that supported it, Labor Stage, became the most commercially successful in the country; and finally, unlike the other authors, John Wexley enjoyed a reputation as a professional playwright on social themes. His connection with leftist theatrical groups was long-standing and derived from a politically active theatrical family. His papers in the State Historical Society of Wisconsin chronicle a theatrical career closely tied to American social movements and issues of the 1920s, '30s, '40s and '50s.

Born in New York on September 14, 1907, Wexley carved out a distinguished career as a playwright and screenplay writer. After attending Cornell University and New York University, he "followed in the footsteps of his uncle, Maurice Schwartz, the Yiddish actor" and appeared in *The Dybbuk* at the Neighborhood Playhouse in New York. He went on to work with Eva Le Gallienne's Civic Repertory Theater during its first season. *The Last Mile,* his first full-length play, was produced in 1930. This exposé of prison conditions on Death Row featured Spencer Tracy and received high praise from New York critics; Burns Mantle included it in the 1929–30 Best Plays series. Wexley followed *The Last Mile* with *Steel* in 1931, but the latter production closed after fourteen performances. However, his script had not gone unnoticed. *Steel* underwent major revisions and reemerged for a successful run in

1937 as the premiere production of Labor Stage, the theatrical arm of the International Ladies' Garment Workers' Union. A discussion of both productions shapes this chapter. In the intervening years Wexley wrote *They Shall Not Die*, a play about racism and the notorious Scottsboro trial, produced successfully by the Theatre Guild. For a time he worked for the Federal Theatre Project as a playreader, where, engaged on a consultative basis, he reviewed scripts submitted for production consideration. It was in this capacity that he read *Altars of Steel* by Thomas Hall Rogers and recommended that it not be produced.

During the mid-1930s he began to establish himself as a screenwriter for Warner Brothers, and his commitment to social issues surfaced in the screenplays he wrote. During the 1930s and 40s, his films featured such stars as Humphrey Bogart, James Cagney, Edward G. Robinson, and Ann Sheridan. In these years he wrote *The Amazing Dr. Clittterhouse* (1938), *Angels With Dirty Faces* (1938), *Confessions of a Nazi Spy* (1939), *City for Conquest* (1940), *Hangmen Also Die* (1943), *Cornered* (1945), and *The Long Night* (1947). His association with leftist issues and politics did not go without repercussions. His name was cited in testimony during the infamous congressional communist witchhunt conducted by the House Un-American Activities Committee in 1947 and 1953, which resulted in Wexley and many others being blacklisted by the motion picture industry. He continued writing pseudononymously for a few years, all the while researching and writing on social issues. In the 1950s, moved by the trial of Julius and Ethel Rosenberg, he set out to treat the case dramatically. However, the material obtained from court transcripts and interviews never saw the stage; it became *The Judgement of Julius and Ethel Rosenberg*, a book published in 1955. John Wexley died in 1985, leaving behind a rich repository of papers. This collection stands as a testament to his career and to plays and playwrights who bravely attempted to use the theatre to address social issues and effect social change during a turbulent and paranoid period in our nation's history[2].

Even though the two-week run of *Steel* closed inauspiciously in early December 1931, it attracted attention within organized labor. Some who viewed the play recognized its propagandistic potential. It took six years, but *Steel*, radically altered, came back as a featured production of one of the most significant labor theatre groups in American theatrical history, Labor Stage. Labor Stage was part of a larger movement of workers' theatre groups, whose surge to prominence in the 1930s was phenomenal. By 1934 there were four hundred workers' theatre groups forming a theatrical fraternity under the national banner of The League of Workers Theatres[3]. Labor Stage grew out of a worker education movement that had its origins in the 1920s and was endorsed by various unions under the American Federation of Labor throughout the 1930s. One of the more popular vehicles for worker education could be found in the activities of the union "dramatic organizations." Such groups served a dual purpose: on one hand, as amateur drama clubs, they promoted a spirit of camaraderie among workers participating in productions; while on the other, they had a more important function of continuing union indoctrination of workers in the leisure hours. Labor Stage, sponsored by the International Ladies' Garment Workers' Union, was one such organization. An ILGWU Executive Board Report records; "In the Summer of 1935, a plan to organize a genuine labor theatre, supported and directed by trade unions, was promulgated by a group closely allied to the ILGWU and its educational work . . . As the plan developed Labor Stage, Inc. came into being." The AFL convention held in December 1935 approved a plan to form a "labor stage group to meet the needs of large scale labor pageants, celebrations and spectacular mass meetings"[4].

Gary L. Smith provides insight into the formation of Labor Stage. His research reveals that David Dubinsky, president of the ILGWU, had long supported the efforts of Mark Starr and Fannia Cohn in the Education Department which promoted and advocated an "attitude of education as recreation." Dubinsky, who knew of Louis Schaffer, then a labor reporter for *The Jewish Daily Forward*, pressured Starr to hire Schaffer to head the recreational division of the Education Department. Schaffer, a promoter with close ties to the Yiddish Theatre, had "grandiose plans for a larger labor theatre." He organized the drama group, known first as the ILGWU Players, using garment workers from Locals 10 and 22. Local 10, the Cutters Union, would feature prominently in the production of *Steel*. Ultimately, Schaffer promoted the creation of Labor Stage to AFL president William Green. Schaffer, in turn, hired Mark Schweid to head the Drama Department. Schweid established a precedent for hiring theatrical professionals, be they designers or actors, to participate in union productions. Through his acquaintance with Schweid, Herbert Weinman, who created the role of Joe in the 1931 production of *Steel*, was hired to act in a mass recitation piece being prepared by the ILGWU Players[5].

Once Labor Stage was established, with the full support of the AFL, a home was needed for the fledgling drama group, and the ILGWU "acquired a long lease on the old Princess Theatre [at] 39th Street near Sixth Avenue, in the theatrical district near Times Square." Under Schaffer's management the whole building underwent renovation. The top floors became studios for drama and dance recitals, while the theatre was refurbished and expanded to hold nearly six hundred. The Labor Stage Studios were given an official public dedication January 11, 1936. It took nearly a year for the company to prepare its first "serious" dramatic presentation, but after a two-month rehearsal period in the fall of 1936, John Wexley's *Steel* rose from the ashes of the 1931 production to play to full houses throughout 1937[6].

The play was a resounding success. There were favorable reviews in the leftist papers, accolades for the cast and the director, and consistent praise for the cultural innovation of Labor Stage and its manager, Louis Schaffer. Schaffer, an adept promoter, brought together three talented artists who at various times had allied themselves with the leftist theatre movement in New York during the 1920s and '30s: John Wexley, whose political leanings were clearly evident in his works; Mark Schweid, who had acted in Elmer Rice's anti-Nazi play, *Judgement Day*, and whose work for the Theatre Guild established him as an actor of merit; and Sointu Syrjala, a skilled set designer whose work included the sets for *Stevedore* and *Precedent*, a play based on the Mooney case. This sensitivity to the suffering of downtrodden groups helped shape the production scheme of Labor Stage's first play.

Schaffer and Julius Hochman, president of Labor Stage, extended an invitation to David Dubinsky, president of the ILGWU, to attend the opening night of the *Steel*, Sunday, January 17th. Correspondence in the Dubinsky papers indicates that he accepted and was in attendance opening night.[7] The program that evening was not informative; it said nothing about the play-wright, the actors, or the play's political position. It contained only incidental announcements about an ILGWU playwrighting contest and the ILGWU Cultural Hour held Saturday afternoons. The program eventually evolved into a comprehensive document of political and theatrical propaganda, featuring photographs of reviews, testimonials from ministers, professors, authors, and even a former deputy in the German Reichstag, union puffery, and the 1937 version of the "up close and personal" snippets of cast members that highlighted their union affiliation.

The tone and tenor of Wexley's *Steel* are different unlike those of *Strike!*, *Strike Song*, or *Altars of Steel*. The overriding theme in *Steel* is that of escape. This is not a play where characters initiate change to be able to remain in their homes, persevere, and make a better life. Characters in this play want to escape the industrial setting: they want their children to escape the oppressive mill town life, devoid of sunlight and grass, filled with grime and grayness. Unlike the other scripts, *Steel* focuses not on the unionizing efforts of outside organizers but on the effects of the mill and the unionization drive on specific individuals and their families. It strives for individual empathetic identification rather than collective ideological appeal. In this regard, *Steel* is the most family–oriented of the plays in this study. It asks the audience to recognize in the hopes and dreams of the Raldney family its own aspirations and disappointments in an industrialized state. Unlike *Strike Song* or *Altars of Steel*, which derived their rhetorical clout from the audience's willingness to make regional identifications, or *Strike!*'s attempt to have northern audiences judge negatively southern labor practices, the geographic setting of *Steel* could be anywhere. Its audience is expected to be moved by the plight of individuals denied their dreams by their inability to escape the mill. *Steel* is not a play that canonizes an abused labor force, and in that sense some may see it as less political than the others. It is, nonetheless, a play of social criticism, concentrating on the broader issue of the dehumanization of workers by industry.

Southern workers pitted against northern industrialist featured prominently in the labor plays of the South, which used only a smattering of other ethnic groups to contribute an element of color. In those plays the conflict was between southern labor and northern management. *Steel* showcases the ethnic diversity of northern labor and accurately identifies management's manipulation of these groups to engender xenophobic isolation and foster racial prejudices—individual against individual. Of particular interest in this play is the role of women in the mill town. The few female characters in Wexley's script serve as sensitive, humane contrasts to the mechanistic nature of the mill. As in the textile plays, their characters and lines convert readily to a thematic social refrain of "save the children," but here it translates to preservation of the family as a social unit.

The two productions of Wexley's play in 1931 and then the Labor Stage production in 1937, contained the same thematic concerns, though differently argued and dramatized. The 1937 Labor Stage script is historically notable because of its close association with the ILGWU and for its use by that organization to serve political and pragmatic ends. However, it was the radical nature of the 1931 script that had caught the attention of Louis Schaffer. It is important to understand the roots of this production, and therefore the analysis that follows compares the variations in Wexley's scripts and posits reasons both for the changes made in the ILGWU production and for the effect these changes may have had on the audiences' perception of the issues addressed. Copies of both scripts are held in the archives of the State Historical Society of Wisconsin. The 1931 manuscript, typed by Wexley, contains his handwritten annotations for corrections and changes.

1931 SCRIPT

Wexley felt compelled to add the following disclaimer to his 1931 script: "This play is entirely imaginary. No indication or reference is made of or to any person or persons, organizations, companies, corporations, police, constabulary, that really exist" (Synopsis of Acts: I). While *Steel* is realistic, neither the 1931 or 1937 script is documentary in form, though both refer to historical incidents in labor history, such as the 1919 strike, and to actual practices both on the part of industry and union organizers. From the stage directions it is evident that Wexley worked to create an atmosphere complementary to the arguments made in the play. The '31 stage directions specify props that contribute to an ominous sense of destruction. The front room of the Raldny house is described as "furnished by Grand Rapids via Montgomery Ward's mail-order catalogue. . . . [there is a] mantlepiece with nick-nacks, and a fireplace underneath. . . . Also hanging from a hook are an American World War helmet, a bayonet and a large army automatic crossed on each other." (I:v) In his review of the play, Richard Dana Skinner reminded his readers of Chekhov's rules of relevance in drama: "If a shotgun is hanging on the wall in the first act, it must go off in the last"[8]. Wexley held to this rule.

The motif of noise from the mill is one found in both steel plays in this study, *Altars of Steel* and *Steel*, and in both productions of the latter. The mill becomes the mythological siren, whose luring wail is inescapable. On another level, the mill noise contributes to the hellish atmosphere created by an enormous industrial machine that conditions individuals to respond to a mechanical whistle, calls men to work with whistles, notifies them of accidents with whistles, and sends them home with whistles. Joe, the son in whom Dan invests his hopes, rails against the whistle earlier in the first act of the '31 version than he does in the '37, priming the audience to recognize the intrusiveness of the machine's incessant summonses. The din created by the mill, as an unrelenting seductress, works to create an overlay of tension in these steel plays, which is very different from the non-threatening portrayal of the physical structures of the textile mills. In the steel plays the mill itself takes on a personality much more sinister than that of the textile mills in the strike plays. The mill with its machinery is personified in the steel plays. It becomes a villain unto itself, devouring men in incremental daily sacrifices, where the villains in the textile plays are merely human. The element of a mechanical monster in the steel plays, especially one that has imagistic overtones of "another woman," works to keep the focus tightly on the family unit.

Wexley's earlier script expanded the discussion of "red anarchists" and "bolsheviks" and included exposition about foreigners starting a union. Here, as in the two southern scripts and Blake and Vorse's northern assessment of southern labor, there are subtle appeals for audience regional identification. *Steel* plays to the willingness of New York audiences to defend their own rich ethnic diversity. Group identification and ethnic pride are evident in all the scripts; however, the political associations in the form of the union vary. This is evident in a crucial difference in the *Steel* scripts. In the '31 production Joe Raldney joins the International Workers of the World, the I.W.W. Dan's furious outburst at his son's joining what he considers a subversive organization results in a stroke. As Dan lies paralyzed on the floor, his life seeping from him, Joe is wracked by guilt, thinking he has caused his father's death. A refrain heard several times in the opening scenes had been "show appreciation." As Dan dies, Joe screams at the whistles which summon him to the mill. The '31 script has Joe's chances of attending law school ironically taken from him by Dan's forgetfulness about paying his insurance premium on the policy intended to pay for Joe's schooling; in this version he can merely hope to attend a technical school. In the later production Joe defiantly chooses to remain at the mill, jeopardizing his chance for education and escape but righteously working to protect the workers. The first version places the pivotal scene of the father's death in the home, making the play more of a drama of domestic upheaval, whereas the ILGWU production puts more emphasis on the labor movement and the oppressiveness of industry. In both versions the physical toll exacted by the mill surfaces in several characters and pieces of dialogue. There is an ominous tiredness that consumes Joe as he describes work in the flues. His description of the hellish atmosphere that causes high blood pressure and ultimately kills is very evocative in the '31 script and portends Joe's defeat; in the later production, he will be victorious.

Joe is much more a "radical reactionary" in the first play, than a careful, ethical man studying the law to use it against those who oppress in the second. Wexley's scripts are the least documentary of all those addressed in this study, but the '31 version contains a greater discussion of the 1919 steel strike and chronicles the abuses suffered by workers in that strike. The tenor of scenes and dialogue is more militant. Joe advocates violence early in the '31 version in a passionate rallying speech:

Joe: Cossacks! State police! Connely's detectives! Why did they do all that? Why did they arrest strikers right in this town by the hundreds for smiling at the soldiers; for trying to buy food at the strikers' grocery; for walkin' on the street? Why? I'll tell you why. To terrorize us. To weaken our spines; to suck out our guts. . . . like Tony says; to make us give in and go back to work. Well, Tony's right. The 1919 strike was lost because we didn't fight. . . . we were afraid. Men, if it comes to a strike, I'm for returning violence with violence, bullets with dynamite; I'm for the real stuff, for guns, for arson, for murder, anything that'll make us win . . . anything that'll give us a bit of the good in life. . . . a decent wage and a human existence. . . . (2:12, '31).

Confrontations between Joe and his brother-in-law, Steve, display this same militance on both sides of the issue—union and management. Steve points to radical actions taken by those influenced by "European books," and the script includes more instances of name-calling using "bolsheviks" and "socialists" pejoratively. He blames Joe for his (Steve's) being "blacklisted and spied on" because of Joe's association with socialists. He charges that Joe killed their father "with Bolsheviky talk" and asserts that Joe's politics would ruin the family. Joe's rage manifests itself in speeches that reinforce his emotional commitment and obsession but that fail to raise him to a level of leader. The earlier script portrays Joe as a worker caught up blindly in an ideology, whereas the later play allows his intellect to govern. His response to Steve in the '31 version, though a powerful indictment of industry, places him on fanatical fringe. Wexley's stage directions indicate this.

Joe: (He speaks with a peculiar intensity, they [Steve and Mela] just stare at him) Why, you'll never leave this place Steve Dugan! You're a slave to your machine. They ripped the guts out of you with their rollers. You like to sweat for them. You love it. They made you love it. They told you it was a man's work, they told you that steel is the nation, that the whole world needs it, they made you proud of it. Sure steel is the nation. We are steel, we are becoming steel. . . . Our flesh and bones and hearts go into it . . . steel. *(He is surprised at what he has said)* We are steel *(He sort of shakes himself, but the thought fascinates him and he mumbles again)* We are becoming steel. . . . (2:16, '31).

Though Wexley left himself every opening to proselytize against the industry, he did not develop this line in the earlier play but chose instead to turn it back on itself as a domestic drama. This passionate speech could have been developed effectively into a moral rationale for the cause of unionism; instead, Wexley has Skinny interrupt it by announcing that Betty, Joe's lover, has fainted at the library. Wexley abandons the political to turn the audience's attention to personal morality. Betty is pregnant with Joe's child. It is revealed that she sought an abortion, but, rejected by one physician who feared going to jail, she found another who was willing to try to induce a miscarriage with drugs. This results in her death. Joe's moral rectitude is severely shaken in the '31 version, and this became an issue with one reviewer of the production, who criticized the character for his selfishness. Joe and Betty are not married in this version, and, although he honorably vows to marry her, he undercuts his own ethos with lame justifications, saying:

Joe: I ain't a machine. I had to live . . . didn't I? I gotta have something nice in life too. Something. I needed something with beauty, something to love . . . and Betty was beautiful to me. She was life and blood for me. . . . I could never thank her enough (2:21, '31).

What started as an ideological argument between Joe and Steve deteriorates into a domestic squabble with Steve angrily claiming that he won't support Joe's child. The scene ends with Joe's scornful allusion to an earlier discussion of violence towards blacks—"I suppose I ought to thank God I'm not a nigger. (2:23, '31). Ironically, in this version Betty and the baby die; the later version keeps the focus on the organizing efforts, supported by Malloy, Betty, and the workers. In the '37 version her pregnancy is announced towards the end of the second act, as is her secret marriage to Joe, but these are incidental to the political focus and provide emotional shading to Joe's character as a leader.

In both versions, as the play moves into the third act, Wexley affords the audience a glimpse of steel management. In the '31 script, Joe has more lines directly analyzing managerial motivation and their attempt to play one ethnic group off on others to create suspicion and engender racism through self-imposed segregation. Of all the labor scripts, this one addresses this kind of industrial manipulation most directly and exposes it to the audience for criticism. However, Wexley chooses to have Joe reveal this within the confines of the family home.

Joe: I was readin' a book the other day. Listen to this, Mela. You know the old Romans . . . you remember from school . . . Well, they once had a law put up in their Senate. It was to make all their slaves, there were millions of 'em to wear some sort of badge . . . to show they were slaves. Well, there was one smart Senator . . . and he said the law was stupid; cause if they did that, then the slaves could easily see that they were superior in numbers and would revolt. Understand? And that's what's happening today. They tell Steve and the others like him that they're not workers but bosses. . . .that they're different; they're Americans, not hunkies. They tell 'em they're skilled mechanics not dumb laborers. . . . that they're white and better than the niggers. . . . and they believe it. Sure, Steve believes it and thousands like him. . . . you see their plan: they separate us, they make us weak. . . they even imported the men from different countries for that reason . . . Slavs, Serbs, Dagoes, Swedes, Irish, and Greeks, so we wouldn't understand each other, so we'd fight and be weak. Huh, it's a joke. They hire one-half of us to kill the other half (3:4,'31).

In the first production Wexley thought it important to extend the metaphor of men being turned into heartless steel, devoid of emotion, and contrast it with Joe's completely emotional posture. His pathos and the rationale for striking are tied to emotional issues by a poignant speech by a laborer named Anderson, who relates the death of his two-year-old child, and his remorse that he saw the child only while she slept because of his shifts in the rolling mill. The resolve to strike is transformed into a free speech issue when the strikers are served injunction papers prohibiting them from assembling. As Joe moves to go to assist the picketers on the strike line, Wexley again indicates the extreme nature of Joe's commitment with the description: "He turns from Mela and looks ahead of him, almost with the expression of some Hebrew prophet, almost with a fanatical tremolo in his voice" (3:8). The violent undercurrent and militancy is reinforced with references to the Klan, repeated references to "red agitators," and graphic descriptions of violence directed towards strikers.

The earlier production is quick to highlight the violence of the strike. Joe returns home with his head broken, barely able to stand. When troopers come looking for Joe, he emerges from hiding to confront the legal issue of their not having a warrant. As the tension escalates, Melania, Joe's sister, takes the army revolver that has been so prominent in each scene and waves it hysterically. She takes control of the room with her own violence, shooting one of the troopers at point-blank range, killing him. Mela verbally attacks and condemns her husband: "You're not Steve . . . my husband. No! You're a machine. With no heart, no soul, no nothing. . . . you're something else. . . . [Y]ou've become . . . steel! (3:18). Wexley makes the play even more despairing by placing Steve alone on the stage after his wife's arrest to hear the mill whistle blow: "Steve's head turns toward the window, then slowly turns back to the body, he sees the lunch-pail lying near Johnston, fallen to the floor . . . and bends over and picks it up and places it on the table and the . . . curtain descends" (3:18, '31). The clear sense given the audience is that he will return to the mill which beckons him. All has been lost in this early version—life, family, love, children, hope.

The violence of the 1919 strike is remembered bitterly in both plays. Their tone in reference to the labor war is different from that taken in the two textile plays. It is harsher, more desperate, more despairing. There are no labor songs in the steel plays as there are in the textile plays. Wexley's *Steel*, in both versions, is the one play of the four that advocates, even encourages, violence by the workers. It is, conceivably, this final scene, with its clear mandate for labor violence, that caused Goldstein to label *Steel* the "most militant" play of the 1930s.

Though the first run of the play in November 1931 at the Times Square Theatre was short, Wexley's reputation was such that the *Steel* attracted the notice of Brooks Atkinson of the *New York Times* and Richard Dana Skinner of *Commonweal*. Both began their reviews by noting Wexley's success in *The Last Mile*, which had catapulted Spencer Tracy to stardom, but they were unwilling or unable to find as much merit in *Steel*. Skinner took umbrage at the moral weakness in Joe's character in this early version: "[Wexley] has made his hero something of a coward and a great deal of a cad, inasmuch as he seduces his brother-in-law's sister on the plea that he 'needs some joy in life.'" He viewed Joe as a "neurotic radical" and found Wexley's handling of his theme "ineffective," "clumsy," and "amateurish." Skinner's review was short, but in it one hears the conservative echoes of Dan's admonition to Joe, "show appreciation." Offended that Wexley's play is so anti-industry, Skinner chastised:

At one moment he seems to be tirading against capitalism at large, but by the next what he is really complaining about is the nature of the work itself. He objects to the everlasting whistle which calls the men back to the mills as if that were somehow a symbol of capitalistic methods. . . . If he is attacking the idea of work for the Communistic state, he has quite failed to make out a case. The play is just one long succession of growls and groans against every aspect of life in one of the big steel towns.[9]

Atkinson's review analyzed the play in light of its propagandistic tendencies, a concern he would address in his reviews throughout the decade. Labeling it "an overwrought propaganda play," he assessed the merits of the script within a critical context of what he believed propaganda plays should do, how they succeeded, and how they failed. He noted that "like most propaganda plays, it lacks the reticence that would make it convincing; . . . It curses and sentimentalizes and spouts turgid proletarian verse. And yet it cannot be casually dismissed as a piece of hokum playwrighting." For Atkinson, it is not until the last act that the propagandistic elements begin to function fully, and then he cited the enthusiastic audience response of as proof that the play had strength:

When the wounded striker's sister shot the detective last evening one of the proletarians in the gallery cried out: 'Shoot all of them!' Apparently Mr. Wexley's play was succeeding. . . . Since they [propaganda plays] have a moral purpose, they should be uncommonly moral about expressing it. . . . There remains that a brutal last act which excited the comrade in the gallery and which sobered this restless column considerably. By the time Mr. Wexley had translated his propaganda into sound theatrical action. To see a wounded man hounded by his destroyers, to see his defenselessness used against him, is to see something that is inflammatory inside the theatre as well as outside. If you are a willing theatre-goer you are likely to conclude that something ought to be done about it. Propaganda plays are rather pathetic when they are bad theatre. When they are good theatre they are flaming propaganda. . . . But he has chosen a provocative topic; and when he puts it in terms of theatrical action, as he does toward the end, he raises the blood-pressure of theatregoing[10].

THE 1937 SCRIPT

The atmosphere created in the 1931 version of *Steel* is quite different from that of the 1937 ILGWU production. Wexley painted a pessimistic picture in the '31 script, poignantly recounting the unnecessary death of children in his dialogue. The '37 text allowed a greater sense of optimism in its unwillingness to have pregnancies terminated or mothers die, and in its dialogue that reinforces Joe's determination to escape the mill environment, and go to law school. This optimism, in large measure, accounts for the new version's success when produced. The audience then was left with a sense of hope and commitment, where the '31 script left it with a family broken by an unconquerable industry. Characters in the first production declared decisively, "Steel is the nation." Yet this rallying slogan lost its efficacy when confronted with another accusation, that men were turning into steel. The transformation of men into steel in the crucible of an all-consuming industry was the central metaphor. The vigorous strength of the industry is implicit in the '37 text—but the silent conviction that workers—workers in all their ethnic diversity, are the nation overpowers the machine. The optimism that the workers will succeed in initiating change and in humanizing that which has treated them inhumanely is an important concept in these scripts, which reflect the sensibilities of the socially conscious Depression era. The weapons that hung on the wall so prominently in the interior scene are not evident in the ILGWU version of the script. In his first draft Wexley editorialized more in his description of the mill and its omnipresent noises, comparing the din to "the grinding of tremendous teeth; the Gargantuan chewing on a gigantic cud by some Brobdingnagian cow" (I:vi). The '37 description is pared down to "a low undertone of sounds. . . .These are the varied sounds of the steel-mills, all combined into one . . . into one heavy deep tone" (1:3).

The living room of the Raldney home is realistically and evocatively described in both versions. Here Dan Raldney plays cribbage with "Skinny," another mill worker, not unlike Henry Morris in *Strike Song*. There is a comic element to Skinny that allows his prophetic commentary to slip by innocuously. In the very first scene the audience learns through Skinny that the rolling mill is a place where men drop dead of high blood pressure because of the unrelenting heat—a significant detail. Dan works in the rolling mill because the pay is better, but he fears Skinny will reveal the physical hazards of the work to his son, Joe. Dan works so Joe can escape the life of the mill by going to law school. These details are very similar in both scripts.

Two motifs surface in the early scenes of the '37 script. The first relates to ethnic prejudices which will be evidenced throughout the play and which find voice in Skinny's comments about a Jewish jeweler and the "Polacks" who reside at his boarding house. The second motif finds expression in the continual contrast between the mill town and the country. This imagery is embedded in the commentary of Melania, Dan's daughter, whose return from a picnic carrying flowers leads to comments on the impossibility of growing such flowers in the smoke and soot of the mill town. Her comments subtly and nostalgically paint an agrarian utopia existing away from the mill town, where everything is different, even the sounds: "There wasn't any noise from the mill" (1:12). Her lines are reminiscent of those in the textile plays, where the hills hold the hope of refuge. Mela's dream is to buy acreage in New Mexico, but her fear centers on her husband's succumbing to the mill. She worries that he will "get into a rut and stay here . . . like all the others" and abandon their dream of land in New Mexico. But the inability to escape the psychological as well as physical bonds of the mill become evident in Steve's assertion that he did not want to go into the mill rolling steel: "it was just natural," his father and brothers had done it, and "the whole town worked there" (1:14). Working in the mill became a rite of passage, an exertion of individual manhood, a prostituted enterprise from which there was no escape.

Like the women in the *Strike!* and *Strike Song*, Melania displays a stereotypical feminine reliance on, and a willingness to believe in, premonition and superstition. She sees Steve as "a sort of bridge for her to leave" and that she was meant to meet him; somehow it was devised by God. Women in these labor plays hold to an elementary intuitiveness and a predisposition to place faith in outside forces, both good and evil, that control the lives of their husbands. Superstition becomes legitimized, and thus the darkness and dangers of mill life take on a different cast as the audience is asked to give credence to beliefs in supernatural darkness and a force of evil not easily vanquished by card-bearing union knights. It is interesting to observe how quickly industrial management grows horns in these plays. There is an ethnic element of the *strega*, mountain witch, in these plays. Superstitious beliefs provide an impetus for the audience to consider forces of good and evil beyond those created by labor and management. The unnaturalness of men working in the bowels of a giant machine, in unhealthy environments, in hell on earth, and being lured there zombie-like by the call of sirens and whistles, resounds strongly in these superstitions. Truth is embedded in the intuitive feelings of nurturing women in these plays.

The union conflict in the first scene establishes sides when the conversation turns to buying stock in the Pan American Steel company. Steve has bought shares, Joe has not. Steve is a company man and the elected representative from his shop. Steve's union, the company-run union, is obviously favored by the mill management that created it. Steve loyally defends, in language demonstrating his complete faith in the company, managerial salaries against Joe's criticisms. A laborer speaking the company line carries the dramatic image of a man brainwashed, a man possessed by industrial demons. The contrast between Joe, the advocate for the real labor union, who speaks on behalf of the workers, and Steve, who is afraid to ask questions because he does not want to get in "wrong with the super," demarcates the savior from the scoundrel. This discussion which includes Steve buying stock in the company and ends with his defense of mill managers, is not elaborated upon in the '31 script to the same extent as in the '37.

In the '37 production Jim Malloy is a minor character who acts as Joe's mentor. It is he who instructs Joe about corporate malfeasance and whose teachings Joe repeats righteously and verbatim. These offer an interesting parallel to Steve's verbatim defense of management. Both are true believers who give themselves to conflicting industrial religions. Joe's messianic qualities become more clearly defined as he relates his desire to be a lawyer to "get into those courts and see that steel workers get a decent break and a fair deal" (1:23). Steve refers to Malloy as a "radical lawyer" because of Malloy's association with the Congress of Industrial Organizations, the CIO. Skinny's revelation that CIO organizers from Pittsburgh are seeking entrance to the mill allows Wexley the opportunity to allude to actual mill practices.

As the plant gateman, Skinny is required to carry pictures of CIO organizers in order to identify and prevent them entering the plant. Such details do not provide literal documentary evidence, but they do contribute to the credibility of Wexley's arguments by demonstrating that he knew industry procedures. The revelation that Joe is fraternizing with CIO organizers (rather than the I.W.W organizers of the earlier script) prompts Dan to recount poignantly how he had hitched his wagon to the union and marched out in the great steel strike of 1919 and how his wife starved to death trying to save the family. This leads to his impassioned plea for Joe to abandon his association with the CIO, ending with the refrain "show appreciation" (1:24–25).

The later version has Dan die, a victim of the oppressive heat of the rolling mill. Tensions mount in the interior mill scenes, such as those at the roller's bench, where an exchange between workers and Steve, their company representative, indicate their dissatisfaction with his representation. The image of pent-up pressure needing a release is conveyed strongly. Wexley, again, presents the issue in quasi-documentary terms, this time allowing the discussion to focus on the complaint of the company's using men for part-time rather than "steady work." This was an issue in several industries in the 1930s. The volatile combination of ethnic groups in the mills comes home in a discussion between Yart, a Pole, and Tony, an Italian. Their conversation is peppered with such derogatory racial epiteths as "wop," "dago," and "polak," is centered on Yart's insistence that Tony join the CIO. The playwright uses parallel arguments, and as labor, in the characters of Yart and Tony, argue, the labor leaders, Joe and Steve, argue over the union. The debilitating physical demands of mill work surface again as Steve reveals that Dan's eligibility for a pension makes it unnecessary for him to continue in the rolling mill; something other than money drives him. The revelation of Dan's high blood pressure underscores the dangers of the rolling mill environment. Dan works so Joe can escape. There is a mythical sense of doom, of lost opportunities and a solitary chance for escape in the words of the father who admonishes his son to leave for school as planned. As in the earlier version, Dan dies of a "paralytic stroke to the brain," but the '37 production has the roller foreman substitute Joe for his father. Symbolically, Joe takes Dan's gloves and shoes and assumes his father's place in the rolling mill. The act ends with Joe watching the body being carried off and saying, "I'll roll steel for you, pop" (1:2:15). The audience recognizes full well that the window of opportunity is now closed. The rite of passage has been enacted once again.

The political criticisms in the play are developed more fully in the second act. In the opening scene of act two in the '37 production, critical commentaries are carried in the dialogue of the women. The scene takes place in Dan's home, now shared by Steve, Melania, and Joe. To this home comes Betty. Betty is Steve's sister, but more important to plot development in this version, she is secretly married to Joe and carrying his child. In the opening of the scene she criticizes the town newspaper: "Everyday there's a sermon against the labor unions and Bolsheviks and all that gold from Moscow" (2:3). Her comments reinforce a perception that the press is against labor. This is a marked contrast to the perception in the southern textile plays, which presented the press as being northern, liberal, sympathetic to the cause of the strikers, and anti-management. There is an important difference between the press in this play and that depicted in the southern labor plays. The newspaper in *Steel* is referred to as a Hearst-owned enterprise, a choice of facts on Wexley's part that would have clear political implications and carry with it implicit criticism readily perceived by a labor audience (2:4). Betty's participation in the organizing campaign, distributing union leaflets for Joe, is contrasted with Mela's naive optimism that Steve will be promoted if "he's careful." This is completely different from Wexley's earlier version of this scene, in which Joe reads Betty his poetic musings on the physical and spiritual darkness of the mills. The emphasis on the escape motif is more pronounced, more futile, in the earlier play than in its revival.

As the scene progresses a union meeting in the Raldney living room highlights the diverse ethnic mix of workers who arrive to support the union. Italians, Slovaks, Poles, Irishmen, and Germans file into the scene. The exploitation of the immigrant groups by the mills is evidenced in the exposition that informs the audience of the strategic segregation of the groups in the mill. Different groups work in different parts of the mill, a tactic used by management to keep the groups separate and to prevent a unified labor force (2:13–15). Wexley, again, dramatizes an actual industry tactic without employing documentary evidence. Malloy asserts that the 1919 strike was hampered by an inability to communicate between the various ethnic groups. Few of the laborers could speak English, and the organizers could not speak other languages. In this speech Wexley again uses factual detail to support his arguments without using literal documentary evidence. When Malloy reveals that his office has been ransacked by someone looking for signed union cards, Joe offers to keep the cards at his house. The revelation that Joe and Betty are married leads to an altercation between Joe and Steve. As in the textile strike plays, it becomes apparent that the union splits families—kin against kin. However, in this instance Steve does not report Joe's union meeting, out of respect for Betty's pregnancy, thus saving Joe's job. The scene ends with Steve shouting about "labor racketeers" and Joe rejoining snidely that Steve was parroting the last "Hearst editorial" (2:30).

The first scene of the final act in the '37 ILGWU production is quite different from the earlier version. The general manager's office of Pan American Steel is prepared for a meeting of the Committee on Wages of the Employee Representation Plan. Present are Mr. Miller, the general manager, Mr. Roberts, the plant superintendent and chairman of the committee, and steel workers Jim Donovan, "Big Pete," Charley Yart, Steve Dugan, Carl Strouss, and others. The hypocritical motivations of the managers become clear as their speeches reveal their intent to manipulate. Miller's transparent attempts to identify with workers by apologizing for missing the annual company picnic shifts the ground as to the purpose of the meeting. The disrespect for worker intellect, the condescension, and the underestimation of workers on multiple levels emerges in his lines:

You know we are all working for one cause that is, pleasure in our daily occupation, and with it, earnings that give us a substantial living. The Pan American Steel Company prides itself on these annual picnics. Now, I trust that you men are ignoring the subversive agitation being spread by this so called Steel Worker's Organizing Committee. We have perfect confidence that our employees are wise enough to avoid these radical agitators with their racketeering union dues, and appreciate the sincere efforts by our Employee Representation Plan. Our company has proven itself a generous champion of labor, LOYAL labor . . . by announcing last month the glorious Vacation Plan, and it flings that plan as a challenge into the teeth of unscrupulous agitators. I trust your meeting today will concern itself with discussion on this Vacation Plan which we are so justifiably proud of. (3:1–2)

Recognizing that the speech shifts focus away from the issue and sets a new agenda, Donovan tries to introduces a discussion on increased wages. He is ruled "out of order," but the workers in this script are not to be underestimated. Having mastered parliamentary procedure, they make a motion to discuss wages, which is seconded. Donovan makes a motion to raise wages by 20 percent, which again is called "out of order;" Charley Yart, however, informs the group that the motion is "ok" and seconds it. Management becomes enraged that labor has learned the formal parliamentary rules previously used to obfuscate, manipulate, and control. Wexley intimates through example that the balance and control of power begins to shift when workers of all nationalities take it upon themselves to learn. Steve's detention by managers leaves him with a choice of either being "with them or against them." Miller outlines the rhetorical tactics that Steve should employ with the rolling mill crew, a tactic that played on the prejudices directed in all these plays towards foreigners and towards lower-class whites—"hunkies," in this play. The labor plays attack prejudice, but generally not racial prejudice; they tend to illuminate the prejudices ingrained in a capitalistic class system where "haves" discriminate against the "have nots." The textbook extrapolation read by Joe earlier in the script, outlining how one group is pitted against another, is transformed into a dramatic exchange exposing the covert operations of the managers against the workers. The class structure of the mills is laid bare in all the plays in this study, both steel and textile. The strategy used to divide (through appeals to prejudice, suspicion, and jealousy) then conquer (by firing card-carrying union members, often identified by rival group members) was pernicious and it codified gang-like alliances that Wexley conveys accurately. Miller's strategy is articulated simply:

Show them that if they join this union and it calls a strike, it means a mob of more or less unskilled labor, foreigners and hunkies . . . walking out. But it also means that they can force your rollers to walk out with them. Walk out on high-wage jobs to support their demands on low-wage jobs! Another thing. They make suckers out of you fellows with union dues . . . because a percentage for dues on your wages means real money whereas they pay only a couple of cents. . . . [A]ll I need is fifty or sixty of those signed-up cards, with the names of the men who joined up with 'em. That's all I need. What we have to face is that we're sitting on top of a roaring furnace and we haven't got a damper to shut off the draft. I don't even dare fire this Donovan who raised all that hell before. But give me fifty, sixty names on union cards and I've got 'm red-handed! Then I fire 'em one by one! Worry em to death. Each one not knowing when his turn's next. I'll put the fear of God and Pan American in those bastard hunkies . . . . If I can do that no man will dare to sign a card, 'cause he won't know if the card goes to their Pittsburgh headquarters or straight to me. They won't trust their own brothers then." (3:1–10)

Ironically, women take control in the later version, and from a social history perspective, the 1937 version of *Steel* offers a rare glimpse of the role of women in the union organizing effort in the North. While women are featured in the southern plays about textiles because of their presence in the workforce, *Steel* is one of the few instances where the importance of women to northern labor unions is dramatized in a commercial production. The play underscores the threat to the security of the family posed by both the industry and the union. Workers from all ethnic groups feared that unless they "showed appreciation" they would lose their jobs; "appreciation" translated into an unquestioning loyalty to the company. The union asked workers to place their jobs, their livelihood, the food for their children, in jeopardy. Resistance to the union often came from within the home—from the wives of workers.

Wexley's revised version of the script addresses this in an accurate and revealing manner. It reveals the role of women in the mill towns, both as impediments to unionization and as recruiters. In one scene in the Raldney house, Betty and Mela discuss union activity. Betty informs Mela that she and Joe plan to recruit what she calls the "kitchen scabs." ("Kitchen scab," it will be recalled, was a pejorative term for women who prevented their husbands from joining the union for fear of losing money and job security for their families.) In many mill towns they stood as a formidable obstacle to organizing efforts. The problem of unifying of diverse ethnic groups surfaces again in the discussion of kitchen scabs. Unless the organizers were polyglots, their efforts were futile. The need to convince the wives of ethnic workers in their own language is dramatized by Wexley in his script when Betty enlists native speakers: Mrs. Dooshenko to speak to the Slovak ladies, Mrs. Jarrouse to speak to the Italian housewives, and even Mela, to speak to the Hungarian women. In his script the emphasis rests on women persuading women that the union will be good for their families. Wexley employs a much more effective emotional appeal in this scene, showing the "little people" rising to confront the captains of industry with their courage and ingenuity. There is still an emphasis on family, but only as a social issue. The second production steers clear of domestic arguments that plagued the 1931 production and keeps the focus clearly on the labor movement and the benefits it accrued for individuals and their families.

The '37 production enjoyed a stronger conclusion by giving the audience moral and ideological reversals. While Joe waits for Malloy to arrive to pick up the signed union cards, Skinny arrives with news that the mill is facing a 97 percent layoff in the spring so that the rolling mill can be converted to automated rollers. Steve is astounded. His betrayal by management becomes sadly clear in his recognition that this new process will mean "they don't need any roller to know HOW to roll it . . . to set the wheels right, to feel the gauges with the tongs . . . to figger out its heat." Skinny replies blithely; "Nuthin! It's all automatic. That's why they were sayin they'll fire more than ninety outa every hundred men in the mill. . . . Jeez, You'll be lucky if they let you stick around to be one of the oilers" (3:2).

Worried that Malloy has not retrieved the signed union cards, Joe and Betty search for him, only to find that he has been arrested. Joe is about to leave to take the cards to Pittsburgh himself when he is stopped by detectives at his door. They enter and arrest him for "criminal syndicalism." During the final scene the betrayed Steve turns on a detective, grabs his gun, and commandeers the guns from the other detectives. Steve is now in control. The warrant for arrest is revealed as fraudulent, and Steve sends Joe to Pittsburgh. Steve and Mela replace Joe and Betty in the union cause. Steve signs a union card in a symbolic gesture of defiance. Accompanied by two other workers, as the play concludes, Steve advances menacingly to beat the detectives so that they "never crawl back to this town again." The '37 version, like the first, ends with the clear promise of violence against the industry and its representatives.

THE PROMOTION STRATEGY OF LABOR STAGE

Steel was both an artistic and public relations victory for the fledgling Labor Stage. Even though the play received good press in the *New York Post*, and *Daily News*, the *New York Times* failed to review the play, though Brooks Atkinson had reviewed the 1931 production. Possibly the production's close association with organized labor, or the fact that Labor Stage was viewed as an amateur production group, prevented Atkinson from reviewing the new version. Nonetheless, Louis Schaffer used in the expanded program notes excerpts from the many reviews and letters he received about the play as proof of its effectiveness. He cited twenty-five testimonials, drawn from *The Day, The Ledger, La Stampa Libera, Justice, The New York Teacher, People's Press,* and *New Theatre and Film,* to list but a few.

Some of the first reviews appeared in *The Daily Worker.* Charles E. Dexter saw the play as a perfect vehicle for unionization efforts and called on the garment workers to sacrifice their jobs to take the play to the steel centers. He praised the actors of Local 10 of the ILGWU, calling them "the standard bearers of the social theatre movement" and went on to encourage them to tour the production. "I know it will be difficult for them to respond to the suggestion that they drop their own workaday tools and go forth to present this problem to the steel workers of Pittsburgh and Duquesne, and Youngstown and Homestead and Chicago and other steel centers, but this is their duty at this moment"[11].

The reviews and commentary on *Steel* were sustained for months, partially through genuine public interest and partially through the public-relations finesse of Schaffer, who monitored the "attitudes" of the left and right-wing press towards Labor Stage and who anticipated political criticism, particularly allegations of communist ties, before they surfaced. Schaffer knew that in order to succeed Labor Stage needed to emphasize its pro-labor rhetoric. He knew too that the general public would accept a pro-union stance but not a pro-communist one. Advance publicity about the play rarely appeared in the daily New York papers. *Steel's* opening received coverage in the leftist press, whose reviewers praised the play; the *American Federationist* ran a condensed version of the script the month the play opened. But reviews were not forthcoming either in the *New York Times,* as noted, or in other, more conservative publications that had reviewed the production in 1931, or even in the more conservative labor publications. *Steel* was a play embraced by the political left. In a letter written to David Dubinsky two months after the play's premiere, Schaffer outlined his concerns about coverage of the play and intimated that Dubinsky should intercede:

I want to call your attention to another situation which is developing in connection with the activities of my department. I know that what it will lead to will be distasteful to you. I refer to the attitude that the left and right wing press has towards our work. I sensed this attitude a long time ago, but lately, with the attention that the production of "Steel" has received and with the increase in activity of our athletic department, the attitude has made itself felt more strongly. The right wing, or so-called Old Guard, labor press has given us almost no attention at all. This lack of interest in us was partly attributable to petty considerations, but mostly, it can be laid to their inefficiency and general neglect of new movements. The left wing press, on the other hand, is alert, very aggressive, and very anxious to wedge itself into the labor movement through whatever cracks there are. It eagerly gives space to all our activities. The outside world, therefore, gets a picture of us as definitely allied with the left-wing movement. To mention a few concrete examples. . . "Steel," favorably reviewed in *The Daily Worker* and the *Freiheit* and receiving two follow-up articles from the same papers, received only a single review from the *Forward*—a sympathetic one due to the fact that the reviewer happened to be Dr. Fogelman—and that was the end of 'Steel' so far as that paper was concerned. None of our releases ever found its way into print in the *Forward*. A similar neglect manifested itself in the field of the weekly English press. *The Socialist Call* has given us two glowing articles on 'Steel,' while to date the *New Leader* has still to sent its regular reviewer to see "Steel" and write a piece on it. After my making several requests, a young man who gave a brief notice to the play was sent, but we couldn't even include his write-up in our circular. I could go on citing any number of instances, but that would make this letter too lengthy. I believe something should be done to straighten out this situation, for while our friends of the right wing have done very little of a constructive nature, they have the capacity, for a lot of squawking and intriguing; and I know that ultimately they'll raise the cry that we have aligned ourselves with the Communists[12].

Schaffer's plan to garner support for the production was well conceived. He invited union leaders from across the country to attend the premiere performance of Labor Stage. They responded with interest, and more importantly, their presence at the premiere. Along with David Dubinsky, on that opening night, Clinton S. Golden, the Northeast Regional director of the Steel Workers Organizing Committee headquartered in Pittsburgh, was in attendance. After seeing the production, Golden wrote to Schaffer to tell him how impressed he was with the play. In the letter he mentions a conversation with David McDonald, Secretary-Treasurer of the SWOC, who expressed interest in seeing the play but who also "promised . . . to try to get President Lewis and John Brophy to . . . witness it." It is Golden's letter that formally broached the idea of a touring company of *Steel*. He saw the play as an asset in the organizing campaign and envisioned it touring "to fifteen or twenty steel towns in the Northeastern Region" where, he anticipated, "a considerable number of tickets could be sold"[13]. The proposal itself may have been orchestrated by Schaffer, who was ready to act on it immediately and exploit it fully.

Within days of receiving Golden's letter, Schaffer arranged for a copy of it to appear in *The Daily Worker*, which heralded the CIO's financial support of the tour. The article noted that the organizing meeting had been called by the New Theatre League under the sponsorship of Will Geer, Mark Starr, and Mark Marvin. At this meeting a Labor Theatre Committee for Touring 'Steel' was formed and a detailed plan devised[14]. Within two weeks of Golden's letter a brief article appeared in *The Daily Worker* that was notable for two reasons. First, it demonstrated Schaffer's ability as a promoter; second, it provided evidence that another show had been touring industrial areas with similar proselytizing intent—Albert Bein's *Let Freedom Ring*, a play about textile workers and the Gastonia strike; the play referred to by J. O. Bailey in his correspondence (See chapter 1).

The Daily Worker outlined a tour of *Steel* planned for all steel centers of New Jersey, Pennsylvania, Michigan, Ohio, and Illinois[15]. Schaffer's committee acted with astounding speed and expediency. Its recommendations, laid out in a tour prospectus contained in the Wexley papers, chronicled in both pragmatic and philosophical detail the backstage orchestration of theatre for political ends. This three-page document, a public relations schematic, targeted a specific non-theatre-going, labor audience. Four objectives were delineated:

1. The object of the Labor Theatre Committee for Touring "Steel" is to show this play to the largest number of steel workers in the steel centers, and thus further the objective of the CIO campaign in steel.

2. Since the projected tour is not geared for profit, but for educational purposes, we must make it possible for the lowest paid steel worker to see it. Hence, the play must be presented at prices which will compete with the average movie admission price,—from 25 to 50 [cents], depending on the locality. This will necessarily mean a low gross income, and the difference between this expected income and the cost of presenting the play, must be provided for in the form of contributions.

3. Whenever possible, the presentation of the play will be tied up with a specific local organizational activity, such as conventions, meetings, rallies, etc.

4. The tour should take place sometime between March and the end of May—for six to eight consecutive weeks.

Tour costs were estimated at approximately $10,450.00, with the total gross income expected to be $5,250.00. The anticipated deficit stood at $5,200.00. This the committee hoped to subvent by holding three conferences to gain the financial and advertising support deemed necessary for the tour[16].

The prospectus indicated that the first conference would be held in New York on February 28 and that invitations had already been sent. The second and third conferences were to be in Pittsburgh and Chicago before March 7, 1937. Schaffer planned to issue simultaneously invitations to labor and fraternal and cultural groups that would be accompanied by a request for donations and pledges to underwrite possible losses. Each group was expected to cooperate with the committee in negotiating bookings "so that the expected income of $150 a performance becomes a reality." Local arrangements committees would coordinate activities with the tour committee, based in New York. The financial and public relations duties were delegated to a "booker" who would arrive in designated tour cities four weeks prior to the performances. A primary responsibility of this position was to guarantee receipt of $150 from the local committee. Small towns would be asked for a "much smaller guarantee," while the larger cities would have to make up the difference. The booker would be followed by an "advance man" about a week before the performance, who would help the local committee with publicity and make all final arrangements for the performance. The production itself would arrive with a business manager authorized to settle all financial matters with the local committees. Hoping to avoid rental fees for public theatres, high school auditoriums, and halls became the sites of choice.

The proposed tour was ambitious. Thirty-one cities between Pennsylvania and Illinois were designated as tour stops. This translated to approximately six cities per week. The itinerary called for minimally two open dates per week which would be kept free in order to fill in other towns as the need and opportunity arose. The tour was to begin in Bethlehem or Allentown, Pennsylvania and end in Peoria, Illinois. All the major steel centers were listed as production sites. They included: [17]

Bethlehem and/or Allentown, Pa.	Cleveland, Ohio
Philadelphia, Pa.	Columbus, Ohio
Baltimore, Md.	Portsmouth, Ohio
Reading, Pa.	Toledo, Ohio
Lebanon, Pa.	Akron, Ohio
Altoona, Pa.	Gary, Ind.
Johnstown, Pa.	Hammond, Ind.
Pittsburgh, Pa.	Chicago, Ill.
Ambridge, Pa.	Waukegan, Ill.
Aliquipa, Pa.	Milwaukee, Wis.
McKesport, Pa.	St. Louis, Mo.
Braddock, Pa.	Granite City, Ill.
New Castle, Pa.	Davenport, Ill.
Lowell, Ohio.	Peoria, Ill.
Youngstown, Ohio	Detroit, Mich.
Canton, Ohio	

A letter sent February 18, 1937, to potential supporters all over the country urged their participation in a planning conference, on February 28 at Labor Stage. There, two accredited representatives sent by local groups would meet with representatives of the Steel Workers Organizing Committee, view a scene from *Steel*, and meet with members of the Committee for Touring 'Steel.' The committee comprised an impressive group of individuals from several leftist theatre organizations in New York. A listing of committee members as it appeared on the February 18 letter included Mark Starr (chairman), John

Howard Lawson (vice chairman), Mark Marvin (secretary), Louis Schaffer (treasurer), Sylvia Regan (executive secreary), John O'Shaughnessy and Rose Keane of the Actors Repertory Company, S. Lifshitz and M. Goldstein of the Artef Theatre, Kumar Goshal of the Brooklyn Progressive Players, Tucker P. Smith of Brookwood Labor College, Barrett H. Clark, of Dramatists Play Service, Mark Schweid and Charles Friedman of Labor Stage, Will Geer of the *Let Freedom Ring* touring company, John Bonn and Ben Irwin of the New Theatre League, Emanuel Raices of Rebel Arts, Lem Ward of the Theatre Union, and also Anita Block, Max Lerner, Ernest L. Meyer, Spencer Miller and Paul and Claire Sifton[18].

While plans were underway for the tour, Schaffer kept the production company active and before the public eye with additional performances in Brooklyn. Because the cast was composed of ILGWU members, who participated in Labor Stage as an extra activity above and beyond their everyday jobs, *Steel* was initially performed only on weekends. However, announcements for the Brooklyn run at the Brighton Theatre indicated that Schaffer had even more ambitious plans for the amateur cast. An article in *The Daily Worker* noted the proposed change, revealing: "It will run at this house all week with a matinee on Saturday. Up to now STEEL has been played only on Sundays but due to popular demand it will start now for a continuous run according to Mr. Louis Schaffer, Manager of Labor Stage. . . . He expects "Steel" to have a long run in New York; in addition he expects to send out two touring companies in the steel areas[19].

Two days later Ernest L. Meyer, reviewer for the *New York Post*, praised the play and commented on the sacrifices made by workers in the cast:

It was not merely because the play was powerful that I was impressed. It was also because I was just as deeply moved by the members of the cast and the conditions under which the play was produced. For every member of the cast was an amateur and a member of the International Ladies' Garment Workers' Union. And for six months of rehearsals these amateurs left their offices and shops, hurried to the theatre before supper, went through the sweat and tension that is part of all dramatic rehearsals, and came home late, hungry and exhausted. The results justify their sacrifice. 'Steel,' produced on Broadway some five years ago and now revised to meet the changing conditions, is the most convincing polemic in favor of industrial unions and against company unions that I have ever witnessed. It is planned to have traveling companies present the play in the steel and mining centers of the country. And I miss my guess if the play does not woo more converts to the C.I.O. than a thousand bales of printed propaganda and a dozen speeches by John Lewis. It is ably produced by workers and for workers, and no worker can possibly misunderstand its implications or withstand its impact[20].

Despite grandiose plans for a national tour, headlines touting CIO support, and the innovative nature of an union-supported theatrical company competing with the commercial theatre, Louis Schaffer and the Labor Theatre Committee for Touring "Steel," made one serious error; they failed to take their own labor force into account. This was a labor force highly attuned to managerial excesses, a labor force that knew how to respond: the cast of *Steel* went on strike! The first public hint of dissension in the ranks had come March 12, less than two weeks after *The Post* had extolled the virtues of the altruistic cast. *The Daily Worker* wrote that "despite pledges of financial aid from the C.I.O." the Local 10 production would continue for just three weeks. The review cited "uncertainty as to the necessity of a strike play . . . when negotiations are underway between the C.I.O. and some of the steel companies." Yet the real reason for the crumbling of Schaffer's plan is revealed in the reviewer's closing comments: "the cutters of Local 10, ILGWU are working hard in shops during the day, now that this is the height of the season, and are too tired to go into action daily"[21].

Notice of a strike that halted production came in *The Daily Worker* the following day:

Labor Stage Inc. the theatrical organization initiated by trade unions, is being plagued by a sit-down strike these days, the members of its acting company, the ILGWU Players, refusing to leave their cutting and sewing machines for nightly appearances in 'Steel,' the current offering of the organization. The worker actors say their jobs, as opposed to their avocations, come first. It is the busy season in the needle trades and they cannot, . . . play every evening[22].

The labor dispute was resolved by early May, but disquietude prevailed. Still, the Labor Stage players met their obligations and performed as the featured attraction at the twenty-third national convention of the ILGWU, May 5, 1937, in Atlantic City.

The program prepared for this convention was cleverly self-serving, simultaneously lionizing the ILGWU and promoting the interests of Labor Stage. A letter from the cast of *Steel* reminded delegates that the decision made by the ILGWU to enlarge the scope of the educational, cultural and recreational work of the union had resulted in the production of *Steel*, and it slyly assured them that money spent on the renovations of the Princess Theatre to transform it into Labor Stage had been well spent. The actors wrote that the facilities at Committee Hall in the Chelsea Hotel were not "nearly so ideal . . . as they are in our own beautiful and comfortable little theatre, Labor Stage"[23].

The program prepared for this production provides a case study of ILGWU self-promotion. John Wexley is described as a man who had virtually spent his life in steel mills. The mythos perpetuated in the program notes was that Wexley had worked in a steel mill as a boy and had "gathered his material not from books or newspapers, but from life." He knew "workers, unions, rolling mills and C.I.O. from personal experience." His summer of 1936 was spent visiting mills, attending union meetings, and talking to hundreds of workers as he went into the field with CIO organizers; "He was on the spot while labor history was in the making." This field work purportedly changed Wexley's perspective and caused him to abandon the earlier version of *Steel*. "In short," it claimed, "the new 'Steel' is a play written to order for Labor Stage. Incidentally, it is the first play about the C.I.O. " The program came replete with pictures of the Labor Stage and a photograph of a crowd purportedly waiting to see 'Steel,' accompanied by the claims that "over ten thousand persons have already seen this timely drama since its opening in January." and (hyperbolically) that "'Steel' is not only the lowest priced show in New York, but the only labor play"[24].

The validity of the assertion depends on how one defines "labor play." *Steel* was certainly the only play at the time produced by organized labor, but it was not the only one that had labor and industry as a thematic concern. Other plays in New York treating these themes during the spring of 1937 were *Power*, the Federal Theatre Project's controversial production that dramatized and satirized utility monopolies in the United States, *Stevedore*, about longshoremen; *Let Freedom Ring*, Bein's play about the textile industry; and Toller's, *The Machine Wreckers*. The theatrical fare in New York reflected a strong interest in labor problems that season.

Despite Labor Stage's public position that everything was progressing without difficulty, in reality by the end of May in-house problems and lack of support by the union locals were threatening the production. On May 21, Schaffer wrote to David Dubinsky complaining that few locals had arranged either a benefit or a theatre party to attend *Steel*. He provided Dubinsky with a tally of the house receipts up through May, reporting that "the total income by the end of this month will be about $6,000; all we have received from the above locals is about $800.00." To his brief financial report, which he submitted to Dubinsky "for the sake of the record," Schaffer attached a copy of a letter he sent to all locals of the ILGWU. In it he had chided the locals for not supporting the production, claiming that only five of fifty performances had been supported by union locals[25]. Schaffer wrote his letter on new Labor Stage stationary, whose letterhead displayed the production list of Labor Stage. *Steel* is listed as the 1936–37 production and the play which was to give Labor Stage its greatest commercial success; *Pins and Needles*, which was in rehearsal as *Steel* was ending its run, is listed as the 1937–38 production.

Schaffer was not the only person connected with *Steel* to write to the President of the ILGWU. The same week Dubinsky received Schaffer's missive, he received another from Mark Schweid, the director of *Steel*. Schweid wrote to Dubinsky because Schaffer had fired him. Schaffer's vision of Labor Stage as a major producing organization coupled with his abrasive personality, were causing problems for the company in the late Thirties. Mark

Starr characterized him as "a take-charge, adrenalin-loaded organizer. He took too little time to explain his ideas and his only philosophy was to try something different, better and bigger." Schweid's letter indicated that Schaffer lacked tact. He recounted to Dubinsky how Schaffer, "now preferring someone else, . . . put a blunt stop to my job, without giving me a single day's notice." Dubinsky responded almost immediately, assuring him that because of his acquaintance with Schweid, and "not as a matter of policy," that he would look into the matter. Schweid did not get his job back, the controversy over which probably centered on the direction of *Pins and Needles*. He did, however, receive a settlement of accounts by the end of June, 1937. His letter of June 28 closed his association with Labor Stage. His letter is of interest because it refers to other productions supported by the ILGWU that preceded *Steel*. Schweid recounts: "In my profession I cannot afford to burn bridges behind me; in particular one which I had a fair share in building. It is, therefore, needless for me to say, that I stand ready at any time to work for the International. I began with the Mass-Recital 'In the Factory' at the Hippodrome, and finished with the full-length production of 'Steel.' In between lie performances of one-act plays from Passaic to Baltimore, and the 1936 Celebration on the Polo Grounds. That is not a bad record, and that is what we all go by in this world"[26].

A number of things were happening at this time. Interest in *Steel* among members of Local 10 seemed to be waning. The cast's restive spirit was problematic. Schaffer, looking to expand the production and support of Labor Stage to other unions, had, according to Sointu Syrjala, "allowed another play to be done in Studio B of the Labor Stage; this was a revue that a group hoped would become a Broadway show. When the group rehearsing the revue failed to secure financial backing for a Broadway production, "Schaffer decided (in the Summer of 1937) to have the amateur garment workers do it under the direction of Charles Friedman." This production, which was *Pins and Needles*, "roared on and roared on" and replaced *Steel* as Labor Stage's showcase production. When this happened, all efforts turned to promoting *Pins and Needles*, and there is little evidence to show that the proposed tour of *Steel* ever materialized[27].

Steel was a milestone production for Labor Stage. It was its first attempt at a serious dramatic production illuminating the problems of labor. Never before had organized labor supported theatre for "educational purposes" in so public a forum. Labor Stage expanded the activities of its education and recreation department to make use of the theatre to proselytize. In its attempt to use the theatre to champion the cause of labor and promote its interests, Labor Stage and the production of *Steel* set precedents. Unfortunately, the premiere production of Labor Stage was overshadowed by the spectacle and comedy of *Pins and Needles*, a play opportunistically absorbed by Labor

Stage, not created for it.

Steel was a genuine attempt by an American labor organization to use the theatre systematically to promote its philosophy and meet its ends. Trends in the late Thirties led several groups to consider national theatre companies that would use the theatre for propagandistic ends. Labor Stage, the New Theatre League, and the Federal Theatre Project are examples of groups with a vision of the theatre as a voice for social change. The congressional closing of the Federal Theatre Project in 1939, on allegations of communistic leanings, had a chilling effect on all these groups. We forget the deleterious effect of decisions made under Martin Dies, Chairman of the House Un-American Activities Committee during the 1930s, and we forget too that blacklists created in the '30s were as destructive to the entertainment industry as those resulting from the HUAC hearings under Joseph McCarthy. Serious leftist drama faded with the coming of the 1940s, and with it faded the idealism of a theatrical movement committed to social change and justice.

NOTES

1. Malcolm Goldstein, *The Political Stage: American Drama and Theater of the Great Depression* (New York: Oxford University Press, 1974), p. 135.

2. "Biography," John Wexley (1907–1985) Papers, 1929–1963, U.S. Mss. 77AN, The State Historical Society of Wisconsin, Madison, Wis.

3. Mark Marwin, "Workers' Theatre Marches," *New Masses* 11 (8 May 1934): 29. Cited in Daniel Freidman, "A Brief Description of the Worker's Theatre Movement of the Thirties," *Theatre for Working-Class Audiences in the United States, 1830–1980,* Bruce A. McConachie and Daniel Friedman, eds. (Westport, Conn: Greenwood Press, 1985), p. 112.

4. "Report of the General Executive Board to the Twenty-third Convention of the International Ladies' Garment Workers' Union," 3 May 1937, p. 175, International Ladies' Garment Workers' Union Records, Labor Management Documentation Center, Cornell University; and Max D. Danis, *The World of David Dubinsky* (New York: World Publishing Company, 1957), p. 124, cited in Gary L. Smith, "The International Ladies' Garment Workers' Union's Labor Stage, a Propagandistic Venture," unpub. diss., Kent State University, 1975, p. 2.

5. Mark Starr, "A Trade Union Pioneers in Education: The Educational Programs and Activities of the ILGWU," *American Federationist,* 43 (January 1936): 54–56; Benjamin Stolberg, *Tailor's Progress; The Story of a Famous Union and the Men Who Made it* (Garden City, N.Y.: Doubleday, Doran and Company, Inc., 1944), pp. 294, 296; letter, Mark Starr to Gary L. Smith, July 22, 1974; "Labor Ventures Into Drama," *Pins and Needles Scrapbook* #1 (1938), ILGWU Education Office, p. 1, cited in Smith, pp. 49, 53, 54, 59, 60, 61.

6. "Report of the General Executive Board May 3, 1937: 176,

7. Letter, Julius Hochman and Louis Schaffer to David Dubinsky, January 12, 1937, Box 79 Folder 3, International Ladies' Garment Workers' Union Records, David

Dubinsky Papers. Labor-Management Documentation Center, Cornell University.

8. Richard Dana Skinner, "Steel," *Commonweal* 15 (December 9, 1931): 160–61.

9. Skinner.

10. J. Brooks Atkinson, "Making Men of Steel," *The New York Times*, November 19, 1931: 26:5.

11. Charles E. Dexter, "Three Plays of Social Value Restore Vigor to the Stage," *The Daily Worker* (20 January 1937): 7.

12. Letter, Louis Schaffer to David Dubinsky, March 15, 1937, Box 79 Folder 3, International Ladies' Garment Workers' Union Records, David Dubinsky Papers.

13. Letter, Clinton S. Golden to Louis Schaffer, January 25, 1937, John Wexley Papers, 1929–1963, Correspondence, Box 2, Folder 8, The State Historical Society of Wisconsin, Madison, Wis.

14. "C.I.O. Pledges Support to Drama About Lives of Steel Workers," *The Daily Worker*, 1 February 1937: 7.

15. "Actors Plan Tour," *The Daily Worker*, 6 February 1937: 9.

16. Prospectus, Labor Theatre Committee for Touring "Steel," John Wexley Papers, Box 2, Folder 11, The State Historical Society of Wisconsin, Madison, Wis.

17. Prospectus. Box 2, Folder 11.

18. Letter Mark Starr to All Labor, Fraternal and Cultural Groups, February 18, 1937, Correspondence, John Wexley Papers, Box 2 Folder 8, The State Historical Society of Wisconsin, Madison, Wis.

19. "'Steel' at Brighton," *The Daily Worker*, 22 February 1937: 7.

20. Ernest L. Meyer, "As the Crow Flies, *The New York Post*, 24 February 1937, n.p. Clipping in John Wexley Papers, Box 2, Folder 10, The State Historical Society of Wisconsin, Madison, Wis.

21. "Detroit Strikes Spur Theatre Movement Into New Activity," *The Daily Worker*, 12 March 1937: 7.

22. "Busy Season Halts 'Steel,'" *The Daily Worker*, 13, March 1937: 7.

23. Letter in Program Notes of Steel, Presented at the 23rd Convention of the International Ladies' Garment Workers' Union, May 5, 1937, Chelsea Hotel, Atlantic City, N.J., in International Ladies' Garment Workers' Union Records, Labor Management Documentation Center, Cornell University.

24. "Notes about the Author," in Program Notes of *Steel*, presented at the 23rd Convention of the International Ladies' Garment Workers' Union.

25. Letters, Louis Schaffer to David Dubinsky, with attachment, Louis Schaffer to All Locals of the International, May 21, 1937, International Ladies' Garment Workers' Union Records. David Dubinsky Papers, Box 79, Folder 3.

26. Letter, Mark Starr to Gary L. Smith, July 22, 1974, in Smith, p. 181; and letter. Mark Schweid to David Dubinsky, June 28, 1937, International Ladies' Garment Workers' Union Records. David Dubinsky Papers, Box 79, Folder 3.

27. "Interview with Mr. Sointu Syrjala" in Smith, p. 166.

CHAPTER 6

The Legacy of American Labor Plays

In the several years it took to complete this book, the world political scene changed significantly. Most astonishing for those who lived through the Cold War was the political collapse of the Soviet Union. At their birthplace, their homeland, the political ideologies that came to be known as communism, socialism, Marxism, and Leninism, are dead as we move toward the end of the twentieth century. With them have died the governing philosophies of most of the radical labor struggles in the United States. As a powerful political movement, Soviet Marxism is but a fading memory. Today's political radicals will be drawn towards other movements, as those movements coalesce in populist efforts. However, analysts and scholars interested in the political left will be continually drawn to the historic examples of leftist art from the 1920s and 1930s, for they provide the symbols of political utopias. Leftist art, whether plays, paintings, music, or propagandistic posters, embodies the idealism born of this need for social improvement. In their artistic expressions political movements provide models and reinforce a strongly held faith in the efficacy of protest and change. Radicals, and more specifically youthful radicals, draw on movements that offer a romantic return to utopian ideological solutions.

One might rightly ask, why would anyone today want to read these plays? Certainly their polemical positions are not endorsed with the fervor displayed when they were performed five decades ago. Why the plays bear reading today lies more in the pieties of the scripts than in their precise political aims. Their political proposals are not as interesting as their moral exhortations. These plays are didactic politically *and* morally. In their respect for the worker, the laborer, the common man and woman, they transcend the modern political movements that spawned them. Their universality manifests itself most persuasively in the moral integrity of the characters.

Labor scripts provide a prototype of an indigenous American morality play; the distinctions between good and evil, right and wrong, are clearcut, even though they are drawn along political lines. The theatrical devices they use remind the audience of its own moral positions which carry strong emotional significance bordering on the religious. The incorporation of labor songs in many, though not all, of the plays to stir audience emotions and heighten fervor and resolve, is analogous to singing hymns or civil rights songs, to fortify pre-existing beliefs in the audience. The music contains spiritual and patriotic elements. Even the singing of the communist *Internationale*, a song not universally embraced by American labor, glorifies the worker. It speaks to the virtues of the common man—the laborer—and in this way crosses political and philosophical lines to appeal to all that the audience would find intrinsically American. The plays speak for more than a political philosophy that some workers of the period would have found repugnant; they articulate and dramatize a pride in the American labor force that embodies our national virtues. The scenes of the leftist plays reflected American virtues as encompassing a strong work ethic, ethnic and regional pride, and a belief that the inviolable rights of the individual stand above any form of political or industrial pressure and prerogative.

The plays exemplify traditional American folkloric elements of man struggling against the machine. In them one finds the heroic underpinnings of John Henry, Joe Magarac, and Paul Bunyan, all of whom at one time stood up to American industry in contests of strength and endurance. The heroes of the labor plays are the union organizers and labor leaders, who stand as men against the combined engines of American corporations. They usually combine such elements of American popular culture as melodrama and variations of well known folk songs that solidifies their appeal to a large audience even though they may not stand the test of "great art."

The mixture of songs and heroic elements harkens back to another age of storytelling, and this is why the audience appreciation and acclaim for the plays at the time they were produced far exceeded the assessment of modern critics. These plays are part of the American cultural heritage—our unique mythos—that pits the individual against powerful machines, and integrity against corporate power. They are, for this reason, worthy of study. The metaphors changed as the United States moved into the twentieth century, but the "steel-driving man" of John Henry and the steel-laborer of Joe Magarac have been reincarnated in the union organizers of Fer and in their female counterpart, Ella May Wiggins[1].

The answer to the question of why would anyone want to read these plays today has at its heart an explanation of the relevance of the old—old values, old movements, old politics, old theatrical forms. Paradoxically, the answer can be best understood by examining the "language of the new" that encompasses the movements out of which these plays grew. The "newness" with which issues, problems, and events were treated artistically led these plays to gain notoriety at the time of their productions.

In placing these plays within a historical context one is tempted to identify them immediately with the labor movement, but with which aspect of the labor movement, Marxist, socialist, communist, liberationist, trade unionist, etc., it is not so easy to identify. Separating the influences of one movement from another is like trying to isolate the artistic effectiveness of individual colors in a painting. There were unquestionably other movements whose development in the early part of the twentieth century bear noting for their influence on the individuals who created these plays. What have been termed "the progressive movement," "the leftist movement," or "the proletarian movement" certainly influenced perceptions of labor, and their identification with the labor movement and literary representations of labor in the United States is beyond dispute. Isolating the political and cultural incidents that led to "radical" departures in mainstream American art and literature is a formidable, if not impossible, task. Identifying "radical" artists and "radical" art is not as difficult. While some prefer the label "revolutionary," it is nonetheless justifiable to claim that the plays studied in this book fall within the rubric of "radical" art, or at the very least might be called "radical" artistic responses to a burgeoning industrial society that, from the artists' perspective, threatened American life. They were not, except in Wexley's 1937 production of *Steel*, directly tied to labor unions but were, rather, artistic responses to labor problems, one step removed from labor itself.

The influences of many movements can be identified in the development of "labor plays." What Adele Heller and Lois Rudnick label "the cultural movement," which began in 1915 and resulted immediately in the creation of the Provincetown Players in Provincetown, Massachusetts, should not be overlooked as a seminal influence on American playwrights, novelists, and artists working throughout the 1920s. In the classification of these plays the term "new theatre" comes readily to mind; yet "new theatre" is a term Heller and Rudnick directly link with the cultural movement, along with "new politics," "new woman," "new psychology," and "new art." They recognize and address the "pragmatic and utopian natures" of the reformers who rose to lead the radical proponents of these movements. They contend that, unlike the "orthodox Marxists" of other movements, influential individuals in the cultural movement supported "a revolution devoted as much to play and self-expression as it . . . [was] to labor unionization and redistribution of wealth"[2].

The artistic emphasis of the movement growing out of political ideology was formalized in the success in the 1920s and 1930s of the John Reed Clubs, which was the artistic arm of the American Communist Party. Members became involved in the publication of the "new magazines, production of the "new films," and the mounting of "new plays" by groups with names like the "New Playwrights Theatre." Others not intimately involved in the formation of these groups but who expressed interest and support through their own works came to receive their own "new" appellation; leftist writers like Langston Hughes, for instance became labeled as "new negroes." Interest in the arts propagated into all areas and what had been established as the League of Workers Theatres in 1932 had to change its name to "New Theatre League" a few years later.

Not all left-wing writers were card-carrying members of the American Communist Party. Daniel Aaron points out that only a small fraction were actually party members and prefers to call the "considerably larger number" of those involved in the movement "fellow travelers." Aaron refers to the communist leanings of leftist writers as a form of "literary insurgency" and casts these writers in terms that evoke heroic virtues, calling them "rebels," "radical intellectuals," and plain "radicals" who carried the banner of social criticism forward in the great literary wars of the 1930s[3].

For decades American theatrical historians have pointed to European influences that changed American drama into the "new theatre" that is so much discussed. Heller says that the this notion of a "new" theatre "borrowed much of its impetus from the European 'little theatres' in France, Germany, England, and Russia. . . ." Jay Williams points to a specific incident in 1926, the International Theatre Exhibition in New York, it showcased the innovative work of European directors and "as an indirect result . . . brought together four earnest, rebellious theatre people . . . John Howard Lawson, EmJo Basshe, Michael Gold and Francis Faragoh"[4].

While not discounting that assessment completely, this study offers a convincing alternative view: that this "new theatre" was not a complete assimilation and Americanization of modern European techniques but a reconstitution and modernization of an American theatrical staple—the melodrama—and as such these plays represent a unique American perspective on industrialization, labor, and the working classes in several industries. The documentary nature of the scripts is uniquely American in its depiction of court scenes, and in the use of journalistic accounts of strikes. The plays here, and others written in the genre we now refer to as "labor plays," praise the mainstays of American labor politics: equality and justice achieved through personal participation. While the plays in this study offer depictions of two industries, steel and textiles, a wealth of material exists written by workers attending sessions and camps sponsored by the labor colleges. These scripts treat other industries with similar techniques of documentary detail, corporate villains, and heroic organizers.

Labor scripts ask the audience to make ethical judgments. Ethical criticism, as Wayne Booth explains in *The Company We Keep, an Ethics of Fiction*, concerns itself with the questions regarding what a piece of literature may *do* to the reader or audience. Labor scripts overtly tried to move the audience not only to an ethical judgment, but to action. When one considers the ethical dilemmas contained in the scripts, the ethical conflicts, and the decisions made by characters on abstract, value-laden grounds, then one begins to see the literature as a series of labor parables intended to teach moral lessons transferable beyond the movements to life itself. What the plays lack in scintillation for modern audiences they compensate for in sincerity. As moral arguments they offer tribute to the humanity of an industrial workforce. They continually dramatize the individual's endurance and resilience challenged by the power either of the machine or the machine state. There are, says Booth, no neutral terms in ethical appraisals, and "ethical criticism will make explicit those appraisals that are implicit"[5]. This study illuminates the implicit ethical judgments being supported by the plays, judgments that may be obscure to modern readers who lack familiarity with the politics of the labor movement generally and the specific controversies involved in strikes and industries represented in these plays.

Booth chooses an epigraph from John Gardner to set the tone of his first chapter, "Relocating Ethical Criticism": "Art is civilization's single most significant device for learning what must be affirmed and what must be denied"[6]. The texts examined here ask the audience to affirm the value of the individual over the machine, to affirm the integrity of personal consciousness over corporate power, and to deny technocratic solutions that transform individual workers into labor units in an impersonal system of scientific management. Such affirmations remind present readers of the supremacy of the individual even in an age when they interact with machines and correspond with unseen colleagues through voice mail, electronic mail, the Internet, and the host of other technological innovations that remove us from the soul of those with whom we purport to speak and share our thoughts electronically. Do these scripts have something to say to modern labor-lore specialists, theatre historians, or literary scholars? Yes. Quite simply, they poignantly affirm the value of work and the value of the individual. They are not perfect scripts, but they are powerful.

Strike Song, Strike!, Altars of Steel, and *Steel* responded artistically to regional political and social problems in the 1930s. They dramatized the dismal economic conditions of the period, made radical ideological arguments for worker organization, and sounded a call for national change. They are Depression-era plays that grew out of the experience of workers in North Carolina and Alabama, and Massachusetts and New York, all treating the same theme—the exploitation of American labor by industrial management. The scripts are not unbiased, nor do they seek to provide a balanced argument. Rather, each constructs a moral argument that attempts to alter the consciousness of the audience toward labor issues and to invite them to take action. The playwrights gave dramatic form to the idealistic philosophies of leftist groups seeking pragmatic, if not utopian, solutions to industrial problems. The plays champion the rights of labor, dignify the national workforce, highlight its ethnic diversity, and instruct popular audiences in labor issues. They are didactic; their intent was to educate the American public and to rekindle in their audiences a belief in the worker as the backbone of the industrial state. They are epideictic in their celebration of regional values and in their praise of exemplary characters, both used to forge emotional alliances with the audience. Their ability to elicit strong empathetic responses was the basis for their success. Audiences were asked to recognize and identify with the deeply held values of their specific regions or groups. They were asked to judge labor conditions in the court of modern history as jury members, as citizens, and as members of specific ethnic groups that held to cultural as well as regional predispositions and attitudes. The southern steel workers dramatized in *Altars of Steel* accepted paternalism in industry as part of their regional work ethic, while Wexley's steel workers in *Steel* respected the father as family head but would never have accepted a metaphor that depicted the mill or its managers as part of a sympathetic and trustworthy family unit.

The strong religious imagery associated with the union in the southern scripts is remarkable in its consistency. *Strike!*, though written by northern authors, still manifested a strong element of religious symbology, because of its southern theme. Audiences were asked continually to see the union as a means to economic salvation. The union became a surrogate religion in these scripts which envision labor leaders as saviors. Contrasts of good and evil, of righteousness and injustice worked compellingly in these scripts. Northern industrial leaders were depicted as devils, while northern organizers were saviors. Crusading metaphors are equally obvious, especially in the textile scripts, where children were employed in the campaign of conversion. Labor songs used in the textile scripts functioned as hymns sung to the honor and glory of American labor. Faith in the union became, in effect, faith in a divine power. Considering the fundamentalist nature of southern religious faith, it would seem that this appeal for unquestioning faith in the union would have raised the specter of a secular religion, which southern audiences would reject, but this did not happen. Rather, the appeal rested on the audience's willingness to believe in itself as a group and to place its faith in the concerted, organized efforts of southern workers acting on behalf of the South. As in any discussion of religion, the audience tended to accept that which it already believed in, the South, as a distinctive and autonomous culture.

Modern readers may charge that the plays were parochial and time-bound, and in many respects, they were. But, in large measure, this was their intent. The plays examined in this study were written with specific audiences in mind. Bailey and Rogers knew southern labor, while Vorse and Wexley knew the prejudices and pieties of northern audiences, and of labor audiences. Yet they did have certain similarities: All were militant in varying degrees, all promoted a melodramatic mythos of virtuous labor struggling against the inhumane practices of evil management, all targeted a working-class audience, and all were connected with significant amateur theatre groups in this country. The plays were not unlike WPA murals painted during the 1930s as part of the public arts program; they sentimentalized and enoblized American labor. And like the WPA murals occasionally uncovered today in post offices and government buildings from Los Angeles to Atlanta, they had a richness in color and detail that caught the unique character of Americans working in a specific region and in a specific industry associated with that region. The artistic intent of the murals commissioned for public buildings was to reinforce individual and regional pride, and to inspire nationalism and patriotism. It is striking how often these murals depicted the industry and workforce of the region. Just as the WPA murals were part of a larger movement in American art, so too were these labor plays. Each uniquely exemplifies social issues that influenced many forms of American art during the Thirties.

The plays discussed here fall under various generic headings: social drama, social realism, documentary drama, leftist drama, New Deal drama, Marxist drama, communist drama, labor drama. But they are first and foremost indigenous American drama, treating indigenous American themes of individual rights and institutional responsibilities. They are part of a larger body of dramatic literature that examines American labor. Thomas Greenfield's study *Work and the Work Ethic in American Drama 1920–1970* postulates that of all the recurring themes in modern American drama, "the most prevalent and most intriguing is the one surrounding the American and his work." The dramatic treatment of the American worker encompasses conflicts in the workplace as wells as the problems that evolve in the individual's attitudes towards the work itself[7]. Greenfield does not include *Strike! Song, Strike, Altars of Steel*, or *Steel* in his study. By and large, they have been forgotten. They have not remained in the repertories of modern producing companies, as have plays like *Waiting for Lefty*, and their titles have slipped from our memories. Yet they were successful when they were produced—they had an effect. Audiences were moved, industries responded. These plays touched nerves and elicited reactions in industries and communities that recognized themselves in the dramatic reenactment of labor issues.

This study has generated for me several hypotheses and suppositions about political plays and producing organizations of this period. These plays have something to teach us about the use of the theatre for political ends and the documentary reenactment of historical events before an audience that knows those events. I believe the plays represented here are part of a larger movement in the American theatre, in which American playwrights employed documentary techniques not usually credited to American drama used by the Federal Theatre Project. Studies of the development of documentary theatre tend to focus on European drama from the agit-prop plays of the Blue Blouses through the works of Joan Littlewood or Peter Cheesman.

Little attention has been given the use of documentary detail in American scripts. Such documentary evidence, incorporated into dialogue and plot, was used more often by more American playwrights of this period than has been recognized. Moreover, the use of documentary detail in American plays seems to have developed as part of a regional, often amateur, grass-roots response to social problems. These plays are evidence that the Federal Theatre Project was not itself the genesis of many of the experimental documentary techniques it employed, as some critics maintain, but was rather the conduit by which the innovations devised, in fact, by American playwrights, came to national attention. The Federal Theatre Project drew upon many sources. Its playwrights, playreaders, actors, and directors were associated with production companies ranging from the Brookwood Labor College to Fred Koch's Carolina Playmakers.

Subsequent studies are likely to reveal material supporting a revisionist notion that the American political theatre of the 1930s was not as reliant on its European counterparts as we have been led to believe, but was in a formative stage, evolving its own distinctive dramatic genre, that was to be aborted with the closing of the Federal Theatre Project. Evidence indicates that during the 1930s in the United States numerous documentary plays were written and produced treating indigenous problems with characteristically American style. Investigations of other plays displaying this documentary impulse need to be undertaken so that their conclusions can be compared; I suspect that examination of plays written and produced in the labor colleges as part of the labor educational movement will discover a prominent documentary quality in the scripts. There are scores of labor plays shelved in collections throughout the nation that merit reexamination by theatre historians and social and literary critics.

I suspect too that examining plays about American labor will be reveal that there were women writing labor plays, women whose works have languished unnoticed in labor archives and theatre collections. The role of women playwrights and their treatment of social themes has not been adequately investigated. Many of these women were amateurs, trying to give artistic expression to problems that affected them and their families. But some, I suspect, were writers of prominence like Mary Heaton Vorse, who turned to drama for an efficacious means to an end—the persuasion of their audience through palatable and pleasurable means. When I began this study I did not know the work of Mary Heaton Vorse, whom I came to recognize as the most significant writer of those examined here. At some point I found myself asking how had I missed her. Why did I not know her work? In the editor's introduction to *Rebel Pen: The Writings of Mary Heaton Vorse*, Dee Garrison provides an answer:

Essentially, Vorse's work did not survive her. With the advent of Big Labor, her literary reputation became nonexistent. With the beginning of the Cold War, her style of politics was forcibly quieted. With the ascendance of the Feminine Mystique, her generation of fighters lay largely forgotten. But no matter. Mary Vorse perfectly understood the process of the momentary extinction of her work—for all her life and all her writing had centered upon the relationship between individual and society. . . . She was confident that her experience had lessons to teach another generation. She fully expected to be studied and understood. Her life had carried exceptional impact. Her ideas would endure[8].

Mary Heaton Vorse's ideas have indeed endured, as have those ideas of Loretta Carroll Bailey, John Wexley, Thomas Hall Rogers, and William Dorsey Blake. They, like Vorse, wrote about the individual and society. Notably, both Bailey and Vorse sought artistic collaboration with men for their scripts, Loretta Bailey with her husband, and Mary Vorse with Blake. Their plays particularly addressed the role of women in a specific industry, textiles. Subsequent researchers will probably find a number of plays that focus on problems in the textile industry in both the North and South, an industry that was dominated by a female workforce. Yet much is to be learned from Wexley's accurate portrayal of the problems that affected women and children in steel towns, and of the role of women in northern organizing efforts. Examination of labor scripts will release the voices of women in American labor: voices of women authors and characters within their scripts. The lines given female characters in these plays reveal the social and political roles of women in the labor force. The body of literature written in the labor colleges may well shed new light on artistic expression by and about women in industry. I think that the examination of labor scripts will reveal that the problems of many industries were dramatized, not just those of textiles or steel, and that many of the concerns focused on industrial effects on individual health and well-being, and on the collective effects of family life in mill towns owned and operated by impersonal, often absent, corporate entities. Other plays might have gone beyond the documentary detail about the use of "clacker," a managerial attempt to force workers to relinquish their wages in the company store. There may have been other dramatizations of the economic enslavement of American workers by companies that eliminated freedom of choice in housing, purchases, recreation, education, and even religion (as evidenced by the character of the mill-paid preacher in *Strike!*).

Research into labor scripts will probably reveal innovative production choices in design and staging. The two steel scripts in this study advanced arguments both intellectually, in the dialogue, and visually in the set designs, that speak to the dehumanization of man by machine: to the individual succumbing to the hellish atmosphere created by giant machines, sucking the life and soul from workers. The futuristic set design for *Altars of Steel* extending beyond the proscenium curtain, in effect, demanded the audience consider the hardness, the coldness, the impenetrability, of steel and, thus, the industry.

Not all acting companies, however, had the security of federal funding for their productions. Most emerged from university or labor groups hampered by limited resources, buoyed only by unlimited commitment. Most, no doubt, employed innovative approaches to traditional theatrical conventions to advance their political arguments. Like the techniques used in the plays examined here, one will likely find strong elements of spectacle, song, choral readings, sound effects, and choreographed masses. It can be hypothesized that regional identification and character types will be found to have been employed to forge ties with their audiences, which, it was presumed knew the history of the labor wars in this country. The four scripts here repeatedly drew from specific regional and national perceptions about American labor, and this gave them their distinctly American character. These scripts were unique treatments of clearly delineated contemporary problems. The intent of the plays was to move their audiences to compassion for the worker, lead them to implement change through organization and legislation, rather than revolt or violent protest.

Researchers need to examine labor plays as contemporary social commentary. One must be cautious in making generalizations based on the examination of four plays treating two specific industries, but evidence suggests that the plays in this study are, in fact, representative of American labor plays of the Depression era. Even though these plays darkly chronicle the abuses inflicted upon men, women, and children in American mills, they do not damn national industrial efforts. In each looms a regional pride, and within each is a poignant commitment to the value and dignity of labor and industry in specific regions and industries. The four scripts examined here symbolize the militance of American labor toward two particularly exploitative industries. They depict the intolerance and manipulation of various ethnic groups by industrial managers, and they ask the audience to condemn the managers for their callousness and indifference. Each in its own way lays bare the central tensions of labor strife in this country by presenting empirical evidence and then blending it into emotionally charged dramatic vignettes. This combination contributes to the uniqueness of the scripts and underscores their significance in American studies. The labor scripts of the 1930s deserve even more detailed study than that which has been attempted here. The corpus of works that constitute American political theatre will reveal when adequately studied,that as a distinct genre its roots run much deeper in our national consciousness than has been recognized or acknowledged. This study uncovers one stratum of a many-layered body of theatrical and social history. The politically inspired plays of the 1930s were icons of an American culture shaped by economic, social and moral turmoil. The significance of these scripts should not be underestimated, nor should the innovative artistry of the playwrights who brought the labor wars to the American public be overlooked. Used polemically, the theatre of this period employed empirical and documentary evidence and emotional appeals to press moral arguments. The labor plays and the playwrights that dramatized American labor reveal an important facet of our national heritage. They are cultural artifacts that tell us today about ourselves—what we were and what we have become.

NOTES

1. For a very pertinent discussion of the role of song in strikes and a discussion of such folk heroes as John Henry, see Archie Green, *Wobblies, Pile Butts and Other Heroes: Laborlore Explorations* (Urbana: University of Illinois Press, 1993), p. 1.

2. Adele Heller and Lois Rudnick, eds., *1915, The Cultural Movement: The New Politics, the New Woman, the New Psychology, the New Art & New Theatre in America* (New Brunswick, N.J.: Rutgers University Press, 1991), pp. 1–11.

3. Daniel Aaron, *Writers on the Left: Episodes in American Literary Communism* (New York: Harcourt, Brace & World, Inc. 1961), pp. ix, 5.

4. Jay Williams, *Stage Left* (New York: Charles Scribner's Sons, 1974), p. 19.

5. Wayne Booth, *The Company We Keep: An Ethics of Fiction* (Berkeley: University of California Press, 1988), p. 9.

6. Booth, p. 1.

7. Thomas Allen Greenfield, *Work and the Work Ethic in American Drama 1920-1970* (Columbia, Mo., and London: University of Missouri Press, 1982), p. 3.

8. Dee Garrison, *Rebel Pen: The Writings of Mary Heaton Vorse* (New York: Monthly Review Press, 1985), p. 9.

Bibliography

Aaron, Daniel. *Writers on the Left: Episodes in American Literary Communism.* New York: Harcourt, Brace and World, Inc., 1961.

Atkinson, Brooks. "Making Men of Steel. *The New York Times.* November 1931.

The Atlanta Constitution, March–April 1937.

The Atlantan Georgian, March–April 1937.

Bailey, James Osler. Correspondence to Paul Green. Paul Green Papers, Southern Historical Collection, University of North Carolina Library, Chapel Hill, N.C.

Bailey, Loretta Carroll. Letter to Nancy Bailey Rich, 3 July 1982.

____, and James Osler Bailey. *Strike Song.* North Carolina Collection, University of North Carolina Library, Chapel Hill, N.C.

Berkin, Carol Ruth. "Women's Life." Charles Reagan Wilson and William Ferris, eds. *Encyclopedia of Southern Culture.* Chapel Hill, N.C.: 1989.

Bigsby, C. W. E. "A View From East Anglia." *American Quarterly,* 41 (March 1989): 131–132

Blake, William Dorsey. "Stray Shots at the Sissy Theme." *Theatre Magazine* (October 1928).

____. Correspondence and Papers Cherry County Playhouse Collection. Billy Rose Theatre Collection, New York Public Library, New York, N.Y.

____. *Strike!: A Play in a Prologue and Fourteen Scenes.* Library of Congress, Washington, D.C.

____. *Strike!!! A Play in a Prologue; Thirteen Scenes, and an Epilogue.* Mary Heaton Vorse Collection, Archives of Labor and Urban Affairs, Wayne State University, Detroit, Mich.

Booth, Wayne. *The Company We Keep: An Ethics of Fiction.* Berkeley: University of California Press, 1988.

Boston Evening Transcript, December 1932.

Boston Sunday Globe, December 1932.

Brandon, Betty. "Women in Politics." Charles Reagan Wilson and William Ferris, eds. *Encyclopedia of Southern Culture.* Chapel Hill: University of North Carolina Press, 1989.

Brown, Richard Harvey. *Society as Text: Essays on Rhetoric, Reason and Reality.* Chicago: University of Chicago Press, 1988.

Campbell, Paul Newell. "The Rhetoric of Theatre." *Southern Speech Communication Journal* 48 (Fall 1982): 11–21.

Clurman, Harold, ed. *Famous American Plays of the 1930s.* New York: Dell Publishing, 1959.

Corbin, David. "Workers' Wives." Charles Reagan Wilson and William Ferris, eds. *Encyclopedia of Southern Culture.* Chapel Hill: University of North Carolina Press, 1989.

The Daily Worker, January–March 1937.

Danis, Max D. *The World of David Dubinsky.* New York: World Publishing Company, 1957.

De Cassers, Benjamin. "Has the Drama Gone Sissy?" *Theatre Magazine* (August 1928).

Deutsch, Helen and Hanau, Stella. *The Provincetown: A Story of the Theatre.* New York: Farrar and Rinehart, Inc., 1931.

Dexter, Charles E. "Three Plays of Social Value Restore Vigor to the Stage." *The Daily Worker,* January 1937.

Dubinsky, David. Correspondence. David Dubinsky Papers, Labor Management Documentation Center, Cornell University, Ithaca, N.Y.

Duffy, Susan and Duffy, Bernard K. "Anti-Nazi Drama in the United States 1934–41." *Essays in Theatre,* 4 (November 1985):41.

Flanagan, Hallie. *Arena: The History of the Federal Theatre.* New York: Benjamin Blom, 1940.

Frederickson, Mary. "Working Women." Charles Reagan Wilson and William Ferris, eds. *Encyclopedia of Southern Culture.* Chapel Hill: University of North Carolina Press, 1989.

Garrison, Dee. *Rebel Pen: The Writings of Mary Heaton Vorse.* New York: Monthly Review Press, 1985.

Goldstein, Malcolm. *The Political Stage: American Drama and Theater of the Great Depression.* New York: Oxford University Press, 1974.

Graves, John Temple. "This Morning." *Birmingham Age-Herald,* 7 October 1936.

Gray, Richard. *Writing the South: Ideas of an American Region.* New York: Cambridge University Press, 1986.

Green, Archie. *Wobblies, Pile Butts, and Other Heroes: Laborlore Explorations.* Urbana: University of Illinois Press, 1993.

Greenfield, Thomas Allen. *Work and the Work Ethic in American Drama 1920–1970.* Columbia, Mo. and London: University of Missouri Press, 1982.

Heller, Adele and Rudnick, Lois. eds. *1915, The Cultural Movement: the New Politics, the New Woman, the New Psychology, the New Art & New Theatre in America.* New Brunswick, N.J.: Rutgers University Press, 1991.

Herring, Harriet L. "The Industrial Worker." W. T. Couch, ed. *Culture in the South.* Chapel Hill: University of North Carolina Press, 1935.

Himmelstein, Morgan. *Drama Was a Weapon.* New Brunswick, N.J.: Rutgers University Press, 1963.

Ingalls, Robert P. "Industrial Violence." Charles Reagan Wilson and William Ferris, eds. *Encyclopedia of Southern Culture.* Chapel Hill: University of North Carolina Press, 1989.

International Ladies' Garment Workers' Union Records. Labor Management Documentation Center, Cornell University, Ithaca, N.Y.

Jones, Anne Goodwyn. "Belles and Ladies." Charles Reagan Wilson and William Ferris eds. *Encyclopedia of Southern Culture.* Chapel Hill: University of North Carolina Press, 1989.

Koch, Frederick H., Ed. *Carolina Folk Plays*. New York: Holt and Company, 1941.
____. Correspondence to Rosamond Gilder. Billy Rose Theatre Collection, New York
    Public Library.
Larkin, Margaret. "Ella May's Songs." *The Nation*, 129 (October 1929): 382.
Lavery, Emmett. "The Flexible Stage." Unpublished manuscript, Federal Theatre Project
    Collection, Library of Congress, Washington, D.C.
Leff, Michael and Sachs, Andrew. "Words the Most Like Things: Iconicity and the
    Rhetorical Text." *Western Journal of Speech Communication,* 54 (Summer
    1990): 256.
Levine, Ira A. *Left Wing Dramatic Theory in American Theatre*. Ann Arbor: University
    of Michigan Press, 1985.
Lightfoot, William E. "Murder Legends." Charles Reagan Wilson and William Ferris,
    eds. *Encyclopedia of Southern Culture*. Chapel Hill: University of North
    Carolina Press, 1989.
Malone, Bill C. "Protest Music." Charles Reagan Wilson and William Ferris, eds.
    Encyclopedia of Southern Culture. Chapel Hill: University of North Carolina
    Press, 1989.
Marwin, Mark. "Workers' Theatre Marches." *New Masses,* 11 (May 1934): 29.
Matthews, John Michael. "Virginius Dabney, John Temple Graves, and What Happened
    to Southern Liberalism." *Mississippi Quarterly, The Journal of Southern
    Culture*, 45 (Fall 1992): 367–405.
McConachie, Bruce A. and Friedman, Daniel. *Theatre for Working-Class Audiences in
    the United States, 1830–1980.* Westport: Greenwood Press, 1985.
Miami Daily News, March 1938.
Miami Herald, March 1938.
Mitchell, Boradus. "A Survey of Industry." W. T. Couch, ed. *Culture in the South.*
    Chapel Hill: University of North Carolina Press, 1935.
Nannes, Caspar H. *Politics in the American Drama*. Washington: The Catholic
    University of America Press, 1960.
"Playreader Reports." Federal Theatre Project Collection, Library of Congress.
Prentis, Albert. "Basic Principles." *Workers' Theatre,* 1 (May 1931): 1.
Rabkin, Gerald. *Drama and Commitment: Politics in the American Theatre of the
    Thirties*. Bloomington: Indiana University Press, 1964.
Rich, Nancy Bailey. Letter to Susan Duffy, 22 June 1989.
Rogers, Thomas Hall. *Altars of Steel*. Federal Theatre Project Collection, 1936, Library
    of Congress.
Skinner, Richard Dana. "Steel." *Commonweal*, 15: 160–61.
Smiley, Sam. *The Drama of Attack: Didactic Plays of the American Depression.*
    Columbia: University of Missouri Press, 1972.
Smith, Gary L. "The International Ladies' Garment Workers' Union's Labor Stage, A
    Propagandistic Venture." Ph.D. dissertation, Kent State University, 1975.
Smith, Susan Harris. "Generic Hegemony: American Drama and the Canon." *American
    Quarterly*, 41 (March 1989): 116.
Starr, Mark. "A Trade Union Pioneers in Education: The Educational Programs
    and Activities of the ILGWU." *American Federationist,* 43 (January
    1936):54–56.

Stewart, Charles; Smith, Craig, and Denton, Robert E. Persuasion and Social Movements. Prospect Heights, Ill.: Waveland Press Inc., 1984.

Stolberg, Benjamin. *Tailor's Progress: The Story of a Famous Union and the Men Who Made It.* Garden City, N.Y.: Doubleday, Doran and Company, Inc., 1944.

"The Strike Song." *Southern Textile Bulletin* (December 1931).

Thatcher, Molly Day. "Drama in Dixie." *New Theatre and Film* (October 1934).

Theatre of the Thirties Collection. Special Collections, George Mason University, Fairfax, Va.

Theatre Workshop, April 1937.

"Their Latest Effort." *Southern Textile Bulletin* (January 1932).

Vorse, Mary Heaton. *Time and the Town, A Provincetown Chronicle* New York: Dial Press, 1942.

_____. Correspondence. Mary Heaton Vorse Collection. Archives of Labor and Urban Affairs, Walter P. Reuther Library, Wayne State University, Detroit, Mich.

_____. Daily Notes. Mary Heaton Vorse Collection, Archives of Labor and Urban Affairs, Walter P. Reuther Library, Wayne State University, Detroit, Mich.

Ware, Caroline F. *The Cultural Approach to History.* Port Washington, N.Y.: Kennikat Press, 1940.

Watson, Goodwin. "Clio and Psyche: Some Interrelations of Psychology and History." *The Cultural Approach to History.* Caroline F. Ware, ed. Port Washington, N.Y.: Kennikat Press, 1940.

Weiner, Lynn. "Aunt Molly Jackson." Charles Reagan Wilson and William Ferris, eds. *Encyclopedia of Southern Culture.* Chapel Hill: University of North Carolina Press, 1989.

Wexley, John. John Wexley Papers, State Historical Society of Wisconsin, Madison Wisconsin.

Williams, Jay. *Stage Left.* New York: Charles Scribner's Sons, 1974.

Yellen, Samuel. *American Labor Struggles.* New York: S.A. Russell, 1936.

Index

Aaron, Daniel, 140

absentee ownership, 8, 82, 85, 90, 105, 82

Agee, James, 26

agitation-propaganda plays (agit-prop), 20, 31, 52, 144

Altars of Steel, 10,12-14, 18, 20, 81-85, 94-97, 99-106, 110, 112, 142, 146

American Communist Party, 139, 140

American Federation of Labor, (AFL) 13-16, 27, 31-33, 35, 36, 39, 42, 44, 52, 57, 58, 60, 97, 100, 101, 103, 105, 109-111, 114, 121, 123-125, 127, 135, 137-140, 141-143, 144-151

Andrew Sachs, 19, 23

Atkinson, Brooks, 118

Atlanta, 10, 14, 84, 85, 89, 94, 96-98, 100-102, 105, 107, 143, 148

Atlanta Constitution, 10, 96, 97, 101, 107, 148

Atlanta Georgian, 10, 96-98,100, 101, 107

Atlanta Theatre Guild, 85

Bailey, J.O., 5, 7, 13, 14, 17, 26-29, 38, 39, 44-46, 49, 57, 58, 90, 145, 148, 150

Bailey, Loretta Carroll, 5, 7, 13, 14, 17, 26-29, 38, 39, 44-46, 49, 57, 58, 90, 145, 148, 150

Bein, Alfred, 26, 129, 133

Bigsby, C. W. E., 11

Black Masks, 37

Blake, William Dorsey, 5, 14, 26, 35, 57, 59, 148

Booth, Wayne, 140

Brown, Richard Harvey, 8

Campbell, Paul Newell, 11

Carolina Playmakers, 3, 5, 9, 10, 17, 25, 27-36, 38, 40, 58, 69, 74, 141, 144, 148-151

Cheesman, Peter, 22

"clacker," 92

Clurman, Harold, 21, 23

Collier, Tarleton, 98, 99

Committee of 100, 37, 69

company store, 92

company town, 16

Congress of Industrial Organizations (CIO), 3, 8, 14, 18, 42, 62, 90, 121, 150, 151

Couch, William T., 28

Cradle Will Rock, 109

Cultural movement, 1, 5, 8, 9, 12, 14, 17, 18, 37, 9, 40, 43, 44, 67, 68, 70, 82, 94, 112, 129, 138, 139, 142

Daily Worker, 127

David Dubinsky, 111, 112, 127, 128, 133, 149

Dies Committee, 21

Dies, Martin, 135

documentary detail, 10, 14, 15,
20, 26, 32, 34, 38, 71, 74, 86, 90,
140, 143-145
documentary techniques, 20, 31,
32, 58, 144
documentary theatre, 15, 52, 144
Dos Passos, John, 18, 51, 61
Dubinsky, David, 111, 133

European influences, 20, 115,
140, 144

Federal Theatre Project, 3, 6, 12,
15, 18, 20, 32, 33, 58-62, 74,
81-85, 89, 98, 99, 101-103, 105,
110, 133, 144
Federal Theatre Project in the
South, 105,
Flanagan, Hallie, 12, 33, 81, 96

Garrison, Dee, 145
Gastonia Textile Strike of 1929,
5-7, 9, 13, 15, 16, 20, 25, 26,
29, 30, 34, 36, 38, 40, 42, 44,
50, 52, 57, 62, 64, 65, 72, 73,
129
Geddes, Virgil, 58
Gold, Michael, 58, 61
Goldstein, Macolm, 109
Graham, Hedley Gordon, 83
Graves, John Temple, 81, 82, 84,
105, 106, 150
Great Steel Strike of 1919, 7,
122
Green, Paul, 27, 28, 32, 33, 54,
58, 59, 63, 96, 147, 148
Greenfield, Thomas, 143

Harris Smith, Susan, 20
Haymarket riots, 7
Heller, Adele, 139
Herring, Harriet, 40, 44
Hochman, Julius, 112
House Un-American Activities
Committee, 110, 135
Hughes, Langston, 18, 35, 61,
140

Ingalls, Robert, 25
International Ladies' Garment
Workers' Union (ILGWU), 12,
109, 111-113, 115, 119, 120,
123, 127, 131-134
International Workers of the World
(I.W.W.), 67, 114

John Reed Clubs, 139
Judgement of Julius and Ethel
Rosenberg, 110

Kazan, Elia, 20
"kitchen scabs," 6, 14, 17, 125
Koch, Frederick H., 27

Labor colleges, 33, 140, 144,
145,
Labor scripts, 138
Labor songs, 35, 39, 138
Labor Stage, 6, 109-112, 126,
132-134
Labor Theatre Committee for
Touring Steel, 129
Labor wars, 17
The Last Mile, 16, 48, 50, 73, 84,
89, 100, 109-110, 114, 118, 119,
123
Lavery, Emmett, 59
League of Workers Theatres, 111
Leff, Michael, 19
Leftist art, 30, 33, 137, 140, 143
Leftist political theatre, 22
Lentz, Josef, 83, 104
Let Freedom Ring, 26, 33, 129,
131, 133, 129
Living Newspapers, 6, 15

The Machine Wreckers, 133
Miami Daily News, 103
Miami Federal Theatre, 102
Miami Herald, 103
music, 10, 37, 48-49, 85, 137

Nannes, Caspar, 21
National Recovery Administration, 3, 6, 7, 21, 26, 27, 33,

38, 42, 45, 57, 59, 68, 81, 86,
95, 98, 103, 111, 132, 138, 141,
142, 144, 146
Negro Little Theatre, 30
New Deal, 6, 7, 82,
New theatre, 14, 22, 26, 51, 127,
128, 131, 135, 139, 140, 139
New Theatre League, 14, 26, 128,
131, 135, 140, 128, 135
New York Times, 3, 12, 22, 23,
27, 31, 33, 58-60, 62, 64, 83, 84,
85, 94, 96, 101, 106, 107, 109,
110, 112, 114, 118, 126, 127,
129-131, 133, 140, 141, 148

Paternalism, 39
Pins and Needles, 133-135
Political theatre, 12, 15, 27, 52,
144, 146
Power, 5, 6, 15, 32, 34, 41, 43,
46, 48, 49, 57, 59, 62, 88, 95,
100, 104, 124, 133, 138, 141,
142
Prentis, Albert, 18, 23
Provincetown Players, 58, 60,
139

religious imagery, 13, 38, 40,
41, 43, 46, 49, 65-67, 70, 87, 93,
138, 142
Rice, Elmer, 20
Rich, Nancy Bailey, 28
Rogers, Thomas Hall, 6, 7, 14,
18, 81, 84, 92, 110
Rudnick, Lois, 139,

Sachs, Andrew, 19, 150
Schaffer, Louis 111-113, 127-129,
131-134
Schweid, Mark, 111, 112, 133,
134
Seydell, Mildred, 98-101
Skinner, Richard Dana, 114, 118
Smith, Gary L., 111
Southern liberalism, 12-15, 17,
25-27, 32-37, 39-44, 46, 50, 57,
65, 66, 67-69, 72-74, 81, 82-94,

97, 99-101, 104, 105, 113, 114,
123, 125, 142, 143, 148
Southern Textile Bulletin, 35, 50
Starr, Mark, 111, 131,
Steel, 5-10, 12-14, 16-18, 20, 26,
33, 40, 81-105, 109-134, 140
143, 145, 146, 148
Stevedore, 109, 133
"stretch-outs," 40
Strike!, 5, 11, 57, 58, 60-62, 64,
73, 94, 112, 113, 120, 132, 143,
145
Strike Song, 5, 10, 13, 26-27, 30,
32 36, 38-41, 43, 45, 49-52, 65,
69, 70, 74, 75, 85, 94, 112, 120
Strike songs, 38

Thatcher, Molly, 30-31
They Shall Not Die, 110
Toller, Ernst, 133

union organizers, 13

Vorse, Mary Heaton, 5, 7, 11,
13, 14, 18, 20, 26, 57, 58, 60-
64, 66, 67, 70, 71, 74, 94, 114,
143-145
Waiting For Lefty, 8, 31, 109,
143
Ware, Caroline, 8, 9, 16, 23
Wexley, John, 6, 7, 14, 17, 18,
20, 26, 33, 84, 109, 112, 113,
118, 122, 123, 133, 139, 142,
145
Wiggins, Ella May, 7, 15, 26, 34,
38, 51, 54, 57, 64, 65
Williams, Jay, 75, 140
Wobblies, 67, 68, 71
women, role of in plays, 9, 13,
14, 17, 26, 41-43, 47, 48, 65,
66, 68-71, 93, 99, 102, 113,
120-122, 125, 126, 144, 145
women as labor leaders, 14, 41-
43, 66, 69, 99
women, union efforts, 48, 66,
120, 125
Worker Education Movement, 111

Workers' Theatre, 12, 14, 18, 75,
     77, 107, 109-111, 131
Works Progress Administration,
     (WPA) 7, 18, 70, 85, 88, 98,
     101-103, 143
WPA murals, 7, 18, 143

Yellen, Samuel, 34, 76

About the Author

SUSAN DUFFY is Professor of Speech Communication at California Polytechnic State University. Her research interests focus on propagandistic uses of the theatre by leftist groups in the 1920s–1940s. She has published *Shirley Chisholm: A Bibliography of Writings By and About Her* (1988), and *The Political Left in the American Theatre of the 1930's: A Bibliographic Sourcebook* (1992).

ISBN 0-313-29861-0

90000>

EAN

9 780313 298615

HARDCOVER BAR CODE